THE
PHOENIX
AREA
GOLF GUIDE

Written by Daniel Wexler

Published by MT III Golf Media
El Segundo, CA   USA
Midd23@aol.com

Also by Daniel Wexler:

The Missing Links: America's Greatest Lost Golf Courses and Holes

Lost Links: Forgotten Treasures From Golf's Golden Age

The Golfer's Library: A Reader's Guide to Three Centuries of Golf Literature

The Book of Golfers: A Biographical History of the Royal & Ancient Game

The World Atlas of Golf (with Michael Clayton, Ran Morrissett, et al)

The Black Book

The American Private Golf Club Guide

The American Golf Resort Guide

The New York Metro Area Golf Guide

The Southern California Golf Guide

The Southeast Florida Golf Guide

The Phoenix Area Golf Guide

The Tropical Golf Guide

MT III Golf Media

In addition to producing our comprehensive golf course guidebooks ("The Black Book"), MT III Golf Media also offers customized public relations and promotional materials for public courses, resorts and private clubs. Please visit us at www.danielwexler.com.

TABLE OF CONTENTS

INTRODUCTION

By no means is this the first guidebook ever penned covering the golf courses of a particular region of the United States; such volumes are, in fact, fairly common, both in major metropolitan areas and destination locales readily identifiable as golfing hotbeds.

The Black Book, however, is different.

To begin with, this volume includes every facility within reasonable driving distance of Phoenix for which verifiable information was available at the time of its writing. From the ritziest private club to the tiniest nine-hole par 3, every course in Maricopa, Pinal, Gila, Yavapai and Counties is included, save for a handful in the far southern reaches of Pinal County that are generally considered a part of suburban Tucson.

Second, these volumes are about the golf courses – their layouts, histories, architectural evolutions, great (and not-so-great) holes, and whatever other salient points come to mind on a course-by-course basis. What they are *not* about is all manner of ancillary items that often clog mainstream guidebooks. There will, for example, be no discussions of food, tennis facilities, nearby hotels or the quality of beverage cart service. These books are for avid, serious golfers; the course is what matters here.

But perhaps most importantly, these guidebooks are intended to live up to a pithy little phrase of my own creation:

"Candid, but not opinionated."

And this to me is the heart of the undertaking because what the golf world does not need is another book calling every layout a "gem," or passing off regurgitated public relations copy as insightful descriptive material. The goal of The Black Book, then, is to provide an accurate picture of each course's overall attributes based upon a mix of objective factors (e.g., style of design, USGA ratings and slope, invasiveness of hazards, etc.), and a consensus of less formalized ones (various published rankings and commentaries), while at the same time minimizing any personal preferences relative to designer, style, region or period. This goal is furthered by the book's use of our exclusive Collectability Rating (see page 3), a unique evaluation method that essentially measures how desirable a "get" each facility is for the discerning golfer's personal list of courses played.

As for The Black Book's accuracy, while periodic renovations of courses are inevitable, numerous sources have been utilized in order to present the most accurate information possible at the time of writing. One notable point, however, concerns individual hole yardages and course ratings. Where possible, the information herein comes directly from the courses themselves, generally via website. Failing this, it has been culled from either regional golf associations or the USGA's national database – sources which often show minor differences based on a variety of factors. Hole yardages can vary similarly, often due only to a recent re-measuring, or the addition of new tees. Therefore while the numbers presented are deemed substantially accurate, the occasional minor variance is unavoidable. And also unavoidable, particularly in golf's present economic climate, is the occasional variance in course classification, often in the form of traditionally private clubs allowing limited outside play. Thus, how a course is classified, while usually reliably accurate, is always subject to potential change.

Regarding "ratings" in the larger sense, at the end of each applicable entry are a course's current rankings in the three American publications that perform this service, *Golf* Magazine (biennial domestic and worldwide top 100s), *Golf Digest* (biennial domestic top 200, state-by-state rankings and top 100 public) and *Golfweek* (annual top 200s for both modern and classic layouts, plus resort courses). They are abbreviated as G, GD and GW respectively.

Now, a final, note regarding bias and perspective.

As mentioned above, the great majority of the material presented herein is *objective* – the scale and style of a course's bunkering, or the statement that a layout measures 7,700 yards, or has been hugely altered since the Golden Age, are all impartial facts and not matters of opinion. But to the extent that one's personal tastes must inevitably poke around at the edges, it seems only fair to lay out my own, as follows:

1) I place an enormous emphasis on strategic design. Being able to hit a golf ball solidly is one important skill that the game requires; being able to think one's way around a well-conceived layout is an entirely different one. For me, the game is infinitely more engaging when both are fully in play.

2) I place a similar level of emphasis on variety, because even the greatest hole would get dull if played repeatedly. Courses with varied lengths and strategic challenges are, to me, much more appealing.

3) I prefer my golf relatively gimmick-free. Granted, this is a somewhat more subjective area, but generally speaking, 700-yard par 5s and artificial waterfalls in the middle of deserts tend not to inspire.

4) Ambience and setting count – not, perhaps, in assessing the strategic merits of a layout, but certainly in weighing the overall experience.

Obviously, readers may disagree with any or all of these perspectives – indeed, that's part of what makes a book like this fun – but either way, at least you'll know which comments might best be taken with a grain of salt when our tastes differ.

Safe travels!

DW

COLLECTABILITY RATING

Among the many qualities that make golf unique, none stands out further than the endless variety of its playing fields. Indeed, for most avid golfers, the chance to experience the game's vast array of courses – layouts built by all sorts of designers, in all manner of styles and settings – represents the lynchpin of golf's visceral, lifelong appeal.

In this light, we are all, in effect, collectors of golf courses, hoping to add as many significant facilities to our personal portfolios as time and circumstance will allow. It is with such an acquisitive sense in mind that The Black Book employs its original Collectability Rating, a one-to-five diamond scale which assesses each profiled facility's relative importance to the golfer's personal collection, based upon the following criteria:

1) The general perception of a course's overall quality as determined by various published rankings and commentaries, both national and regional.

2) A course's historical significance, measured primarily in terms of major competitions held, as well as period or social prominence/prestige, famous professionals or members, etc.

3) A course's architectural significance, judged by its design pedigree, its place within a particular designer's portfolio and, for older facilities, how much of their original layout remains in play.

4) An especially high (or low) degree of scenery or golfing ambience.

Each club's rating appears in the initial line of its entry, and can be defined as follows:

One of the game's absolute elite. A must-see.

An internationally prominent facility. Well worth a special visit.

A nationally prominent facility. First-class design and/or major history.

A regionally prominent facility, often worth traveling for.

A significant facility worth finding, should one be in the neighborhood.

A stronger facility offering flashes of notable design or history.

A mid-range facility, perhaps standing out in a narrow market.

A basic facility, but one rated somewhat above the mundane.

♦

It beats a driving range.

PROMINENT ARCHITECTS OF
THE PHOENIX AREA

The following are the course designers who have left the largest footprints upon the golfing landscape of the Phoenix Area, having built at least five courses in the region. Courses are referred to by their current names and are listed chronologically, with only those which remain in existence being included. Lists include only new courses or renovations large enough in scope to make the architect the new designer of record.

William P. & William F. Bell – A former agricultural student, Canonsburg, Pennsylvania native William Park Bell (1886-1953) moved to Southern California in 1911, initially becoming caddie master at Annandale Country Club, then greenkeeper at the Pasadena Golf Club. He entered the field of golf course architecture by working as a construction foreman on several of William Watson's area designs, then eventually started his own practice in 1920.

Bell enjoyed considerable success as a solo act, eventually chalking up more than 75 new designs, several of the best of which (the original El Caballero CC, Midwick CC and The Royal Palms CC) met their demise circa World War II. But despite this considerable résumé, Bell's enduring fame lies more in the loose partnership that he formed with Golden Age giant George C. Thomas, Jr. during the 1920s. Beginning with a 1925 redesign of Santa Barbara's La Cumbre Country Club, Bell would collaborate on seven Thomas projects (including Riviera, Bel-Air and the Los Angeles Country Club), with Thomas himself crediting Bell with a high level of creative input. Despite this, Bell has often been viewed simply as Thomas's sidekick – a falsehood borne out by early photographs which illustrate that the famous "Thomas bunkering style" was more rooted in Bell's pre-collaboration form than Thomas's own.

Bell's son William Francis (1918-1984) entered the family business after graduating from the University of Southern California, eventually taking over the firm upon his father's 1953 passing. Somewhat less creative in his work, he nonetheless became, by the late 1950s, *the* name in California design, completing more than 75 layouts throughout the state, the most famous being 2008 U.S. Open venue Torrey Pines.

The Bells in the Phoenix Area:	
William P. Bell	
Arizona Biltmore GC (Adobe) – Phoenix	1928
Encanto GC – Phoenix	1935
William P. Bell & William F. Bell	
Mesa CC – Mesa	1949
Wickenburg CC – Wickenburg (9)	1949
William F. Bell	
Encanto GC – Phoenix (9, Executive)	1952
Grand Canyon University GC – Phoenix	1961
Papago GC – Phoenix	1963

Milton Coggins – Milt Coggins (1902-1994) took a circuitous route into the field of golf course design, initially owning a sporting goods store during the Depression, then playing tennis professionally for more than a decade. Eventually becoming golf professional at Phoenix's Encanto Golf Course, he moved gradually into the field of course design by the late 1950s. Though Coggins made the occasional out-of-state cameo, the great majority of his work was in Arizona, where he was born and lived for most of his life.

Milton Coggins in the Phoenix Area:	
Sun City (North) – Sun City	1960
Coronado GC – Scottsdale (9, Executive) (w/G. Nash & J. Hardin)	1961
Sun City (South) – Sun City	1962
Sun City CC – Sun City	1967
Sun City (Lakes West) – Sun City	1968
Rio Verde CC (Quail Run) – Rio Verde	1971
Rio Verde CC (White Wing) – Rio Verde	1971
Paradise Valley Park GC – Phoenix (9, Executive)	1972
Prescott G&CC	1972
Sunland Village GC – Mesa (Executive) (w/G. Nash & J. Hardin)	1975
Sunland Village East GC – Mesa (Executive)	1987

Tom Fazio – Standing among the biggest names in modern golf course design, Tom Fazio (b.1945) has been in the business since 1962 when he began working for his ex-PGA Tour Player uncle George. The firm enjoyed a good deal of success as Tom gradually replaced the aging George as its centerpiece, with much of "their" later output being more on the order of solo designs. Despite stylistically awkward alterations of Golden Age classics Inverness (1979) and Oak Hill (1980), it would, perhaps ironically, be Fazio's polished aesthetics that would ultimately lead him to stardom, and by the early 1980s he was turning out attractive, often spectacular-looking courses from coast to coast.

Frequently appearing more difficult than they actually played, such layouts became a favorite of real estate and resort developers – though plenty of private clubs dot the Fazio résumé as well. A strong believer in moving tons of earth, Fazio has prided himself on being able to build "quality" golf holes on virtually any terrain – an expensive philosophy but one which yielded Las Vegas's famed Shadow Creek, whose construction upon once-barren desert rates among the great accomplishments in the history of course design.

Though Fazio's layouts have frequently drawn lavish praise upon opening, a perceived emphasis on aesthetics over tactical excellence has made their staying power atop many rankings fleeting, and among Major championships, only the 1987 PGA has ever visited a Fazio-designed course.

Tom Fazio in the Phoenix Area:	
Sun City (Willowcreek) – Sun City (w/G. Fazio)	1974
Sun City (Willowbrook) – Sun City (w/G. Fazio) (Executive)	1974
Estancia C - Scottsdale	1995
Grayhawk GC (Raptor) – Scottsdale	1995
Mirabel – Scottsdale	2001
Whisper Rock GC (Upper) – Scottsdale	2005

Jeff Hardin & Greg Nash – An Arizona native, Jeff Hardin (b.1933) graduated from the University of Arizona in 1959 and soon went to work as a civil engineer for the Del Webb Company, spending more than a decade collaborating with a variety of architects on the corporation's course design projects. Hardin hung out his own design shingle in 1972 and quickly hired another Del Webb employee, Greg Nash (b.1949), who was also a fellow U of A graduate and an up-and-coming designer in his own right.

Their partnership would last for 11 years before Nash eventually went out on his own in 1983, later teaming up with Billy Casper on a number of projects. Though credits sometimes vary as to which projects were completed by which partner (or both), their association proved a fruitful one, particularly within their home state, where the overwhelming majority of their work was completed. Few of their courses have ever been rated among Arizona's elite but they are, by a comfortable margin, the most prolific designers ever to work in the Phoenix/Scottsdale area.

Jeff Hardin & Greg Nash in the Phoenix Area:	
Jeff Hardin & Greg Nash	
Sun City (Quail Run) – Sun City (9, Executive)	1977
Villa de Paz GC – Phoenix	1977
Hillcrest GC – Sun City West	1978
Los Caballeros GC – Wickenburg	1979
Paradise Valley Park GC – Phoenix (Add 9, Executive)	1986
Jeff Hardin	
Sun City (Lakes East) – Sun City (Executive)	1970
Palmbrook CC – Sun City	1972
Sun City (Riverview) – Sun City	1972
Greg Nash	
Union Hills CC – Sun City	1974
Continental GC – Scottsdale (Executive)	1978
Prairie Pines – Peoria (Executive)	1978
Sun City West (Pebblebrook) – Sun City	1979
Sun City West (Stardust) – Sun City (Executive)	1980
Gold Canyon G Resort (Sidewinder) – Gold Canyon	1982
Briarwood CC – Sun City West	1983
Sun Lakes (Cottonwood) – Sun Lakes	1983
Roadhaven GC – Apache Junction (9, Par 3)	1984
Leisure World CC (Coyote Run) – Mesa	1985
Sun City West (Grandview) – Sun City	1985
Superstition Springs GC – Mesa	1986
Sun City West (Echo Mesa) – Sun City (Executive)	1987
Great Eagle GC – Surprise (Add 9)	1989
Sun City West (Trail Ridge) – Sun City	1991
Sun City West (Deer Valley) – Sun City (w/B. Casper)	1994
Terravita – Scottsdale (w/B. Casper)	1994
Sun City West (Desert Trails) – Sun City (Executive) (w/B. Casper)	1995
Sun City Grand (Desert Springs) – Surprise	1996
Sun City Grand (Granite North) – Surprise (w/B. Casper)	1997
Sun City Grand (Granite South) – Surprise (w/B. Casper)	1997
Anthem G&CC (Persimmon) – Anthem	1999
Sun City Grand (Cimarron) – Surprise	2003
Sundance GC – Buckeye	2003
Anthem G&CC (Ironwood) – Anthem	2004
Corte Bella GC – Sun City West	2004
Mission Royale GC - Casa Grande	2004

Ken Kavanaugh – An Illinois native, Ken Kavanaugh (b.1952) attended both Southern Illinois University and Arizona State before getting a landscape architecture degree from the University of Arizona in 1976. While overseeing construction of Fred Enke Municipal Golf Course for the City of Tucson, he discovered his true calling to be course design and – with enviable confidence – embarked on a solo career thereafter. Though he has found regular work elsewhere, Kavanaugh's practice has been mostly an Arizona-centric affair since its establishment.

Ken Kavanaugh in the Phoenix Area:	
Gold Canyon G Resort (Dinosaur Mountain) – Gold Canyon	1986
Great Eagle GC – Surprise (9)	1986
Westbrook Village GC (Vistas) – Peoria	1990

Ken Kavanaugh Cont'd.

Club West GC – Phoenix (w/B. Whitcomb)	1993
Gold Canyon G Resort (Sidewinder) – Gold Canyon (add 9)	1998
Longbow GC – Mesa	2003
Verde River G & Social C – Rio Verde	2006

Red Lawrence – White Plains, New York native Robert F. "Red" Lawrence (1893-1976) got his start in the field of golf design working for Walter Travis during the 1919 building of the Westchester Country Club, then was hired by William Flynn to supervise construction of several Golden Age layouts in Florida. Chief among these were 36 outstanding holes (now deceased) at the Boca Raton Hotel, a legendary period club to which Lawrence latched on as greenkeeper during the doldrums of the Depression.

Not until after World War II did Lawrence enter the design business full-time, initially in Florida and then, during the 1950s, in Arizona. Though he counted more than 25 new designs in his portfolio, Lawrence is best known for the groundbreaking Desert Forest Golf Club, a 1962 layout in Carefree whose numerous forced carries to naturally contoured "island" fairways presaged modern desert design by a good 20 years.

Red Lawrence in the Phoenix Area:

Desert Forest GC - Carefree	1962
Camelback GC (Padre) – Scottsdale	1970
Bellair GC – Glendale (Executive) (w/G. Nash & J. Hardin)	1972
Fountain of the Sun CC – Mesa (Executive)	1972
Dobson Ranch GC – Mesa	1974
The Wigwam G Resort & Spa (Heritage) – Litchfield Park	1974

Jack Nicklaus – By record the greatest golfer of all time, Jack William Nicklaus (b.1940) built a résumé which requires no amplification, his total of 18 professional Major titles (plus two U.S. Amateurs) remaining the game's gold standard. The son of a Columbus, Ohio pharmacist, Nicklaus was an excellent athlete as a youth, starring in basketball and giving up several other sports only when they began to conflict with golf. But as a golfer he was uniquely special, learning to play at the Donald Ross-designed Scioto Country Club and establishing his dominance early and often. Thus some 73 PGA Tour wins later, he turned his focus to a course design business which has surely covered more ground worldwide than any other firm.

Indeed, Nicklaus Design (which includes all manner of family members) has completed over 400 projects in 41 countries on all six inhabited continents, and in 39 American states. Though chided in its early years for building courses that either (A) favored long, high faders (like Jack himself) or (B) were somewhat formulaic, the company's work has seldom failed to be tactically engaging. Indeed, one would be hard pressed to find a Nicklaus layout that doesn't regularly engender a real degree of playing interest.

Jack's most famous designs have included 1974's Muirfield Village Golf Club (built with Desmond Muirhead), Alabama's Shoal Creek (1977), Colorado's Castle Pines (1981) and Kentucky's Valhalla (1986) – all well-established big-event venues. In Arizona, his 1983 design at Scottsdale's Desert Highlands amply demonstrated the possibilities of modern desert golf, with his six courses at Desert Mountain continuing to expand the concept to its fullest.

Jack Nicklaus in the Phoenix Area:

Desert Highlands GC – Scottsdale	1983
Desert Mountain C (Renegade) – Scottsdale	1987
Desert Mountain C (Cochise) – Scottsdale	1988

Jack Nicklaus Cont'd.	
Desert Mountain C (Geronimo) – Scottsdale	1989
Desert Mountain C (Apache) – Scottsdale	1996
Superstition Mountain (Prospector) – Apache Junction	1998
Desert Mountain C (Chiracahua) – Scottsdale	1999
GC of Estrella – Goodyear	1999
Superstition Mountain (Lost Gold) – Apache Junction	1999
Bear Creek G Complex (Bear) – Chandler	2000
Bear Creek G Complex (Cub) – Chandler	2001
Desert Mountain C (Outlaw) – Scottsdale	2003

Gary Panks – A native of Michigan's Upper Peninsula, Gary Panks (b.1941) majored in landscape architecture while starring on the golf team at Michigan State. After graduation he began a long run of jobs as a landscape designer, working for employers as diverse as New York State, the Bureau of Indian Affairs and the Maricopa County Parks Department. In 1978, while residing in Phoenix, he began a second career as a golf course designer, building a practice weighted heavily towards projects within the State of Arizona.

In 1988, he brought aboard two-time Major champion David Graham as a partner, enabling the firm to find work in Graham's native Australia, as well as in Thailand and other farther-flung locales. The partnership ended in 1997 (with Graham joining the Champions Tour) but Panks has continued a strong solo practice, with much of his work still coming in the Phoenix area.

Gary Panks in the Phoenix Area:	
Sun Lakes (Oakwood) – Sun Lakes (27)	1985
Rolling Hills GC – Tempe (Executive)	1987
Sunbird GC – Chandler (Executive)	1987
Sedona G Resort – Sedona	1988
Antelope Hills GC (South) – Prescott	1992
Grayhawk GC (Talon) – Scottsdale (w/D. Graham)	1994
Tonto Verde (Peaks) – Rio Verde (w/D. Graham)	1994
Raven GC – Phoenix	1995
GC at Chaparral Pines – Payson (w/D. Graham)	1997
Falcon Dunes GC – Waddell	1998
Aguila GC – Laveen	1999
Aguila GC – Laveen (Par 3)	1999
Legacy G Resort – Phoenix	1999
Tonto Verde (Ranch) – Rio Verde	1999
FireRock CC – Fountain Hills	2000
Whirlwind GC (Devil's Claw) – Chandler	2000
Seville G&CC – Gilbert	2001
Whirlwind GC (Cat Tail) – Chandler	2002
Trilogy GC at Vistancia – Peoria	2004
Poston Butte GC – Florence	2007

Arthur Jack Snyder – A native of Rosedale, Pennsylvania, Arthur Jack Snyder (1917-2005) came from a golfing background, his father having been trained as a greenkeeper by Emil Loeffler at Oakmont. In addition to operating a landscape design business (his major at Penn State), Snyder himself served as Oakmont's greenkeeper in the early 1950s before moving west and eventually opening his own Arizona-based design firm in 1958. Nearly all of his projects can be found in the Southwest, with most coming in Arizona. He remained active well into his 70s, aided by associate Forrest Richardson, with whom he completed his final Phoenix-area work, the

Coyote Lakes Golf Club, in Surprise, in 1993.

Arthur Jack Snyder in the Phoenix Area:	
Apache Wells CC – Mesa	1962
Arizona City GC – Arizona City	1963
Arizona G Resort & Conference Center – Mesa	1965
Desert Sands GC – Mesa (Executive)	1969
Ken McDonald GC – Tempe	1974
Dave White Municipal GC – Casa Grande	1979
Canyon Mesa GC – Sedona (Executive)	1984
Coyote Lakes GC – Surprise (w/F. Richardson)	1993

Tom Weiskopf & Jay Morrish – Universally hailed as one of the most talented golfers of his era, Massillon, Ohio native Tom Weiskopf (b.1942) starred (two years behind Jack Nicklaus) at Ohio State before going on to win 16 PGA Tour titles, including the 1973 British Open. Indeed, Weiskopf's six-win 1973 was one of decade's strongest single-season campaigns, but while six more official victories remained in his future, he would never again reach that level of dominance. By the mid 1980s, Weiskopf turned his attention to the field of golf course design, eventually entering into a highly successful partnership with Jay Morrish in 1984.

For his part, Morrish (b.1936) was experienced, having worked for Robert Trent Jones, George Fazio, Desmond Muirhead and Jack Nicklaus, with the latter being a 10-year stint in which he also moonlighted with Bob Cupp in a venture known as Golforce. The pairing with Weiskopf would indeed prove fruitful, with the duo producing 23 new designs, many of which received national acclaim. One in particular, Northern Arizona's Forest Highlands, is widely rated among America's top 100 courses, while several others have occasionally found positions on such lists. Though several of Morrish's independent redesign projects have met with mixed reviews, his solo work at Scottsdale's Boulders Resort received universally high period acclaim.

Tom Weiskopf & Jay Morrish in the Phoenix Area:	
Tom Weiskopf & Jay Morrish	
Troon GC – Scottsdale	1985
TPC Scottsdale (Stadium) – Scottsdale	1986
Foothills GC – Phoenix	1987
TPC Scottsdale (Champions) – Scottsdale	1987
Troon North GC (Monument) – Scottsdale	1990
Troon North GC (Pinnacle) – Scottsdale	1996
The Rim GC – Payson	1999
Tom Weiskopf	
Capital Canyon GC – Prescott	1997
Silverleaf – Scottsdale	2002
Seven Canyons – Sedona	2003
Jay Morrish	
Boulders Resort GC (North) – Carefree	1985
Boulders Resort GC (South) – Carefree	1991
Talking Rock GC – Prescott	2002

MARICOPA COUNTY

Alta Mesa Country Club - Mesa   ◆◆½

Dick Phelps   www.altamesagolf.com
1460 North Alta Mesa Dr, Mesa, AZ 85205   (480) 832-3257
            7,100 yds   Par 72   Rating: 73.7 / 134   (1985)

The Alta Mesa Country Club is in many ways a prototypical desert golf course of its
period, being a long (for 1985), essentially flat test marked by eight man-made water
hazards, plenty of flanking waste areas and housing down both sides of nearly every hole.
But despite its formulaic qualities, this Dick Phelps-designed test is not without its
interesting moments, particularly at the 442-yard dogleg-left 13th, an engaging two-
shotter where a narrow sliver of sand-flanked alternate fairway dares the aggressive tee
ball. Also of tactical interest are a pair of lake-bothered tests in the property's northern
reaches, the 559-yard dogleg right 3rd and the 356-yard 4th, where longer hitters might be
tempted to try and slip aggressive drives between left-side sand and right-side water
some 50 yards shy of the green. The outward half also finishes strongly with a trio of
muscular closers: the 247-yard 7th (where several small trees help defend the green), the
428-yard pond-flanked 8th and the 564-yard 9th, where right-side water cuts into the lay-
up zone and also abuts the putting surface. The back nine, which extends southward
across East Brown Road, is the less-engaging half, but in addition to the 13th, includes two
more solid par 4s, the 424-yard dogleg right 11th and the 425-yard finisher.

Ancala Country Club - Scottsdale   ◆◆◆

Perry Dye   www.ancalacc.com
11700 East Via Linda St, Scottsdale, AZ 85259   (480) 391-1000
            6,818 yds   Par 72   Rating: 73.0 / 139   (1990)

Built in the foothills of the McDowell Mountains, on the northeastern side of Scottsdale,
Ancala shakes off the presence of copious housing (and Perry Dye's modern bunkering)
to rate as one of the region's more natural-feeling desert designs. One reason for this is
a noticeable absence of water, for aside from the narrow hazard which separates holes 9
and 18 (a Dye family trademark) no additional lakes were constructed. The result is a
layout where the challenge lies primarily in some steep green contouring, the proximity
of the open desert to numerous landing areas and – though surely unforeseen in 1990 –
several crossing arroyos which, with unchecked advances in modern equipment, can
throttle back bigger hitters by forcing them to lay up off the tee. Though Ancala is not
quite as strategically inclined as many a Dye track, it does possess a strong and varied
collection of par 4s which, going out, include the narrow 466-yard 2nd (the number one
stroke hole), the 357-yard uphill (and tightly bunkered) 6th and the 372-yard 9th, whose
green extends leftward into the aforementioned lake. The back then counters with the
406-yard 10th (where a very long bunker flanks the left side), the 372-yard 13th (whose
fairway is impeded by a centerline bunker), the driveable 304-yard 15th and the 453-yard
18th, a genuinely strong finisher with the lone lake (and a long buffering bunker) running
down the entirety of its right side. This may not be Desert Forest, but despite the
frequent presence of housing, it's closer to natural desert golf than many in the region.

Anthem Golf & Country Club (Persimmon) - Anthem   ♦♦½

Greg Nash   www.clubcorp.com
2708 West Anthem Club Dr, Anthem, AZ 85086   (623) 742-6200
        7,197 yds   Par 72   Rating: 74.6 / 140   (1999)

A sprawling real estate development situated in the Phoenix/Scottsdale area's northern reaches, the Anthem Golf & Country Club sports 36 Greg Nash-designed holes routed spaciously (though among endless rows of homes) beneath Daisy Mountain. The club's older course, the Persimmon, is both long and tough, but also somewhat period desert formulaic, offering predictable entries like the long two-shotter to a bunkerless green (the 460-yard 6th and the 457-yard 12th), the driveable par 4 (the 339-yard 10th) and the obligatory double green, in this case serving holes 9 and 18.   But man-made water hazards are not overly relied upon (they affect only three holes) and there are a fair number of engaging moments, with the front nine's best including the 562-yard downhill 3rd (where back-left water flanks the green), the 408-yard uphill 5th (a dogleg left along an arroyo) and the 409-yard arroyo-fronted 9th. The back includes the 574-yard 16th (where another arroyo, plus a single tiny bunker, menace the second) and the 445-yard 18th (a heavily bunkered, downhill dogleg left), as well as the layout's most memorable overall entry, the aforementioned 10th, whose green angles leftward along a pond.

Anthem Golf & Country Club (Ironwood) - Anthem   ♦♦♦

Greg Nash   www.clubcorp.com
2708 West Anthem Club Dr, Anthem, AZ 85086   (623) 742-6200
        7,231 yds   Par 72   Rating: 74.5 / 144   (2004)

The newer (by five years) of the Anthem Golf & Country Club's two Greg Nash-designed layouts, the Ironwood course plays out of a separate clubhouse to the east and is both the tougher and tactically more engaging test. Though water appears only slightly more often (meaningfully affecting five holes), its presence tends to be more invasive. Likewise Nash's large-of-scale bunkering, which pinches a number of fairways and requires a bit more respect off the tee. Following a wide, counter-clockwise routing to the west, the outward half features the 541-yard downhill 3rd (where the drive angles across the same dry wash that fronts the green), the 220-yard 4th (whose narrow, bunkerless putting surface sits flush against a right-side pond, the 321-yard 7th (driveable across a line of angled bunkers) and the 432-yard uphill 9th, whose green includes a very narrow back section. The back nine opens in distinctive (if contrived) form as the 412-yard 10th and the 217-yard 11th are the rare consecutive holes to have water hugging both the front and back of their tightly guarded putting surfaces. Also notable are the 598-yard 12th (which twists between two small lakes) and the 464-yard 13th, where sand greatly affects the drive but is entirely absent around the green. Similarly strong are the 475-yard 16th (whose narrow target angles along right-side sand) and the 547-yard pond-guarded 18th, where the lay-up zone is divided by rough and a centerline tree.

Arizona Country Club - Phoenix

Ernest Suggs & Willie Wansa   www.azcountryclub.com
5668 East Orange Blossom Lane, Phoenix, AZ 85018   (480) 889-1505
                6,720 yds   Par 72   Rating: 71.9 / 130   (1946)

Though not established until 1946, the Arizona Country Club can claim golf to have been played on its property for longer than any course in Arizona, as the old Ingleside Inn's original nine-hole sand-greened layout debuted here in 1909. The Inn expired during the Depression but some odd remaining features of its site were incorporated into the new postwar course by designers/owners Ernest Suggs and Willie Wansa, who created a flat, mostly open layout marked by a single small lake, and views of nearby Camelback Mountain. Their work has since seen several renovations (most prominently in 1962 by former PGA Tour star and longtime desert resident Johnny Bulla) with today's track being a mature, tree-lined test which includes far greater bunkering and a second, much larger lake. This current version is led by a pair of water-guarded par 5s (the 503-yard 3rd and the 593-yard 10th), each of which is followed by a mid-length par 3 playing across the same hazard. Also notable are stout par 4s like the 455-yard 2nd (played to a narrow, angled green), the 443-yard dogleg right 5th and the 437-yard 17th. Somewhat usurped golf-wise by the area's many newer facilities, the Country Club still boasts a great deal of history; indeed, as a Phoenix Open co-host from 1955-1973, it claims Hall-of-Famers Billy Casper, Julius Boros, Arnold Palmer (twice) and Gene Littler (thrice) among an impressive list of champions. One of the region's most venerable golfing institutions, comfortably.

Arrowhead Country Club - Glendale

Arnold Palmer   www.arrowheadccaz.com
19888 North 73rd Ave, Glendale, AZ 85308   (623) 561-9600
                7,001 yds   Par 72   Rating: 73.1 / 123   (1987)

Situated within a bend of the Agua Fria Freeway, in Phoenix's northwestern suburbs, Arrowhead offers a good-size, moderately difficult Arnold Palmer design flanked at nearly every turn by expansive neighborhoods of single-family houses. In spots the level of tactical interest is lower than one might expect, and the front nine as a whole offers little more than straight ahead desert golf, save for a pair of engaging driving holes, the 433-yard 5th (a sweeping dogleg right around a vast waste bunker) and the 572-yard 6th, which bends leftward, around a lake. The back nine is more interesting, however, due mostly to the more frequent presence of water, which meaningfully affects play on five holes. On the first two, the 446-yard dogleg left 10th and the 206-yard 11th, this presence is more peripheral, and largely out of range of the competent ball striker. But the same cannot be said of three more memorable tests to follow: the 397-yard 13th (a tactically strong entry played to a water-divided split fairway), the 423-yard lake-fronted 17th and the 477-yard par-5 18th, whose green is tucked left, behind both sand and a long pond.

Blackstone Country Club - Peoria

Jim Engh   www.troongolf.com
12101 West Blackstone Dr, Peoria, AZ 85383   (623) 707-8700
                7,089 yds   Par 72   Rating: 73.9 / 143   (2005)

A new millennium facility sitting just south of the Hieroglyphic Mountains, 15 miles northwest of Phoenix, Blackstone features a Jim Engh-designed 18 that is somewhat more subdued than this popular modern designer's stylistic norm. In one sense, this is standard desert golf, replete with the requisite forced carries and the occasional man-made lake to spice things up. But as one might expect of Engh, there is also quite a bit more in play here, for beyond a traditionally limited bunker menu of "tiny and round" and "long, narrow, cape-and-bay," Engh's work invariably carries a clear and engaging strategic bent. Thus while two-shotters like the 442-yard lake-flanked 4th, the 470-yard 5th (featuring a long approach across a dry wash) and the 447-yard 8th are palpably strong, more memorable are entries like the 555-yard 9th (which dares a long second over open desert to a narrow green), the 416-yard 10th (whose fairway is dotted by five zig-zagging pot bunkers) and the 619-yard 11th, a lake-menaced dogleg right. Also notable is a back nine trio which play to another Engh specialty, the very long, *extremely* narrow putting surface: the 203-yard 13th, the 524-yard 14th (a reachable double-dogleg) and the downhill 228-yard 15th, whose green becomes frighteningly slim in its back reaches. The quasi-geometric shaping is certainly not every golfer's cup of tea, but there is more than enough playing interest here to make for a fun and challenging game.

Briarwood Country Club - Sun City West

Greg Nash   www.briarwoodcc.com
20800 North 135th Ave, Sun City West, AZ 85375   (623) 584-5600
                6,576 yds   Par 72   Rating: 71.4 / 129   (1983)

One of several private clubs that operate autonomously within Del Webb's massive Sun City West retirement community, Briarwood was designed by the locally prominent Greg Nash to appeal mostly to recreational golfers. A short layout routed against Sun City's standard housing-lined backdrop (though notably, the houses are generally set well back from the fairways), it opens with a mostly functional front nine whose strongest entries include a pair of sturdy back-and-forth par 4s (the 410-yard 4th and the 426-yard 5th) as well as a reachable pond-guarded par 5, the 505-yard 8th. The more engaging back then follows a narrow out-and-back routing to the east where it offers several holes marginally affected by a wandering, man-made creek. Among the top entries here are the 187-yard tightly bunkered 11th, the 202-yard 14th (which lies adjacent to a pond in which the creek terminates), the 339-yard driveble 15th and the 514-yard 17th, where the creek partially fronts a shallow putting surface. A solid entry among retirement-oriented clubs.

Corte Bella Golf Club - Sun City West

Greg Nash   www.cortebellagolfclub.com
22129 North Mission Dr, Sun City West, AZ 85375   (623) 556-8951
              7,011 yds   Par 72   Rating: 72.5 / 129   (2004)

Another of Sun City West's autonomous private facilities, the Corte Bella Golf Club is also the development's newest, being built by Greg Nash in 2004. Measuring over 7,000 yards, it is a layout less overtly aimed at relaxing retirees – but as a 129 slope suggests, it was hardly intended for PGA Tour play either. The majority of holes are lined on both sides by housing (the exceptions border either the driving range or Deer Valley Road) and are of fairly basic design. Their backbone comes from longer tests like the 448-yard bunkerless 2nd, the 474-yard par-4 7th (a sharp dogleg left around two prominent corner bunkers) and the 607-yard 13th, as well as a pair of strong closers, the tactically sound 571-yard 17th and the heavily bunkered 411-yard 18th. Water appears only twice (man-made ponds guard both the 157-yard 12th and the 367-yard 14th) and is considerably overshadowed by a number of large-scale bunkers – though like the native terrain that often lies beyond them, their affect on play is usually more visual than invasive.

Country Club at DC Ranch - Scottsdale

Scott Miller   www.ccdcranch.com
9290 E Thompson Peak Pkwy, Scottsdale, AZ 85255   (480) 342-7200
              6,888 yds   Par 71   Rating: 73.0 / 135   (1997)

Built by Scott Miller in 1997, the Country Club at DC Ranch is an expansively routed residential layout built upon a site which descends steadily from north to south, along the foothills of the McDowell Mountains. The present course is not completely original, however, having been renovated (mostly in its bunkering) by John Fought and club resident Tom Lehman in 2002. The site's sloping nature is a primary feature early on as the first six holes alternately climb and descend, with favorites including a pair of longer downhill par 4s, the 452-yard dry wash-crossed 2nd and the 451-yard 6th. The strong 218-yard 7th and 462-yard 9th then close out the front side, leading to a back highlighted by a trio of holes which climb significantly into the foothills: the 273-yard 12th (a sharply uphill par 4), the photogenic 128-yard 13th (played across rough terrain to a putting surface buttressed in front by a rock wall) and the 447-yard 14th, which plunges some 200 feet from tee to green. The 475-yard dry wash-crossed 15th rates among the layout's strongest par 4s and kicks off a run of three downhill closers before the terrain reverses at the 439-yard 18th, which plays uphill to a tightly bunkered target. With homes set well back from the fairways, this is a refreshingly spacious layout as residence-oriented facilities go. But while eminently solid and highly scenic, it falls slightly shy of the region's elite in terms of either pure challenge or fundamental playing interest.

Desert Forest Golf Club - Carefree   ◆◆◆◆

Red Lawrence   www.desertforestgolfclub.com
37207 North Mule Train Rd, Carefree, AZ   85377   (480) 488-4589
            7,203 yds   Par 72   Rating: 75.5 / 149   (1962)

The Desert Forest Golf Club enjoys a significant place in the history of course design for it was, by about two decades, the forerunner of the modern target-oriented game that has made golf in the southwestern desert possible. Located 30 miles northeast of Phoenix, in the foothills below Gold Mountain, the course was built on a shoestring by ex-Walter Travis assistant Robert "Red" Lawrence, who simply laid the holes onto the rolling desert floor, reserving his paltry earth moving budget for green complexes and the leveling of tees (thus championing "minimalism" several decades early as well). The result was a set of fairways as natural as any in America, though the surrounding desert vegetation (which has grown out enough in over half a century to frame each hole individually) allows for no aesthetic parallels to links golf whatsoever. Consistent with his other work, Lawrence's bunkering here was limited in both scale and style, with most greens offering little more than a nondescript hazard on either side, and not a fairway bunker to be found. Such a recipe might well add up to uninspiring golf on a lesser site, but Desert Forest has enjoyed a strong national reputation virtually from its inception. Thus it becomes quite interesting to note that in 2013, the club hired former Coore & Crenshaw associate Dave Zinkand to perform a renovation which, beyond re-grassing and the rebuilding of green complexes, including substantial alterations to the bunkering, with numerous hazards being moved or removed as all were re-fashioned with a more rough-edged style. The result is a layout which retains all of what made Lawrence's version special, but which has been improved both tactically an aesthetically. Notably fine challenges are sprinkled throughout, with the front nine initially offering strong entries like the 456-yard uphill 2nd and the 464-yard 5th, an uphill dogleg left and an especially demanding driving hole. The loop's most engaging golf comes at its close, however, and includes the highly engaging 551-yard dogleg right 7th (a tactically rich test daring a long drive across open desert and a second across an angled arroyo), the 231-yard downhill 8th (where Zinkand's revised bunkering includes a tiny centerline hazard) and 533-yard 9th, which descends to a green closely guarded by greatly expanded bunkering. The slightly shorter back nine must, by definition, be highlighted by a pair of holes listed among *Golf* magazine's top 500 in the world, the narrow 466-yard 13th (which climbs to a tightly bunkered putting surface) and the 535-yard 16th, whose fairway is centered by a grand clump of mesquite which, architecturally speaking, was also some two decades ahead of its time.   Beyond these obvious standouts, additional favorites include the 581-yard uphill 11th (whose green sits behind another new centerline bunker), the 329-yard downhill 14th (whose narrow putting surface angles rightward behind sand), the 435-yard downhill 15th and the 467-yard 18th, a rolling, obviously stout finisher. With so little grass existing off of the fairways upon which to entertain galleries, Desert Forest has largely existed outside of the national tournament spotlight, though it has hosted a pair of USGA national championships, the 1990 U.S. Senior Amateur and the 2007 U.S. Women's Mid-Amateur. But regardless of its lower profile, Desert Forest is a unique and challenging golf course of the highest order which, particularly post-renovation, ranks firmly among the Southwest's most original and very best, making it a genuine must-see for course design aficionados.   (**GD**: #197 USA, #9 State   **GW**: #44 Modern)

1	2	3	4	5	6	7	8	9	Out
404	456	168	441	464	371	551	231	533	3619
4	4	3	4	4	4	5	3	5	36
10	11	12	13	14	15	16	17	18	In
392	594	194	466	329	435	535	170	467	3582
4	5	3	4	4	4	5	3	4	36

Desert Highlands Golf Club - Scottsdale ◆◆◆◆

Jack Nicklaus   www.deserthighlandsscottsdale.com
10040 East Happy Valley Rd, Scottsdale, AZ   85255   (480) 419-3745
                7,108 yds   Par 72   Rating: 74.0 / 150   (1983)

It seems appropriate for the Desert Highlands Golf Club to immediately follow Desert Forest, for Jack Nicklaus's work here was really the first step in turning Red Lawrence's early '60s target style into the staple of modern desert golf that it has become – particularly in water-conscious Arizona, where state law limits new courses to only 90 acres of maintained turf. Like most Nicklaus projects, this is not Desert Forest II but rather Desert Forest on Steroids – yet with not a single water hazard in play, it is far less contrived than many an Arizona layout, and it also provides a fairly broad menu of tactically engaging holes. Notably, while virtually every fairway is at least partially flanked by low-density housing, the homes tend to be set well back from the action, often buffered by wide swaths of open sand from which errant shots can be far more readily recovered than from the native desert. From a clubhouse situated on the lower slopes of Pinnacle Peak, the 350-yard opener begins memorably from tees elevated within the rocks before the action picks up at the 580-yard 2nd (where native sand tightly squeezes the lay-up zone) and the 450-yard 3rd, whose approach must carry more open sand to reach a fallaway green. Perhaps most memorable going out, however, are a pair of strong par 4s offering alternate fairways off the tee, the 428-yard 6th (where the more dangerous left-side option is preferred) and the 444-yard 8th, whose tougher right-side choice yields the ideal line of approach. Following the 565-yard uphill 9th (which curls leftward, along/around an endless left-side bunker), the inward half includes three par 3s and three par 5s, and kicks off with the descending 406-yard 10th and the 563-yard 11th, the latter daring a long, uphill second across native terrain in order to get home in two. The 173-yard 12th then joins the 188-ard 7th as par 3s with greens perched closely above large native areas, though the putting surface at the 12th is a quirky one indeed, being wildly shaped, quite narrow (in spots) and offering a number of testing pin placements. The 394-yard 13th would be equally distinctive were it not the club's third alternate-fairway par 4. It is, however, arguably the most engaging of the trio, for its right-side fairway (which requires a 230-yard desert carry from the tips) leaves only a fairly simple pitch, whereas the safer left side yields a second played across a wide dry wash to what from this angle has become a very shallow target indeed. Also memorable is the layout's unconventional finish, which begins with a pair of back-to-back Mutt-and-Jeff par 3s, the 146-yard 15th (whose putting surface pushes against the rocky slopes of Pinnacle Peak) and the 242-yard downhill 16th, a demanding one-shotter and one of the few entries to bring housing close to the line of play. The unusual homeward run then closes with back-to-back par 5s, the 574-yard 17th (a downhill/sidehill test with green set beyond a dry wash) and the 563-yard 18th, which bends leftward along open sand before reaching a mound-and-bunker-protected putting surface. With many holes requiring clear tactical decision-making, Desert Highlands was well-suited to television, and thus hosted the first Skins Game (Nicklaus, Palmer, Player and Watson), a ratings bonanza that briefly vaulted the course as high as 25th in *Golf Digest*'s U.S. top 100. Today, it is usually rated among the top 10 in Arizona, but given its architectural significance and spectacular scenery, this remains among the region's most desirable golfing stops. An innovative Gary Panks-designed 18-hole putting course adjoins.   **(GD**: #182 USA, #7 State   **GW**: #167 Modern**)**

1	2	3	4	5	6	7	8	9	Out
350	580	450	205	419	428	188	444	565	3629
4	5	4	3	4	4	3	4	5	36
10	11	12	13	14	15	16	17	18	In
406	563	173	394	418	146	242	574	563	3479
4	5	3	4	4	3	3	5	5	36

Desert Mountain Club (Renegade) - Scottsdale   ♦♦♦½

Jack Nicklaus   www.desertmountain.com
10333 East Rockaway Hills Dr, Scottsdale, AZ 85262   (480) 595-4000
        7,435 yds   Par 73   Rating: 75.2 / 147   (1987)

One of America's most successful golf/real estate developments, the Desert Mountain Club sits among the foothills of Apache and Lone Mountains, 25 miles north of downtown Scottsdale, and offers a remarkable six courses designed by Jack Nicklaus, all set amidst architecturally attractive low-density housing. The club's initial layout, the Renegade, occupies the property's lower slopes and is famous for introducing a rather bizarre concept: Instead of providing alternate tees for the purpose of flexibility, it offers alternate *greens* – or, frequently, an absolutely gigantic single putting surface with completely separate compartments. Thus allowing the layout's back tees to play to holes with nearly 450 yards worth of difference overall, it may seem a hokey concept, but 30 years later it's still rolling along, partially because there are lots of strong holes present. The non-returning routing forms a huge, clockwise circle, with outgoing favorites including the 449-yard uphill 3rd (whose longer right-side green is angled dangerously above a narrow dry wash), the eminently reachable 531-yard downhill 5th (ditto) and the 480-yard downhill 8th, whose longer green sits beyond more native sand. The 586-yard 10th is a tactically engaging (if complex) three-shotter and paves the way for a back nine led by first the 207-yard pond-crossing 12th and the 495-yard par-4 13th, then over a steadily ascending closing run by the 167-yard 16th (whose huge green is divided by two internal bunkers) and the 568-yard 17th, which plays to alternate fairways off the tee. The dual green concept does at times weigh in as gimmicky, but the Renegade remains widely rated among the state of Arizona's top 25 tests. **(GD**: #17 State)

Desert Mountain Club (Cochise) - Scottsdale   ♦♦♦

Jack Nicklaus   www.desertmountain.com
10333 East Rockaway Hills Dr, Scottsdale, AZ 85262   (480) 595-4000
        7,042 yds   Par 72   Rating: 72.8 / 143   (1988)

Chronologically, Desert Mountain's second course was the Cochise, by far the club's most recognizable layout as it hosted The Tradition (a Champions Tour Major) from 1989-2002. Though not originally intended as a tournament venue, its shorter carries and sporty par-5 finisher (a 511-yarder whose elevated green sits above a dry wash) proved a good fit for the seniors, and so there the event remained, producing a roster of champions that included Trevino, Floyd, Kite, Dr. Gil Morgan (twice) and Jack Nicklaus himself, who won here a remarkable four times. The dry wash-before-green theme was not reserved strictly for the 18th hole, as it earlier appears at the 546-yard 4th (an uphill dogleg left), the 341-yard 6th, the 424-yard uphill 10th and the 523-yard 12th, an uphill three-shotter which dares a long second across the wash, which also partially flanks the right side. Also present (à la the Renegade course) are alternate greens at the 6th and 13th, the latter a downhill par 3 offering two small, desert-surrounded targets measuring 140 and 138 yards. Overall, the standard of design may strike some as less engaging here, though numerous narrow, angled greens (especially at holes 8, 11 and 14) suggest an element of shotmaking on approach. Patently gimmicky, however, is the double island green that serves the 215-yard 7th and 548-yard 15th, a somewhat contrived concept anywhere – and especially so on the side of a mountain in the middle of the Sonoran desert.

Desert Mountain Club (Geronimo) - Scottsdale   ♦♦♦½

Jack Nicklaus   www.desertmountain.com
10333 East Rockaway Hills Dr, Scottsdale, AZ 85262   (480) 595-4000
            7,293 yds   Par 72   Rating: 73.5 / 147   (1989)

The third course to be built at the Desert Mountain Club was the Geronimo, which shares a clubhouse with the Cochise and occupies somewhat steeper terrain immediately west of its older sibling. One of the region's toughest courses, the Geronimo required a fair amount of creativity simply to be constructed over such land, with concessions including the presence of a par-3 finisher (a rarity in the Nicklaus Design portfolio) and an original 14th green so blind as to require a 40-foot flagstick (!) for directional purposes (since completely redesigned). Utilizing another non-returning routing, the front nine initially descends away from the clubhouse and is led by a quartet of strong holes: the 582-yard 1st (which offers a long, left-side desert carry for those hoping to get home in two), the 489-yard par-4 2nd, the 483-yard pond-guarded 5th and the 445-yard 6th, where a large, twisting dry wash affects both drive and approach. The action then kicks up a notch on the back nine, where both the 424-yard 10th and 190-yard 11th (played to an angled, ridgetop green) up the ante immediately with ravine-crossing approaches. The 564-yard downhill 12th then requires a second angled across a vast dry wash, setting up a finish that initially features the 510-yard uphill 15th (where a ravine flanks the right side and a centerline bunker complicates the drive) and the 497-yard 16th, a beast of a par 4 requiring a drive angled across a canyon. The 404-yard 17th (played uphill to a shallow, angled target) seems tame by comparison before the 197-yard 18th descends over a ravine to a green wedged into a rocky hillside beneath the clubhouse.   **(GD**: #13 State)

Desert Mountain Club (Apache) - Scottsdale   ♦♦♦

Jack Nicklaus   www.desertmountain.com
10333 East Rockaway Hills Dr, Scottsdale, AZ 85262   (480) 595-4000
            7,211 yds   Par 72   Rating: 74.1 / 136   (1996)

Desert Mountain's kinder and (somewhat) gentler Apache course is situated east of the club's main entrance road and, though still stretching slightly beyond 7,200 yards, was intended to be more forgiving, featuring some very large greens and bunkering which is both smaller and less invasive. There is, in fact, a fair amount of room to operate here, but the challenge still remains significant, with the lower-lying front nine being led by a trio of strong par 4s: the soundly bunkered 443-yard downhill 2nd, the downhill, dry wash-crossing 475-yard 4th (the layout's number one stroke hole) and the uphill 443-yard 8th, where a well-positioned bunker guards the favored left side of the fairway. The inward half then fans out north of the clubhouse and initially features a pair of strong dry wash-affected par 4s, the 450-yard 10th (where the approach diagonals across the hazard) and the downhill 455-yard 13th, where longer hitters might be tempted to try to carry 300 yards of native terrain to reach a favorably positioned section of right-side fairway. The 462-yard uphill 14th ranks as the layout's number two stroke hole and begins an arduous finish that includes the 182-yard pond-crossing 15th, the semi-blind 226-yard 17th (played to a very large, bunkerless green) and the 551-yard 18th, a peculiar test in that it offers two targets: a primary putting surface set beyond a rocky dry wash and a shorter 496-yard option situated precisely where one would ideally lay up if playing to the longer version. Hardly "Scottish" in character, but a different sort of test from its five siblings.

Desert Mountain Club (Chiracahua) - Scottsdale   ♦♦♦½

Jack Nicklaus   www.desertmountain.com
10333 East Rockaway Hills Dr, Scottsdale, AZ 85262   (480) 595-4000
                7,347 yds   Par 72   Rating: 75.2 / 151   (1999)

Arguably the most demanding of the Desert Mountain Club's six Jack Nicklaus-designed courses, the Chiracahua carries a bit more pretense about it, with phrases like "the Pine Valley of the Desert" initially being bandied about – rather a stretch given its 600 feet of elevation change, and the presence of Desert Forest (which might actually merit such comparisons – if loosely) at the bottom of the hill. Still, this is a highly demanding layout whose non-returning routing initially makes a brief early climb, then a long descent to the 12th green before ascending its way back through a particularly tough closing stretch. A quirky early note is sounded at the 287-yard uphill 2nd, where crossbunkers complicate attempts at driving a green perched near the top of a small canyon. But thereafter, the scale of things expands significantly, with front nine favorites including the 656-yard 3rd (a downhill, dry wash-crossed dogleg right), the descending 230-yard 5th, the 461-yard pond-guarded 7th and the 156-yard 8th, an all-carry test played across an arroyo to a surprisingly large green. The stronger back nine opens with the downhill 482-yard 10th, a brutal two-shotter (and the number one stroke hole) whose small green is perched above a rocky dry wash. Following two more demanding par 4s and a ravine-crossing par 3 (the 206-yard 12th) The run home is then led by the 159-yard 14th (based upon Riviera's famed "doughnut" 6th) as well as uphill entries like the 582-yard 15th (which twice crosses a dry wash), the 516-yard 17th (where a wide arroyo divides the lay-up zone) and the 424-yard dogleg right 18th, whose right side is flanked by a small ravine. (**GD**: #10 State)

Desert Mountain Club (Outlaw) - Scottsdale   ♦♦♦

Jack Nicklaus   www.desertmountain.com
10333 East Rockaway Hills Dr, Scottsdale, AZ 85262   (480) 595-4000
                7,107 yds   Par 72   Rating: 73.5 / 147   (2003)

Desert Mountain's sixth and final Jack Nicklaus-designed course, the Outlaw, opened in 2003, and features a homesite-free design on the huge property's eastern boundary, along the edge of Tonto National Forest. Despite fewer forced carries and numerous smaller bunkers, it may not live up to its "links-like" marketing (it is, after all, situated on a desert mountainside) but it is a friendlier, more traditional layout devoid of man-made water hazards, and one whose vastly more compact routing actually makes walking a realistic possibility. Quirky moments include several shared fairways, a pair of double greens, a gargantuan putting surface at the 338-yard 14th and, most of all, a routing that returns to the clubhouse at the 338-yard driveable 10th rather than the par-5 9th. The significantly longer outward half provides plenty of backbone within its par 4s, first at the 512-yard 3rd (a downhill dogleg left), then later at the 430-yard uphill 7th and the 475-yard 8th, which shares the 7th's fairway as it descends to a shallow, bunker-fronted green. The aforementioned downhill 10th (with its very shallow target) is indeed tempting and kicks off a back nine whose most engaging entries include the similarly driveable 14th (whose massive green extends back nearly 80 yards), the 532-yard uphill 16th (where bunkers divide the lay-up zone) and the demanding 464-yard 18th, which descends to a very long and narrow green angled along a left-side arroyo.

The Estancia Club - Scottsdale ♦♦♦♦

Tom Fazio
27998 North 99th Pl, Scottsdale, AZ   85262
7,314 yds   Par 72   Rating: 74.3 / 148   (1995)

www.estanciaclub.com
(480) 473-4400

Located on the opposite side of Pinnacle Peak from Jack Nicklaus's Desert Highlands, The Estancia Club is a scenic, big-budget Tom Fazio design which has gained great fame over the course of its existence due to how attractively it blends with the mountains, rock formations and cactus that creep at its edges. Marked by low-density housing whose architecture generally mixes equally well with the native landscape, the course is laid out in two separate loops, the nines neatly divided by a mountain ridge which, for the most part, represents the layout's primary strategic component. Though fairly sturdy at 7,314 yards, and carrying a solid-enough 74.3 rating, Estancia has proven itself challenging yet also willing to yield to superior golf, as its course record – a dazzling 58 by Bubba Watson – readily indicates. Play opens with a descending 459-yard par 4 and the layout's first really demanding test, the 240-yard tightly bunkered 3rd is also routed downhill. The 504-yard 4th offers an obvious birdie opportunity before play reaches a run of holes that are substantially affected by the mountain ridge and which, in the main, represent the best run of golf on property. This stretch begins with the beautiful 478-yard 5th, whose elevated tee sits upon a rocky crest, resulting in a downhill drive played to a ribbon of fairway tightly squeezed by a pair of bunkers. Next comes the quirky 369-yard 6th, an uphill test which curls rightward along the base of the ridge, daring a blind drive to the right side of a bunker-divided fairway. The 147-yard 7th descends from the mountainside to a small green guarded by a prominent front-left bunker, and if the 457-yard downhill 8th moves away from the mountain, the 571-yard 9th returns it to a place of prominence as the hole's latter 300 yards curl gently rightward along the escarpment's base. The slightly longer back nine then commences with a pair of short but memorable uphill tests, with the 341-yard 10th climbing to a bunker-fronted green situated upon a rock-and cactus-dotted hillside. However, this serves as little more than a warm-up for the 137-yard 11th, where Fazio's positioning of the putting surface beyond some enormous left-side boulders turned a challenging section of real estate into a true conversation piece. Next up are a pair of strong par 4s, with the 459-yard 12th descending gently to a narrow green angled beyond front-right sand, and the 411-yard 13th playing over a left-to-right-sloping fairway to another well-bunkered target. The 631-yard 14th is the layout's longest hole and, after initially doglegging left around a pair of invasive fairway bunkers, plays to a green guarded left by the property's lone pond – a slightly out-of-place hazard made further incongruous by a greenside bunker which descends into it beach-style. The 453-yard uphill 15th plays over another tightly bunkered fairway to a green protected primarily by a right-side tree, and opens a stretch run which includes the 195-yard 16th, the 584-yard 17th (which doglegs left before tumbling downhill) and the 462-yard 18th, a very demanding uphill dogleg left played to a narrow, right-to-left-angled putting surface. Though undeniably a very fine layout, it can be argued that Estancia occasionally follows the frequent Fazio pattern of scoring a bit better on scenery than strategy. To wit: *Golf* magazine does not include the club among its national top 100, while *Golf Digest* has often rated it between 70th and 100th – buoyed heavily by an "Aesthetic" score somewhere in the 20s. This may not represent an ideal balance, but the place *does* look fantastic... **(GD: #74 USA, #1 State   GW: #31 Modern)**

1	2	3	4	5	6	7	8	9	Out
459	389	240	504	478	369	174	457	571	3641
4	4	3	5	4	4	3	4	5	36
10	11	12	13	14	15	16	17	18	In
341	137	459	411	631	453	195	584	462	3673
4	3	4	4	5	4	3	5	4	36

FireRock Country Club - Fountain Hills

Gary Panks
16000 E FireRock CC Dr, Fountain Hills, AZ 85268
7,001 yds   Par 72   Rating: 73.0 / 134   (2000)

www.firerockcc.com
(480) 836-8100

Anchoring a spacious community of single-family homes situated in the hills northeast of Scottsdale, the FireRock Country Club offers a new millennium Gary Panks design of reasonably high playing interest and challenge. With homesites mostly set well back from the line of play, many holes offer a pleasantly natural feel – and while a lack of flashy strategic questions may detract in an obvious sense, the absence of overcooked hazarding only adds to the rustic appearance. The front nine is the tamer half, and is led by the 403-yard 3rd (a well-bunkered downhill test with water right of the green), the 145-yard 6th (played over native terrain to a narrow target) and the 399-yard mountain-flanked 9th, an arroyo-crossing dogleg right. The back is both longer (3,584 yards) and far more engaging, and is built around a trio of strong par 4s: the 454-yard 10th (whose shallow green sits beyond another arroyo), the 444-yard 13th (which turns leftward, around a large hillside) and especially the 484-yard 15th, where a pond must be carried off the tee and a second water hazard flanks the green's left side. Also notable down the stretch are the 335-yard 14th (driveable, but across/between a collection of five bunkers), the 393-yard 16th (where more water bothers the right side) and the 558-yard 18th, which tumbles downhill to a green set 20 yards beyond one final arroyo.

Leisure World Country Club (Coyote Run) - Mesa

Greg Nash
908 South Power Rd, Mesa, AZ 85206
6,437 yds   Par 73   Rating: 69.7 / 120   (1985)

www.leisureworldgolfarizona.com
(480) 634-4370

Originally built on open farmland in the east Phoenix suburb of Mesa (today the state's third largest city in its own right), Leisure World is an established retirement community whose golf facilities are led by its newer Coyote Run course, a short Greg Nash-designed layout on the development's west side. By no means confusable with the region's many stronger, more modern tests, this is housing-flanked recreational golf whose 69.7 rating speaks directly to its lack of difficulty. Better players will find the occasional engaging entry here but nearly always on a smaller scale, with favorites including pond-bothered par 4s like the 344-yard 1st and the 328-yard 7th, as well as a finishing stretch led by the 214-yard lake-flanked 16th, the 494-yard 17th and the 372-yard 18th, a dogleg right daring a drive across an invasive lake. On the longer side, the 499-yard dogleg left 4th plays to a tightly bunkered green, while the 561-yard 5th runs straightaway to a pond-side putting surface. The club also offers an executive 18 known as Heron Lakes (page 100).

Mesa Country Club - Mesa

William P. & William F. Bell   www.mesacountryclub.com
660 West Fairway Dr, Mesa, AZ 85201   (480) 964-1797
             6,887 yds   Par 72   Rating: 72.5 / 131   (1949)

One of Arizona's most established golfing facilities, the Mesa Country Club was built in 1949 by the Billy Bells, but has been substantially reconfigured since, largely via an Arthur Jack Snyder renovation in 1986. Yet despite such changes, this is a facility which has had time to settle into its landscape, resulting in a mature, tree-lined test which, having been grandfathered past Arizona's 90-acre turf limit, can in spots feel borderline parkland in nature. The layout is short by modern standards but there is plenty of solid golf here, particularly on a much longer par-37 front nine which spends much of its time occupying the higher ground south of the clubhouse. Initially the loop is led by a trio of strong par 4s: the 460-yard 3rd (flanked left by the Tempe Canal), the 422-yard 4th (a sharp dogleg left around trees) and especially the 419-yard 6th, a tough uphill dogleg left of some regional fame. The 198-yard tightly bunkered 7th plays downhill and across a bend of the Canal, while the 546-yard 9th returns home by slipping between a right-side lake and a small pond sitting front-left of the green. The back is both shorter and less engaging, and after the 504-yard 13th (a short par 5 played across the club's entrance road) is led by its trio of par 3s: the 185-yard pond-flanked 11th, the stiff 231-yard 14th and the 154-yard 16th, which descends across the entrance drive to a well-bunkered green.

Mirabel - Scottsdale

Tom Fazio   www.mirabel.com
37401 North Mirabel Club Dr, Scottsdale, AZ 85262   (480) 437-1500
             7,147 yds   Par 71   Rating: 72.8 / 136   (2001)

In a new millennium era of golf development not always marked by economic prudence, Mirabel made for an especially interesting case study. For here, on a moderately sloping tract just south of Desert Mountain, a new ownership group elected to tear up a ready-to-open Greg Norman design (originally called Stonehaven) and bring in Tom Fazio to essentially start from scratch. The result, some $8 million later, is a typically appealing Fazio design – long on highly polished aesthetics, but only moderately stocked with holes of tactically oriented playing interest. But certainly Mirabel offers plenty of engaging golf, with fairways wide enough to encourage the frequent use of the driver, and greens that are often large and well contoured. The front nine lies north of the clubhouse and is led by strong par 4s like the scenic 439-yard 3rd, the demanding 472-yard 4th (whose narrow green angles beyond front-left sand) and the 456-yard into-the-wind 9th. The back forms a clockwise loop to the south and kicks off with an imposing pair of its own, the 449-yard pond-guarded 10th and the scenic 178-yard 11th, where Pinnacle Peak looms in the distance. The finishing stretch is then set up by the soundly bunkered 466-yard 13th before featuring the 423-yard 16th (where sand again affects the tee ball) and the 474-yard 18th, a suitably challenging, uphill closer. By most accounts, the present Mirabel is a measurably better golf course than the tough, very narrow daily fee track which it replaced - but was it worth an extra $8 million when the result, though impressive, isn't even Fazio's highest rated design in Scottsdale? **(GD: #16 State)**

Moon Valley Country Club - Phoenix   ♦♦½

Dick Wilson   www.moonvalleycc.com
151 West Moon Valley Dr, Phoenix, AZ 85023   (602) 942-0000
              7,216 yds   Par 72   Rating: 74.3 / 125   (1959)

Located in an attractive residential neighborhood that was wide open desert at the time of its construction, Moon Valley is one of Arizona's more time-honored clubs, boasting an aesthetic maturity not always found in these parts. Originally a 1959 Dick Wilson design which was partially reconfigured during the late 1980s, the layout was significantly modernized and expanded by Bob Cupp in 1999. Remaining mostly true to Wilson's routing (there was little choice with the houses already in place), Cupp's good-size layout features only a smattering of water, though its presence is certainly felt at the 190-yard 5th, the 412-yard 9th (where both pond and creek front the putting surface), the 396-yard 17th and the 454-yard 18th, a dogleg left with a pond filling the corner. There is enough size and bunkering present to test better players, but with one double green (serving holes 2 and 8), and a huge putting surface at the 9th doubling as the practice green (à la Oakmont), Cupp's work is not without contrivance either. Notably, the LPGA visited from 1987-2003, and it was here, in 2001, that Annika Sorenstam became the first woman ever to card a competitive 59. A bunkerless 18-hole par-3 course (page 101) adjoins.

Paradise Valley Country Club - Paradise Valley   ♦♦♦

Lawrence Hughes   www.paradisevalleycc.com
7101 North Tatum Blvd, Paradise Valley, AZ 85253   (602) 840-8100
              6,887 yds   Par 72   Rating: 73.0 / 132   (1954)

A long-ago *Golf Digest* column once observed that in most major cities, the club generally assumed to be *the* golfing organization of choice usually isn't, that honor instead being reserved for some quieter, less-flashy, older-money facility. Inasmuch as many observers might assume that its unparalleled location and history would make the Phoenix Country Club the region's most prestigious, *Golf Digest* was right, for in area social circles Paradise Valley is widely viewed as *the* place to be. In this light, "less flashy" is not a bad description of the club's Lawrence Hughes-designed layout, a flat and fairly basic desert track which has recently taken a big step forward via a renovation by Bill Coore and Ben Crenshaw. With only a single water hazard in play (a lake which flanks the 401-yard 8th), the renovation focused mostly on enhancing the strategic element of the bunkering, such as the addition of two centerline hazards at the 524-yard 4th, and another in the lay-up zone of the 517-yard 6th. Further, several shorter doglegs now have multiple bunkers strategically guarding their corners (including the 362-yard 7th and the 474-yard par-5 13th) while holes like the lakeside 8th, the 440-yard 11th and the 425-yard 17th all more readily favor approaches played from the hazarded side of their fairways. Pre-dating Arizona's 90-acre turf limit, this is a lush oasis situated beneath scenic Camelback Mountain, and it now possesses a layout more in line with the club's overall experience.

Phoenix Country Club - Phoenix

Harry Collis   www.phoenixcc.org
2901 North 7th St, Phoenix, AZ 85014   (602) 263-5208
                    6,763 yds   Par 71   Rating: 72.6 / 131   (1919)

Any discussion of the history of golf in Arizona must begin with the Phoenix Country Club,
the oldest still-extant course in the Southwest. Though the club was actually playing the
game (on different sites) as early as 1900, this facility dates to 1919 when Harry Collis
managed to shoehorn 18 holes into barely 100 acres in close proximity to the city center.
So small a property has defied expansion, however, so while the course has frequently
been modernized (most recently by John Fought and Tom Lehman in 2002), the club's
run as a PGA Tour host ended in 1986. Its championship history, however, is impressive,
for it stands among a select few to have hosted PGA Tour events in six different decades,
having entertained 37 Phoenix Opens and two Western Opens, and counted among its
champions Hall-of-Famers like two-time winners Nelson, Hogan, Demaret and Mangrum,
as well as Nicklaus, Palmer, Middlecoff, Miller and Bobby Locke. Today a shortish, tree-
lined layout, it is enlivened by several modern-era ponds which particularly affect a trio
of par 3s: the 164-yard 2nd, the 194-yard 13th and the 178-yard 15th. Among the longer
holes, favorites include several tree-narrowed par 4s: the 457-yard 3rd, the 460-yard 10th,
the 444-yard 11th and the 411-yard pond-guarded 17th. Most notable, however, is the
527-yard par-5 18th, a short, pond-flanked centerpiece of winter golf telecasts throughout
the 1970s and '80s which is once again on display nationwide as the Champions Tour has
scheduled their season-ending Charles Schwab Championship here in 2017 and '18.

Pinnacle Peak Country Club - Scottsdale

Dick Turner   www.pp-cc.org
8701 East Pinnacle Peak Rd, Scottsdale, AZ 85255   (480) 585-0385
                    7,095 yds   Par 72   Rating: 74.0 / 131   (1976)

Though more fitting at the time of its opening, Pinnacle Peak's name rings a bit less true
now that Desert Highlands and Estancia have actually been built on the slopes of the
nearby eponymous landmark. Renovated at least twice since its inception (most recently
by Dick Phelps in 1996) it provides a rather different look than most in the neighborhood,
for as another facility old enough to be exempt from Arizona's 90-acre turf limit, its lush
fairways and closely flanking desert-style homes often more resemble Palm Springs than
Scottsdale. But Pinnacle Peak is also a sneaky-tough test whose strongest holes come
towards the close of each nine, including the pond-guarded 400-yard 8th, the similarly
watery 170-yard 9th, and the twisting 588-yard 18th, where water squeezes the left side
on the second shot but ends well shy of the putting surface. On the dryer side, backbone
is provided by longer par 4s like the 431-yard 5th, the 468-yard straightaway 7th, the 439-
yard dogleg left 13th and the 424-yard bunker-squeezed 17th. But while all of this adds up
to a fair degree of challenge, tactically engaging holes are at a premium, all of which
makes this a solid enough layout, but one pegged a notch or two below the area's elite.

Red Mountain Ranch Country Club - Mesa   ◆◆◆

Perry & Pete Dye   www.rmrcc.com
6425 East Teton, Mesa, AZ 85215   (480) 981-6501
                6,795 yds   Par 72   Rating: 73.3 / 144   (1986)

Red Mountain Ranch is one of a generation of courses laid out primarily by a Dye son (Perry claimed full credit for it on an older version of the family website) but which, for obvious marketing reasons, touts itself as being at least partially a product of Pete's legendary hand. The property was a difficult one for flood control/drainage reasons, as well as the high density of its interior housing, and in this light the results are fairly impressive, for Red Mountain Ranch provides considerable challenge without relying upon either backbreaking length or plentiful water hazards to do so. Further, with the exception of the 201-yard 11th (an attractive-but-demanding par 3 played to a green angled rightward into a lake), what water there is appears only on shorter holes, and many greens are only sparingly bunkered. Present, however, is plenty of Dye quirkiness, particularly on holes like the watery, 164-yard 6th, the 201-yard 15th (a dry one-shotter whose wildly shaped putting surface is nonetheless buttressed by railroad ties) and the 413-yard bunkerless 16th, whose narrow green is flanked left by a steep grass fallaway. More "normal" tests include a pair of demanding early par 4s (the 455-yard 1st and the 452-yard 3rd) and two more water-bothered holes on the back nine, the 397-yard 13th (where a lake flanks the fairway's left side) and the 354-yard pond-fronted 18th. Housing-flanked at every turn, but there is some offbeat, often interesting golf present.

Rio Verde Country Club (White Wing) - Rio Verde   ◆½

Milton Coggins   www.rioverdearizona.com
18731 East 4 Peaks Blvd, Rio Verde, AZ 85263   (480) 471-7010
                6,391 yds   Par 71   Rating: 70.5 / 123   (1971)

One half of the 36-hole private segment of a trio of adjacent golfing communities, the Rio Verde Country Club's White Wing course is located 10 miles east of Scottsdale, between McDowell Mountain Regional Park and the Tonto National Forest. Along with its sister Quail Run layout, White Wing was designed by local architect Milton Coggins in 1971, and has thus been around long enough to be lined by housing for the entirety of its routing. It is, on the whole, fairly basic in nature, with eight of its greens entirely unbunkered and only three par 4s exceeding 400 yards. Not surprisingly, this trio collectively rates among the layout's strongest entries, with the 436-yard 5th being a sharp dogleg right, the 456-yard pond-guarded 12th offering enough challenge to fit in almost anywere, and the 423-yard 13th playing to a second straight pond-flanked putting surface. Also notable are the 194-yard tightly bunkered 6th and the 264-yard 11th, a quirkily dangerous two-shotter whose predictably small green backs up flush against a pond.

Rio Verde Country Club (Quail Run) - Rio Verde   ♦½

Milton Coggins   www.rioverdearizona.com
18731 East 4 Peaks Blvd, Rio Verde, AZ   85263   (480) 471-7010
            6,493 yds   Par 72   Rating: 71.0 / 122   (1971)

The other half of the Rio Verde Country Club's 36-hole facility is the Quail Run course which, like the neighboring White Wing layout, was designed by Milton Coggins in 1971. Also housing-lined throughout, Quail Run stretches northward out of the same clubhouse and, though slightly longer, is similar in its recreational, relatively undemanding style. Water is a somewhat greater presence here, however, adding interest at holes like the 432-yard 3rd (where it closely flanks the left side on approach), the 195-yard 4th (which crosses a corner of the same hazard), the 372-yard pond-fronted 13th, and especially the 487-yard 18th, whose lay-up zone is tightly squeezed by a hazard which goes on to flank the right side of the green complex. Also worthy of mention are a pair of par 3s (the 206-yard 2nd - mostly for its size – and the 159-yard pond-flanked 16th) as well as two more invasively bunkered par 5s on the front side, the 458-yard 6th and the 461-yard 9th. Both could easily be converted to strong par 4s, but such doesn't seem to be the M.O. here.

Scottsdale National Golf Club (Mineshaft) - Scottsdale   ♦♦♦½

Jay Morrish & Dick Bailey   www.sngc.com
28490 North 122nd St, Scottsdale, AZ   85262   (480) 443-8868
            7,571 yds   Par 72   Rating: 75.0 / 144   (2003)

Originally known as the Golf Club of Scottsdale, this geographically isolated facility sitting near the base of Fraesfield Mountain was purchased in 2013 by internet magnate and PXG club developer Bob Parsons, who has drawn considerable attention with both his expansion of the facility and reconfiguration of its membership. This, the club's original course, was built by Jay Morrish and Dick Bailey, who chose not to mar such a pristine site with man-made water hazards (though their copious modern bunkering can hardly be called "minimalist"), helping to create one of the more peacefully remote golfing experiences in all of Arizona. Massive par 4s are the rule here, though often with a significant dose of strategy thrown in, such as at the 456-yard 3rd and the 480-yard 4th (both of which feature centerline bunkers off the tee) and the 474-yard 14th, a heavily bunkered dogleg left. The 571-yard 10th offers split fairways off the tee and the 240-yard 12th is bothered by a short-left dry wash, but the back nine was originally marketed mostly around its final four holes, three of which (numbers 15-17) climb into the adjacent foothills. Parsons (with help of ex-Tom Fazio associates Tim Jackson and David Kahn) has made the layout more walking-friendly by filling in an arroyo on the 565-yard uphill 15th – while also adding the deep, railroad tie-buttressed "mineshaft" bunker behind the green after which the layout has been rechristened. Add in the remodeled 488-yard par-4 closer and regardless of ownership, this remains one of the Scottsdale area's toughest (and most housing- and development-free) golfing experiences. **(GD**: #14 State**)**

Scottsdale National Golf Club (Other) - Scottsdale   N/A

Tim Jackson & David Kahn   www.sngc.com
28490 North 122nd St, Scottsdale, AZ 85262   (480) 443-8868

Following his 2013 purchase of the former Golf Club of Scottsdale, former GoDaddy.com boss Bob Parsons expanded the club's acreage significantly, with the biggest chunk being added by the purchase of 223 acres to the west previously slated for development by Desert Mountain creator Lyle Anderson. This enabled Parsons to add both one of the world's quirkiest/most difficult par-3 courses (see page 103) as well as to build what has officially been named The Other Course, a big, rough-edged layout designed by former Tom Fazio associates Tim Jackson and David Kahn. Though not enough information on this brand new layout was available at the time of this writing, early indications are that this it quickly rank among the region's strongest courses, as it incorporates numerous natural dry washes and arroyos (as well as one man-made lake at the par-3 9th) and appears to offer considerable design variety within its 18 demanding holes.

Seville Golf & Country Club - Gilbert   ♦♦½

Gary Panks   www.clubcorp.com
6683 South Clubhouse Dr, Gilbert, AZ 85297   (480) 722-8100
          7,036 yds   Par 72   Rating: 73.1 / 126   (2001)

Featuring a modern Gary Panks design located in Phoenix's far southeastern suburbs, the Seville Golf & Country Club is the anchor of another expansive real estate development, with most fairways lined by the usual rows of single-family homes – though frequently at a comfortable distance. This is also a layout with a touch of the derivative about it, a point driven home by the 146-yard 17th, which is an unambiguous copy of Pete Dye's famed island-green 17th at Florida's TPC Sawgrass. And indeed, to a large degree it is water which defines Seville, for its most interesting holes all feature prominent man-made ponds. Going out these include the 516-yard 5th (where a right-side pond squeezes the lay-up zone), the 430-yard 6th and the 375-yard 7th, where most of the large putting surface sits beyond a front-right lake. Coming home, the dangerous 17th heads a closing trio which also includes the 314-yard 16th (driveable, but with its right side skirting the same lake that houses the 17th) and the 543-yard 18th, where a crossing pond affects the second, and the green angles leftward behind both the pond and a long bunker.

Silverleaf - Scottsdale   ♦♦♦½

Tom Weiskopf   www.silverleafclub.com
19890 North 101ˢᵗ Way, Scottsdale, AZ   85255   (480) 568-1821
                7,322 yds   Par 72   Rating: 74.7 / 149   (2002)

Its clubhouse set discreetly back from East Thompson Peak Parkway, tucked away behind
a small residential neighborhood, Silverleaf is a long but widely varied Tom Weiskopf
design which makes good use of the natural desert terrain while only briefly (at the 418-
yard 13ᵗʰ) employing a single man-made water hazard. As with most of Weiskopf's work,
there is lots of large, strategically oriented bunkering, a circumstance readily visible at
outbound favorites like the 206-yard 5ᵗʰ (a long uphill one-shotter whose angled green is
framed by five bunkers), the 423-yard centerline-bunkered 6ᵗʰ, the 194-yard over-the-
desert 7ᵗʰ and the 569-yard 8ᵗʰ, a fine par 5 played across a barranca to a green angled
between bunkers and more open desert. Coming home the downhill 13ᵗʰ offers several
options off the tee (including driving close to the pond-flanked green), while both the
427-yard 15ᵗʰ and 209-yard 16ᵗʰ hopscotch across some particularly intimidating native
terrain. This sets the stage for an equally tough pair of closers, the 436-yard 17ᵗʰ (whose
green is tucked behind more impeding desert) and the 498-yard 18ᵗʰ, a huge downhill par
4 which tumbles its way across a narrow dry wash to a large, undulating putting surface.
Though not always the first layout mentioned in a list of Weiskopf's top Arizona works,
Silverleaf enjoys more undeveloped desert along its flanks than most in the region. That,
plus a fairly high level of both challenge and variety allow it to hold its own among the
area's best layouts, making for an attractive, worthwhile stop. **(GD**: #11 State**)**

Sun City West (Pebblebrook) - Sun City West   ♦½

Greg Nash   www.rcscw.com
19803 R.H. Johnson Blvd, Sun City West, AZ   85375   (623) 544-6037
                6,410 yds   Par 72   Rating: 70.0 / 120   (1979)

Amidst this sprawling Del Webb-constructed mini-city, a collection of seven private golf
courses are operated by the Recreation Centers of Sun City West, a group composed of
four regulation layouts and three executive facilities. Like all six to follow, the first layout,
the Pebblebrook course, was built by area design stalwart Greg Nash and is narrowly
rated the easiest of the club's regulation courses. It occupies a flattish, oddly shaped
tract hemmed in by housing and was designed mostly to a functional standard, with only
three of its par 4s exceeding 400 yards and its water hazards - though plentiful – seldom
affecting play too closely. The outward half sits west of the clubhouse and offers a run of
four solid tests: the 533-yard tree-narrowed 4ᵗʰ, the 339-yard pond-flanked 5ᵗʰ, the 429-
yard 6ᵗʰ (the number one stroke hole) and the 504-yard 7ᵗʰ, a straightaway entry with
water lurking right of the green. The back nine then lies across 128ᵗʰ Avenue to the east
and features the 510-yard 17ᵗʰ, where a pond pinches the right side of the lay-up zone.

Sun City West (Grandview) - Sun City West   ◆½

Greg Nash   www.rcscw.com
19803 R.H. Johnson Blvd, Sun City West, AZ 85375   (623) 544-6037
           6,775 yds   Par 72   Rating: 72.3 / 129   (1985)

Sun City West's second golf course was the Grandview, whose layout is built partially around the Banner-Del Webb Medical Center where, with its greater length and more imposing bunkering, it is more suitable for the community's better golfers. The 3,405-yard front nine circumnavigates a large residential neighborhood and is anchored by a quartet of solid par 4s: the 400-yard dogleg left 2nd, a pair of bunkerless entries at the 430-yard 5th and the 425-yard 7th, and the tightly bunkered 350-yard 9th. The back then follows a long out-and-back routing to the southeast of Meeker Road, where it opens and closes on high notes with the 336-yard 10th (another well-bunkered test) and the 400-yard 18th, which bends rightward along a huge fairway bunker en route to a small, tightly bunkered triangular green. However, the loop's strongest entries lie at the property's eastern tip, where the 575-yard 13th crosses a creek before bending rightward along a lake and the 421-yard 14th has its fairway divided by a huge centerline bunker.

Sun City West (Trail Ridge) - Sun City West   ◆½

Greg Nash   www.rcscw.com
19803 R.H. Johnson Blvd, Sun City West, AZ 85375   (623) 544-6037
           6,581 yds   Par 72   Rating: 71.2 / 128   (1991)

The 1990s saw the arrival of Sun City West's third regulation-size course, Trail Ridge, which follows a huge (if narrow) clockwise routing through a sea of surrounding homes to the northeast of U.S. Route 60. Another reasonably challenging Greg Nash-designed test, test, Trail Ridge adds an element of flavor by more frequently utilizing native desert terrain along its flanks; indeed, the layout includes only 27 man-made bunkers, and fully one-third of those are reserved for the 353-yard 15th. The desert is seldom really invasive but it often lies closer to the fairway than one might expect, injecting life into holes like the 361-yard 4th (whose fairway is pinched from the right side), 420-yard 10th, the 368-yard 11th (where native sand encroaches from the left) and the 544-yard dry wash-crossed 13th. The finish is also strong, first at the 214-yard 16th (whose narrow green is backed by water), then at the 503-yard 17th (featuring native sand and a deep, very narrow waterside green) and the 415-yard 18th, a straightaway, desert-narrowed closer.

Sun City West (Deer Valley) - Sun City West   ♦½

Greg Nash & Billy Casper   www.rcscw.com
19803 R.H. Johnson Blvd, Sun City West, AZ 85375   (623) 544-6037
            6,547 yds   Par 72   Rating: 70.5 / 122   (1994)

Sun City West's Deer Valley course is one of the community's two private facilities upon
which Greg Nash enlisted the help of Hall-of-Famer Billy Casper to complete the layout's
design – though stylistically, it is little different from Nash's other user-friendly Sun City
creations. Situated along the enormous development's north side, it is – per the Sun City
norm – housing-lined from stem to stern and counts only three lakes meaningfully in
play. However, it does make fairly regular use of the native landscape alongside many
holes as well as some large man-made bunkers – but even so, few entries can truly be
called standouts. The front nine forms a large, counterclockwise circle to the west,
where it offers the 518-yard soundly bunkered 4th, the 209-yard 5th and the 405-yard 6th,
a challenging dogleg left. The back nine then ventures eastward across Deer Valley Road,
where its stronger entries include a pair of pond-bothered tests at the 397-yard 11th and
the 367-yard 12th, as well as the tightly bunkered 535-yard 15th and the 351-yard 18th, a
bunker-lined dogleg right whose green is flanked by one last pond along its right edge.

Tatum Ranch Golf Course - Cave Creek

Bob Cupp   www.tatumranchgc.com
29888 N Tatum Ranch Dr, Cave Creek, AZ 85331   (480) 585-2399
            6,860 yds   Par 72   Rating: 72.4 / 134   (1987)

A mid-size, occasionally interesting layout situated in this small town north of Scottsdale,
Tatum Ranch dates to 1987 and features a desert aesthetic colored both by surrounding
housing and architect Bob Cupp's modern shaping. The odd engaging moment does
appear, however, notably at the 348-yard 7th (which curls rightward, around the club's
lone water hazard), the 151-yard 11th (played diagonally across a dry wash) and the 305-
yard downhill 12th, which offers driving the green (across two prominent bunkers) among
its several tee shot options. But more representative are some long, tough but not
terribly engaging par 4s like the narrow 444-yard 5th (where native sand closely flanks
both sides of the driving zone), the dry wash-crossed 445-yard 10th and, down the
homestretch, the 470-yard 15th (played slightly downhill) and the 467-yard uphill 18th –
which, in its original configuration, was saddled with a predictable/gimmicky double
green shared with the par-3 16th. Cupp did succeed in working a fairly good-size layout
into a compact site, but the resulting back-and-forth nature of the routing is one reason
why this rates a notch or two below the region's very best.

Terravita - Scottsdale   ♦♦½

Greg Nash & Billy Casper
34034 North 69th Way, Scottsdale, AZ 85266
7,075 yds   Par 72   Rating: 73.4 / 142   (1994)

www.terravita.com
(480) 488-3456

Located just across North Scottsdale Road from the famed Boulders Resort, Terravita was a groundbreaking development in 1994, being the Del Webb Company's first project not aimed specifically at the 55-and-over retirement market. Successful enough that its impressive mountain backdrops now frame waves of fairway-side housing, it opens with a front nine that mixes the notable (the sandy 610-yard double dogleg 3rd) with the solid (heavily bunkered two-shotters like the 366-yard 5th and the 358-yard 9th) and the semi-awkward (the 422-yard dry wash-crossed 6th). The back fires its biggest shot immediately at the 442-yard 10th (a pond-guarded dogleg right) before featuring engaging par 5s at the 524-yard dry wash-fronted 12th and the rugged 594-yard 14th, where a tree-dotted native area presses into the right side of the lay-up zone. Also effective are the 439-yard 15th and the 409-yard 18th (whose driving zone is squeezed by a huge right-side bunker), while the faintly awkward is once again visited at the 354-yard dogleg left 17th, a slightly downhill test requiring longer hitters to threaten several left-side houses should they have a go at driving the green. Solid enough stuff, but this is a competitive market.

Troon Golf Club - Scottsdale   ♦♦♦½

Tom Weiskopf & Jay Morrish
25000 North Windy Walk Dr, Scottsdale, AZ 85255
7,041 yds   Par 72   Rating: 73.9 / 146   (1985)

www.trooncc.com
(480) 585-4310

Located immediately east of Desert Highlands, the Troon Golf Club was Tom Weiskopf and Jay Morrish's first architectural collaboration (indeed it was Weiskopf's first design, period) as well as one of the pioneer courses in the Scottsdale golf boom of the 1980s and '90s. Flanked by some low-density housing and substantial elevations, it was a huge hit upon its 1985 arrival – though this was surely due, at least in part, to the newness of the visually striking desert golf concept. The front nine does a long out-and-back north of the clubhouse and is the rather more contrived half, for it includes a double green (serving holes 2 and 7) as well as man-made ponds guarding this green complex, plus those of the 507-yard 8th and the 411-yard 9th. The 460-yard 2nd and 463-yard 6th are the loop's backbone, but somewhat more engaging are the 541-yard 3rd (which twice crosses a prominent dry wash) and the 296-yard 4th, a drive-and-pitch which dares one to thread the needle through some rough native areas. The higher-profile back nine is situated south of East Happy Valley Road and, after opening with the 395-yard split-fairway 10th, features the 440-yard 14th (where a sharp descent separates the driving area from the approach), the attractive 139-yard 15th (which backs up against Troon Mountain) and the 347-yard 16th ("The Gunsight"), whose tee shot is aimed between two rock formations. Also noteworthy is the 629-yard 17th, which crosses a dry wash en route to a shallow centerline-bunkered green. Long gone are the days when *Golf Digest* ranked Troon 41st in the nation and *Golf* magazine rated it 64th in the world (!), but this remains a strong test, and one of the region's more architecturally significant stops. **(GD**: #18 State)

Whisper Rock Golf Club (Lower) - Scottsdale   ♦♦♦½

Phil Mickelson & Gary Stephenson   www.whisperrockgolf.com
32002 North Old Bridge Rd, Scottsdale, AZ   85262   (480) 575-8700
                7,417 yds   Par 72   Rating: 75.0 / 147   (2001)

A trendy new millennium address among PGA Tour pros, the Whisper Rock Golf Club is a low-key 36-hole facility set well back from surrounding roads just south of The Boulders resort. A golf-only club, it began first with its Lower course, a very tough but consistently interesting layout built by Phil Mickelson and former Panks & Graham associate Gary Stephenson at the start of the new millennium. The 496-yard par-4 1st (with approach played diagonally across a dry wash) immediately sets the tone and there are plenty of similarly grand two-shotters to follow, led by the 450-yard 5th (where desert nips at the green's left edge), the 450-yard dogleg right 10th (its putting surface backed by a 15-foot depression), the 486-yard 14th (played to a near island green amidst the scrub) and the 470-yard 16th, where a stonewalled dry wash flanks the left side of the approach. Though the par 3s are arguably the layout's least distinguished component, several huge desert-hopping par 5s are quite another story, led by the 573-yard 8th (where an arroyo fronts the green complex), the 554-yard 11th (whose narrow putting surface angles leftward, behind a large bunker) and especially the 600-yard 18th, where a wide dry wash slashes across the fairway, then continues up the left side. Curiously, while the Lower carries a higher rating and slope than the Upper, and presents at least as many tactical options, it is often the less-honored layout in course rankings – perhaps because the Mickelson/Stephenson pedigree is not quite as marketable as Tom Fazio's? But as "second" courses go, this is very solid stuff.   (**GD**: #172 USA, #5 State   **GW**: #164 Modern**)**

Whisper Rock Golf Club (Upper) - Scottsdale ♦♦♦♦

Tom Fazio   www.whisperrockgolf.com
32002 North Old Bridge Rd, Scottsdale, AZ 85262   (480) 575-8700
        7,550 yds   Par 72   Rating: 74.9 / 145   (2005)

To illustrate the degree the Whisper Rock Golf Club has become a home to professional golfers, it has been estimated that upwards of 30 touring pros (owning at least 11 Major championship trophies) are members, a number of whom can be considered household names. Indeed, a favorite story – not necessarily apocryphal – holds that 2006 U.S. Open champion Geoff Ogilvy once finished 10th in the club championship in the same week he tied for 9th in a PGA Tour event. As noted on the previous page, this is a genuine golf-only facility; swimming pools and tennis courts are entirely absent and housing is limited to a small neighborhood of opulent homes set between the entry gate and the Lower course, plus a single row of homesites adjacent to the 9th fairway of the Upper. With the club having opened around Phil Mickelson's first major design project in 2001, the idea of choosing another outside-the-box architect to lay out the Upper course in 2005 might well have been a realistic one. But instead, the job went to the period's biggest name, Tom Fazio, who answered the bell by producing one of his best-received courses – a tough, man-sized layout tailored more for a PGA Tour-heavy membership than, say, a retirement-oriented facility. While Fazio's trademarked polished aesthetic varies a bit from the somewhat more rustic feel of the Lower course, the Upper also adds a slightly different dimension by utilizing some hillier terrain on the property's northwestern corner, as well as by incorporating a man-made lake significantly into play at the finishing hole. The action opens in a somewhat unforgiving manner as both the 449-yard dogleg left 1st and the 412-yard 2nd feature driving zones tightened by invasive bunkering, while the 394-yard 4th allows the golfer to choose from multiple lines of play among two large bunkers and a wide stretch of left-side desert. The scale of things then picks up as the action moves into the property's eastern reaches, first at the 581-yard 5th (where a centerline bunker just shy of the green complicates aggressive seconds), then at the 487-yard 6th, where one of the layout's wider fairways is lined down its left side by out-of-bounds. The 411-yard bunker-narrowed 7th might be viewed as something of respite before the nine concludes with two more broad-shouldered entries, the 260-yard 8th (whose green angles leftward among a trio of bunkers) and the 608-yard 9th, with its putting surface tucked left, beyond another patch of native sand. The 479-yard 10th is another long, bunker-narrowed two-shotter and sets up what many consider the Upper course's most engaging test, the 179-yard 11th, which plays diagonally across the length of a tree-flanked dry wash. The 603-yard 12th is a strong three-shotter whose uphill approach slips between a pair of rocky outcroppings before the ascent is made to higher ground for two of the layout's shortest tests, the 322-yard 13th (potentially driveable from a tee perched among rocky terrain) and the downhill 169-yard 14th, whose narrow green is angled between sand and another rock-strewn hillside. The closers are then anchored by a pair of huge par 4s, the 512-yard downhill 15th and the 501-yard 18th, a brutal finisher which bends rightward along Fazio's utterly incongruous lake. Many observers may disagree with the magazines which rate the Upper course the stronger layout but regardless, boasting about as much design variety as the desert will allow (sans island greens and other carnival-like stunts), Whisper Rock is, by any measure, the top 36-hole facility in Arizona.   (**GD**: #167 USA, #4 State **GW**: #128 Modern)

1	2	3	4	5	6	7	8	9	Out
449	412	210	394	581	487	411	260	608	3802
4	4	3	4	5	4	4	3	5	36
10	11	12	13	14	15	16	17	18	In
479	179	603	322	169	512	561	422	501	3748
4	3	5	4	3	4	5	4	4	36

Arizona Biltmore Golf Club (Adobe) - Phoenix   ♦♦½

William P. Bell   www.arizonabiltmore.com
2400 East Missouri Ave, Phoenix, AZ 85016   (602) 955-9655
            6,430 yds   Par 71   Rating: 70.2 / 120   (1928)

One of the Southwest's legendary resort hotels, the Arizona Biltmore occupies its own scenic compound in the shadow of Piestewa and Squaw Peaks, just a short drive from downtown Phoenix. Its 36 holes of golf began with 1928's Adobe course, a much-altered Billy Bell design situated on the south side of the hotel. Neither long nor overly difficult, the Adobe occupies mostly flat and open terrain, with the somewhat longer front nine led by strong par 4s like the 412-yard 1st (where a creek and pond flank the right side), the 397-yard pond-fronted 3rd and the 411-yard 5th, as well as the 486-yard par-5 6th, where a centerline bunker impedes the lay-up zone. The shorter back nine opens with the 340-yard dogleg right 10th (where right-side sand raises tactical questions off the tee) and eventually closes with a short but engaging stretch that includes the 512-yard pond-flanked 14th, the 141-yard 16th (played to a quasi-boomerang green), the driveable 311-yard 17th and the 494-yard creek-lined 18th. Though neither overly demanding, nor entirely classic-feeling in a Golden Age sense, the Adobe does boast a bit of history, with the LPGA visiting both from 1963-1965 and 1983-1986, allowing the renowned resort to count Hall-of-Famers Marlene Hagge and Betsy King among its champions.

Arizona Biltmore Golf Club (Links) - Phoenix   ♦♦

William Johnston   www.arizonabiltmore.com
2400 East Missouri Ave, Phoenix, AZ 85016   (602) 955-9655
            6,300 yds   Par 71   Rating: 69.7 / 124   (1978)

The newer half of the Arizona Biltmore's 36 holes, the William Johnston-designed Links course begins with a front nine routed clockwise around the Adobe, separated from it by a neighborhood of affluent single family homes. Though measuring less than 3,000 yards, this loop is occasionally squeezed a bit by adjacent commercial development, but does open with a tricky little par 4 (the 351-yard 1st) and later includes two fairly strong par 5s, the 532-yard water-flanked 2nd and the 529-yard 9th. Requiring a significant cart ride to reach, the more substantial back nine runs lies north of the famed Frank Lloyd Wright-inspired hotel where it wends its way among several residential neighborhoods. Early highlights here include the 549-yard uphill 10th and the 434-yard 13th, a genuinely strong two-shotter with out-of-bounds left and a narrow green angled along right-side sand. The closers are also solid and include the 387-yard dogleg left 16th, the 451-yard downhill 17th and the 521-yard 18th, whose green sits beyond a wide, grassy depression. Though arguably a bit stronger than the neighboring Adobe course, the Links represents pleasant desert golf but without the history of its far longer-running sibling.

Arizona Golf Resort & Conference Center-Mesa   ♦♦½

Arthur Jack Snyder   www.azgolfresort.com
425 South Power Rd, Mesa, AZ 85206   (480) 832-3202
                6,542 yds   Par 71   Rating: 70.8 / 120   (1965)

Dating to 1965, the Arizona Golf Resort is one of the region's older courses, with mature cottonwood and eucalyptus trees (as well as long rows of housing) lining many fairways. But as with so many early desert designs, the golf is seldom more than functional, with variety at a premium; indeed the par 3s all range between 175-217 yards, while the par 5s are similarly wedged between 480-494. The strongest challenges come quickly, with the first four holes including a lake-flanked par 5 (the 494-yard 1st), the layout's longest par 4 (the 445-yard 3rd) and two big one-shotters, the 217-yard 2nd and 226-yard 4th. Thereafter, however, play is largely defined by straight, lightly bunkered holes of only middling interest – leaving the 175-yard 14th (an attractive test played over water to a slightly elevated green) to stand out. Caveat emptor: This course has some of the most invasive cart paths ever built, potentially allowing several longer holes to be shortened via gigantic bounces off paths running literally right up the center of fairways.

Arizona Grand Resort - Phoenix   ♦♦♦½

Forrest Richardson   www.arizonagrandresort.com
8000 S. Arizona Grand Pkwy, Phoenix, AZ 85044   (602) 438-9000
                6,336 yds   Par 71   Rating: 68.8 / 124   (1988)

Formerly known as Phantom Horse, the Arizona Grand Resort lies adjacent to Phoenix's South Mountain Park where it features a golf course in two parts: Its opening eight holes are a neatly manicured bunch largely wedged among homes, the Maricopa Freeway and multiple man-made water hazards. Its final 10, on the other hand, climb into native desert terrain, ultimately shedding the housing (mostly) for some interesting golf. The 387-yard 1st (whose tee sits upon an island that originally housed the 18th green) and the 392-yard pond-guarded 2nd set the tone for the first eight, with its watery, modern vibe being continued at holes like the 362-yard dogleg left 4th and the 211-yard 8th. The desert begins to creep in around the edges at the par-4 9th and 10th before showing up more noticeably at the 535-yard 11th, which teasingly skirts some native terrain. The landscape is embraced even further at the 124-yard 12th, the 538-yard 13th (whose narrow, very long green sits atop a bunker-lined hillside) and the 157-yard 14th, before play closes with a pair of notable entries, the 307-yard 17th (a slightly awkward dogleg right played to another narrow putting surface built into the foothills) and the 241-yard 18th, which plunges 75 feet off a desert hillside to a much larger target.

The Boulders Resort Golf Club (North) - Carefree   ♦♦♦

Jay Morrish   www.bouldersclub.com
34831 N. Tom Darlington Dr, Carefree, AZ 85377   (480) 488-9028
                6,959 yds   Par 72   Rating: 73.3 / 138   (1985)

Doubling as a private residential community, the Boulders Resort was an early player in Arizona's modern golf boom, and is also noteworthy as the lone solo design project completed by Jay Morrish between his stints working for Jack Nicklaus and partnering with Tom Weiskopf. Morrish's 36 holes received plenty of attention during the 1980s, and while his desert stylings may not seem quite as cutting-edge today, the imposing rock formations from which the club draws its name still form a uniquely attractive golfing backdrop. The two courses wander over this distinctive, often housing-flanked terrain, and though they are similar in size and challenge, the longer North carries a slightly higher rating and slope. It initially features a pair of engaging par 5s (the 513-yard 1st and the 548-yard creekbed-fronted 3rd) before playing through a varied front nine led by the 425-yard dogleg left 5th and the 347-yard 9th, whose L-shaped green backs up against sand and a rocky hillside. The much longer back nine opens with stiff par 4s at the 451-yard uphill 10th and the 441-yard 11th, and quickly backs them up with the 457-yard 13th, a stiff, dry wash-fronted test. Following the 183-yard over-water 14th, the finishing run is also quite strong, culminating with the 424-yard 16th (played to another dry wash-fronted putting surface), the downhill 220-yard 17th and the 424-yard 18th, a dogleg right to a green guarded left by both sand and water. **(GW: #128 Resort)**

The Boulders Resort Golf Club (South) - Carefree   ♦♦♦

Jay Morrish   www.bouldersclub.com
34831 N. Tom Darlington Dr, Carefree, AZ 85377   (480) 488-9028
                6,917 yds   Par 71   Rating: 72.9 / 142   (1991)

The Boulders Resort's South course came along six years after its sister North, and while the two layouts measure up relatively equally in most ways, the more scenic South has tended to hold more sway with course raters, if only by a nose. Play opens over four holes which actually sit in the property's northern half, the best of which is the 409-yard 4th, which calls for an approach across a pond-bottomed swale and is rated the number one stroke hole. Thereafter, several of the layout's best holes fall in the middle of the front nine, including the 545-yard split-fairway 5th, the 355-yard 6th (which commences high upon a massive rock formation in spectacular fashion) and the 455-yard dry wash-jumping 8th. Beginning far afield, the inward half bears the quirkiness of including back-to-back par 3s at the 15th and 16th, and is notable mostly for the potentially driveable 348-yard 12th (played between trees and native desert to a heart-shaped green), the 460-yard 17th (which calls for a long, desert-pinched approach) and the 583-yard 18th, a straightaway par 5 whose putting surface angles rightward around a pond. Like many upscale desert courses, the surrounding housing is architecturally harmonious with the landscape, a large aesthetic plus. Further, Morrish elected to introduce man-made water hazards sparingly, giving the entire facility a less-contrived look. Combine this with the presence of several massive rock formations, and the Boulders is able to retain one of the region's most recognizable and attractive resort identities. **(GW: #165 Resort)**

Camelback Golf Club (Padre) - Scottsdale   ♦♦½

Red Lawrence   www.camelbackinn.com
7847 North Mockingbird Lane, Scottsdale, AZ 85259   (480) 596-7050
6,868 yds   Par 72   Rating: 72.3 / 130   (1970)

Affiliated with Marriott's nearby Camelback Inn, the Camelback Golf Club offers a pair of early Arizona layouts built into a rather oddly shaped property three miles south of the Scottsdale Airport. The older Padre course dates to 1970, but Red Lawrence's original version was substantially renovated by Arthur Hills in 1999. Occupying land just north of the clubhouse, it follows a fairly compact routing built around a pair of interior residential neighborhoods and, being old enough to pre-date the state's turf restrictions, offers an appearance rather more manicured than desert-like. The longer front nine features a run of sturdy holes that includes the 553-yard 5th (a gentle dogleg right made interesting by two Hills-era lakes), the 410-yard 7th (which bends leftward around a 100-yard-long bunker) and a pair of watery closers, the 220-yard 8th and 518-yard 9th. The more tightly routed back nine is initially led by the 482-yard par-4 10th and the 508-yard 13th (a dogleg left to a green flanked by right-side water) before closing with a watery trio, the 351-yard 16th (with water at the green's left edge), the 198-yard 17th (ditto) and the 547-yard 18th, a locally prominent finisher whose narrow green is closely flanked by another Hills-designed water hazard. Lawrence's initial version was a functionally bunkered track with far less playing interest, so Hills' modernized version represents a significant step up.

Camelback Golf Club (Ambiente) - Scottsdale   ♦♦♦

Jason Straka   www.camelbackinn.com
7847 North Mockingbird Lane, Scottsdale, AZ 85259   (480) 596-7050
7,225 yds   Par 72   Rating: 74.3 / 139   (1978)

The Camelback Golf Club's second layout began life as a 1978 Arthur Jack Snyder design known as the Indian Bend course, which mostly occupied a narrow swath of land (the Indian Bend Wash) that extends northwestward, seemingly half way to Las Vegas. But in 2013, former Hurdzan & Fry associate Jason Straka performed a comprehensive redesign, building 17 new holes, reestablishing the wash as a more significant hazard, and reducing 200+ acres of maintained turf to around 90. The result was a layout which, after opening with what largely remains the original 1st hole, provides lots of size but also lots of room to use the driver, with the mostly wide fairways offering a fair amount of tactically sound bunkering as well. Going out, featured entries include the 556-yard soundly bunkered 3rd, the 328-yard 5th (driveable, but with water right), the strong 448-yard 6th and the 241-yard 8th, a stiff par 3 with the wash lying right of target. The longer back nine is anchored by its par 4s which initially include the 454-yard 12th and the 393-yard 13th, where tee shots played across a large right-side bunker open the ideal line of approach. The march home briefly encounters a central man-made lake (which can consume sliced tee shots at the 523-yard 16th) before closing with the 445-yard straightaway 17th and the 462-yard 18th, a gentle dogleg right which finishes 450 yards – one final long cart ride – from the clubhouse. Overall, a meaningful improvement over what came before it.

Golf Club at Eagle Mountain - Fountain Hills   ♦♦½

Scott Miller   www.eaglemtn.com
14915 E. Eagle Mountain Pkwy, Fountain Hills, AZ 85268   (480) 816-1234
           6,800 yds   Par 71   Rating: 71.2 / 136   (1996)

Located in Scottsdale's northeastern reaches, the Golf Club at Eagle Mountain is a mid-size test built by local designer Scott Miller to serve a same-named on-site inn. Fanning out to the south, its slightly longer (but far more compact) front nine is the less engaging half – though it is refreshingly free of artificial water hazards, and does include several strong par 4s, notably the 433-yard 2nd (played uphill to a bunkerless green) the 443-yard dogleg right 7th and the 456-yard 9th, a demanding, uphill dogleg left. The back nine then forms a wide clockwise circle to the west where it begins with the 535-yard 10th (played significantly downhill but to a green guarded by five frontal bunkers and a left-side lake) and the 461-yard 11th, another descending entry. As the routing then moves into hillier territory, the action peaks at a pair of shorter holes, the 384-yard 14th (played to a shallow, dry wash-fronted green) and the 129-yard 15th, a mere pitch angled across the same natural hazard. Also notable are the closers, the 345-yard 17th being a potentially driveable par 4 running parallel to Shea Boulevard, and the 18th a 420-yard two-shotter culminating in a waterside green. Though flanked by housing throughout, the club's remote location remains conducive to a fairly unencumbered desert golf experience.

Gainey Ranch Golf Club - Scottsdale   ♦♦½

Brad Benz & Mike Poellet   www.clubcorp.com
7600 East Gainey Club Dr, Scottsdale, AZ 85258   (480) 483-2582
      Arroyo/Lakes: 6,800 yds   Par 72   Rating: 71.9 / 128   (1986)
      Dunes: 3,376 yds   Par 36   Rating: 34.9 / 128   (1986)

An early player in the Scottsdale golf boom, Gainey Ranch has long benefited from a location much closer to civilization than some of the area's later arrivals. Its 27 holes are a fairly balanced group, and wind their way past all manner of housing (plus an on-site Hyatt Regency resort), with the Arroyo/Lakes combination rating the highest by a narrow margin. Not surprisingly, a largely grassed-over arroyo does much to define the former loop, crossing the fairway at the 386-yard 1st, flanking the 404-yard 4th, affecting the second and third shots at the 533-yard 5th, and guarding the inside of the dogleg at the 384-yard 7th. The 173-yard 6th and 555-yard 9th are also notable as the Arroyo's sole water holes, the latter daring a long lake-crossing second. The Lakes nine opens slowly but closes fast, led by the 521-yard 5th (a lake-guarded double dogleg), the similarly watery 410-yard 7th and the 492-yard par-5 9th, whose green juts right, into a pond backed by a geometrically layered waterfall built just beneath the clubhouse. The Dunes nine is the club's shortest (its longest par 4 is the 390-yard 7th) but does offer engaging entries like the 187-yard 4th (played across a huge frontal bunker), the 506-yard 6th (a dogleg right to a very narrow green) and the 550-yard 9th, another dogleg right, this one traversing the grassed-over arroyo. None too difficult a facility overall, but there is enough interesting golf present to entertain the great majority of visitors.

Kierland Golf Club - Scottsdale   ♦♦½

Scott Miller   www.kierlandgolf.com
15636 Clubgate Dr, Scottsdale, AZ 85254   (480) 922-9283
        Ironwood/Acacia: 6,974 yds   Par 72   Rating: 72.8 / 127   (1996)
        Mesquite: 3,478 yds   Par 36   Rating: 36.4 / 126   (1996)

Entertaining guests from the adjoining Weston Resort & Spa, the Kierland Golf Club is an unassuming Scott Miller design featuring three nines of fairly equal style and challenge, all of which opened in 1996. The Ironwood/Acacia combination is the highest rated, with the Ironwood being the club's longest nine but also, arguably, its least engaging. Routed partially around a residential neighborhood in the property's northwestern reaches, it includes five par 4s in excess of 410 yards (led by the 412-yard sand-flanked 6th) as well as two more holes of interest, the well-bunkered 200-yard 5th and the 495-yard par-5 9th, which is guarded by water down the entirety of its right side. The Acacia, meanwhile, is wedged somewhat tightly into the site's northeastern section, where it initially features the strong 448-yard 3rd (with green pinched between bunkers and natural desert) and the narrow, out-of-bounds-flanked 568-yard 5th. Both the 190-yard 6th (with its tough back-right pin) and the 219-yard 8th are solid par 3s, setting up the 531-yard 9th, where left-side water can affect the second and/or third. The Mesquite nine crosses East Greenway Parkway to the south and, after opening with several shorter holes, flexes some muscle at the 521-yard dry wash-fronted 5th, the 468-yard straightaway 7th and the 547-yard 7th, where a large bunker slashes into the preferred left side of the lay-up zone. Also notable is the 427-yard 9th, whose approach must carry a pond and four fronting bunkers.

Legacy Golf Resort - Phoenix   ♦♦½

Gary Panks   www.golflegacyresort.com
6808 South 32nd St, Phoenix, AZ 85040   (602) 305-5550
        6,966 yds   Par 71   Rating: 72.0 / 127   (1999)

Located on a rectangular, housing-oriented site five miles directly south of Sky Harbor Airport, the Legacy Golf Resort features a mid-size Gary Panks-designed layout that utilizes water only sparingly as it wanders through rows of homes and, in its northeast section, resort accommodations. The front nine starts out uneventfully before picking up steam at the 216-yard 4th, then peaking at the 571-yard 6th (a gentle dogleg left enhanced by some well-placed sand), the heavily bunkered 136-yard 7th and the soundly bunkered 442-yard 9th. The par-35 back nine includes a trio of par 3s, though its most memorable holes are the 580-yard 14th (where the layout's lone significant water hazard lies left of the lay-up zone and putting surface) and the 389-yard 16th, where invasive fairway bunkering narrows the favored right side. Among the one-shotters, the 185-yard 15th makes moderate use of the aforementioned lake, while 203-yard 17th plays to a narrow green which bends leftward around a huge bunker). Designed primarily for resort play, there is little that is overly flashy or difficult here, but with many well-positioned fairway bunkers, Panks' work does offer a reasonably high degree of playing interest.

Lookout Mountain Golf Club - Phoenix

William Johnston   www.tapatiocliffshilton.com
11111 North 7th St, Phoenix, AZ 85020   (602) 866-6356
          6,515 yds   Par 71   Rating: 70.0 / 130   (1989)

Built just a long par 4 from the affiliated Pointe Hilton Tapatio Cliffs, Lookout Mountain is one of the stronger works of former PGA Tour journeyman Bill Johnston, its shortish 6,515-yard layout utilizing some significantly undulating terrain to create a large number of tactically interesting holes. The course's routing is of particular interest, for lacking the requisite land immediately adjacent to the resort, Johnston instead used a nearby parcel to house a St Andrews-like parallel 1st and 18th, then a second similar patch (housing the 2nd and 17th) to reach Thunderbird Road, beyond which the remainder of the layout fans out. Golf-wise, the 461-yard par-4 4th gets the ball rolling, after which there follows a run of engaging golf which includes the 515-yard 5th (where a centerline bunker fronts a boomerang green), the stiff 238-yard 6th (angled across some native desert), the 527-yard tree-dotted 7th and the 115-yard 9th, a short pitch to a shallow green benched into a hillside. The back nine kicks off with the steeply downhill 419-yard 10th before peaking at a pair of tactically interesting downhill par 4s, the 417-yard 12th (where longer hitters can drive fairly close to the green across a wide stretch of desert) and the 344-yard dogleg left 14th, another reachable test but one toughened by a shallow green, a prominent tree and, perhaps, some adjacent housing. Curiously, man-made lakes suddenly appear to affect three of the four closers – but the more pressing question of why this rises so far above the rest of Johnston's design portfolio remains anybody's guess.

Los Caballeros Golf Club - Wickenburg

Greg Nash & Jeff Hardin   www.loscaballerosgolf.com
1551 S. Vulture Mine Rd, Wickenburg, AZ 85390   (928) 684-2704
          7,020 yds   Par 72   Rating: 73.1 / 137   (1979)

The Los Caballeros Golf Club is part of an eponymous resort and was built in 1979 upon a rolling site 55 miles northwest of Phoenix, but with its modest, unassuming bunkering and limited use of water, it manages to provide something of a classic feel. At 2,100 feet of altitude, its 7,020 yards aren't quite grueling, but there is plenty of challenging golf here just the same. The shorter front nine lies north of the clubhouse and is somewhat the less engaging half, with notable entries including the 536-yard soundly bunkered 5th, the 578-yard 7th (where a pond eats up nearly the entire lay-up zone, forcing some long approaches) and 213-yard 8th. The back nine, on the other hand, features a long run of solid holes, initially including the 599-yard out-of-bounds-lined 13th (which plays to an elevated green) and the 368-yard dogleg right 14th. The homeward run then ups the ante size-wise, with the 448-yard 16th incorporating a right side pond and several small trees, the 452-yard 17th climbing to a small, bunkerless green, and the 561-yard 18th descending past a lay-up zone sand to an angled, tightly bunkered putting surface. With only limited housing present and a healthy dose of mountain scenery, this is a pleasant desert stop.

McCormick Ranch Golf Club (Palm) - Scottsdale   ♦♦½

Desmond Muirhead   www.mccormickranchgolf.com
7505 East McCormick Pkwy, Scottsdale, AZ 85258   (480) 948-0260
                    7,044 yds   Par 72   Rating: 73.7 / 137   (1972)

Serving the on-site Scottsdale Resort & Conference Center and the immediately adjacent Millennium Hotel, the McCormick Ranch Golf Club features 36 holes built by Desmond Muirhead in the years before his work fell into the abyss of "symbolic" and geometric designs. Both courses wind among housing and several large lakes, with the slightly shorter Palm arguably being the more interesting. It is also, in spots, quite challenging, with the 446-yard lake-flanked 4th and the 214-yard tightly bunkered 5th setting an early tone before the front nine peaks over a particularly watery stretch which includes the 535-yard 7th (where a left-side lake tightly flanks both fairway and green), the 195-yard 8th (whose boomerang green bends left around a larger hazard) and the 408-yard 9th, which plays to either an S-shaped island fairway or a longer, safer option. The back nine lies across McCormick Parkway to the north where a pair of water-flanked par 5s (the 510-yard 12th and the 564-yard 16th) drew one's initial attention, but the loop is equally characterized by solid par 4s playing to angled, tightly bunkered greens like the 420-yard dogleg right 11th, the 448-yard 15th and the 428-yard 18th. Save for the island fairway at the 9th, there is little here that resembles the Desmond Muirhead so many like to ridicule.

McCormick Ranch Golf Club (Pine) - Scottsdale   ♦♦

Desmond Muirhead   www.mccormickranchgolf.com
7505 East McCormick Pkwy, Scottsdale, AZ 85258   (480) 948-0260
                    7,187 yds   Par 72   Rating: 74.4 / 135   (1972)

Though McCormick Ranch's Pine course actually carries a slightly higher rating than the Palm, standout holes are at more of a premium here, at least in part because water is far less frequently in play. Going out, the 390-yard 3rd features a very narrow green angled behind sand, while the 537-yard lakeside 4th and the 419-yard 6th both rely on water for their challenge, but in a manner rather less tactically engaging (or intimidating) than several holes on the Palm. The 211-yard tree- and bunker-guarded 8th is a stronger entry, paving the way for an inward half that initially features the strong 443-yard 11th, where drives flirting with a left-side lake open up a better angle of approach to another narrow putting surface. While holes like the 404-yard 14th and the 517-yard dogleg left 18th are solid enough, the loop's centerpiece is undoubtedly the 470-yard par-4 15th, a bunkerless test which requires sizeable water carries both off the tee and on approach, the latter being played to a large (and somewhat forgiving) island green complex. Fans of Muirhead's work – whomever they may be – will surely enjoy these solid layouts, though both are today largely overshadowed by many newer area facilities.

Orange Tree Golf Resort - Scottsdale

Lawrence Hughes & Johnny Bulla   www.orangetree.com
10601 North 56th St, Scottsdale, AZ 85254   (480) 948-3730
                6,740 yds   Par 72   Rating: 71.1 / 124   (1957)

One of Scottsdale's older golf facilities, Orange Tree sits just north of the Camelback Golf Club and features a 1957 Lawrence Hughes and Johnny Bulla design which, beyond the addition of a lake flanking the 9th and 18th greens (and 50 years of tree growth), is remarkably unaltered. Hughes in particular tended to build straight-ahead, functional courses with limited flair, and this is particularly in evidence on the front nine, where notables are largely limited to the 168-yard bunker-fronted 4th and a pair of water-affected closers, the 414-yard 8th (which is guarded short-left by a pond) and the 376-yard 9th, whose green angles behind the modern-era lake. The inward half is somewhat more engaging, and opens strongly with the 408-yard 11th (where a right-side pond is largely decorative) and the 188-yard 12th, whose front left water hazard is far more invasive. Coming home, the 409-yard 14th is a challenging dogleg right, the 501-yard out-of-bounds-flanked 17th has its approach partially bothered by a prominent left-side tree, and the 403-yard 18th is closely guarded by left-side water over its last 150 yards. Not as challenging as some, but with its maturity, more flavorful than many.

The Phoenician - Scottsdale

Ted Robinson   www.thephoenician.com
6000 East Camelback Rd, Scottsdale, AZ 85251   (480) 941-8200
        Oasis/Desert: 6,282 yds   Par 70   Rating: 69.1 / 128   (1986)
        Canyon: 3,008 yds   Par 35   Rating: 34.9 / 129   (1995)

One of Scottsdale's more opulent addresses, The Phoenician sits on the southern slopes of Camelback Mountain and features 27 shortish holes shoehorned into an oddly shaped site – thus requiring several herculean cart rides to make the routing serviceable. Though laden with Ted Robinson's unnatural water features (as well as the obvious question of why the resort opted for 27 short holes instead of a full-size 18), there is actually quite a bit more of interest here than on many a Robinson design. On the Oasis nine, this is evident at the pond-fronted 518-yard 2nd, the 211-yard 3rd (where an extension of the same hazard flanks the green) and the 379-yard sand-encircled 9th – though the 396-yard 7th, a 90-degree dogleg left with water lying blindly around the corner, is significantly awkward. Usually paired with the Oasis is the Desert, which initially offers the heavily bunkered 505-yard 2nd and the watery 303-yard 3rd before climbing into the foothills for the 443-yard uphill 5th and the downhill 180-yard 6th. The loop peaks, however, at the 502-yard 7th (whose fairway runs along the base of Camelback Mountain to a green tucked into a cove) and the 120-yard 8th, which plays from mountainside tees to a green squeezed between two hotel buildings. The remaining Canyon nine is a disjointed affair on the property's west side which, after six fairly basic holes, closes with the 201-yard pond-flanked 7th, the 132-yard lake-fronted 8th (located – following an extended cart ride – far out by the resort entrance) and the 525-yard 9th, an unwieldy dogleg right with water severely pinching the driving area and fronting the green.

San Marcos Golf Resort - Chandler   ♦♦½

Harry Collis & William Watson   www.sanmarcosresort.com
1 San Marcos Pl, Chandler, AZ 85225   (480) 812-0900
                6,626 yds   Par 72   Rating: 70.7 / 123   (1928)

Occasionally cited as Arizona's first course to play on grass greens (the Phoenix Country Club also makes a strong claim), today's Crowne Plaza San Marcos Resort has been playing on its present site since 1928 – though the club utilized a nearby sand nine as early as 1913. Not so very much has changed since the Roaring '20s, and with three par 5s under 480 yards, there is plenty of room left among the layout's 6,626 yards for some longer par 3s and 4s, most of which play to small, elevated, tightly-bunkered greens. The front nine boasts several of these, including early favorites like the 411-yard opener (a rolling, canal-crossing dogleg right, the unforgiving 212-yard 3rd and especially the 482-yard out-of-bounds-lined 4th. Thereafter, the loop also includes the 421-yard 6th (whose green is especially well bunkered) and the 428-yard dogleg left 7th, as well as the 160-yard 8th, which angles along a modern-era pond. The shorter back nine begins with the 454-yard 10th before downsizing over shorter entries like the 387-yard 11th (another hole which crosses the narrow canal), the watery 147-yard 13th, and the 509-yard 18th, one more canal-crosser, this time with out-of-bounds right. With its often-rolling fairways lined by mature trees, there is more of a classic feel here than at many a desert layout

Talking Stick Golf Club (O'odham) - Scottsdale   ♦♦♦½

Bill Coore & Ben Crenshaw   www.talkingstickgolfclub.com
9998 East Indian Bend, Scottsdale, AZ 85256   (480) 860-2221
                7,133 yds   Par 70   Rating: 72.7 / 125   (1997)

Serving as the primary amenity of the Salt River Pima-Maricopa Indians' adjacent hotel and casino, Talking Stick was a relatively early entry in the Coore & Crenshaw design portfolio, and its 36 fairly compact holes succeed in providing visitors with widely varied golfing experiences. The O'odham course (née the North) is comfortably the higher rated layout (no surprise given that it's 300 yards longer with a par of 70) but is also more consistent with the traditional C&C style, relying upon the land's natural features (as well as some of the region's more interesting green complexes) to create something rather different in Arizona golf. This is apparent early on at the 552-yard 2nd and 450-yard 3rd, both of which hug an arrow-straight left-side out-of-bounds fence and offer ideal angles of approach to tee shots cozied close to the boundary. Even more engaging, however, is the 433-yard 4th, a split-fairway test whose bunker-framed right-side option shortens the hole considerably. The longer back nine then offers several muscular holes of distinction, including the 261-yard par-3 11th and a trio of strong par 4s: the 445-yard dogleg right 14th, the 461-yard 15th and the 471-yard 18th, an obviously demanding finisher. The most engaging test of all, however, is the 392-yard 12th, where drives which reach a sliver of alternate fairway wedged between a dry wash and more out-of-bounds avoid a delicate pitch across the dry wash on the second. Though perhaps not as purely refined as would eventually become the Coore & Crenshaw norm, this is a strong, fun and unique test, and one which makes much out of a flat, mostly featureless site. **(GW: #160 Resort)**

Talking Stick Golf Club (Piipaash) - Scottsdale ◆◆◆

Bill Coore & Ben Crenshaw   www.talkingstickgolfclub.com
9998 East Indian Bend, Scottsdale, AZ 85256   (480) 860-2221
6,833 yds   Par 71   Rating: 72.1 / 127   (1997)

The Talking Stick Golf Club's shorter Piipaash course (née the South) was clearly intended to represent a slightly different golfing style, offering wider, often tree-flanked fairways and – oddly for designers Bill Coore & Ben Crenshaw – artificial water hazards affecting play on five holes. The less-engaging front nine features two huge par 4s (the 471-yard out-of-bounds-lined 5th and the 476-yard dogleg right 8th) but its highlight may well be the simple-yet-thought-provoking 4th, a 327-yarder where a single centerline bunker and out-of-bounds define the direct route to an appropriately tiny green. The back nine then introduces the water, which initially appears in the form of the lake which closely flanks the left side of the 392-yard 11th. A run of noteworthy (and more natural feeling) dry golf immediately follows and features the 441-yard dogleg right 12th, the tightly bunkered 152-yard 13th and especially the 541-yard 14th, whose lay-up zone divides around a long dry wash. The water reappears at the finish, however, first affecting the 548-yard 16th (where it angles across the lay-up zone), then framing the 184-yard 17th and defining the 323-yard 18th, an offbeat, driveable closer which dares a tee ball angled across a lake to a suitably small green wedged between its banks and a pair of left-side bunkers. By any measure, this is very solid "second course" stuff - if a tad less rustic than fans of Coore & Crenshaw have come to expect based on their work in the years since.

TPC Scottsdale (Champions) - Scottsdale ◆◆◆

Tom Weiskopf & Jay Morrish   www.tpc.com/scottsdale
17020 North Hayden Rd, Scottsdale, AZ 85255   (480) 585-4334
7,115 yds   Par 71   Rating: 73.7 / 140   (1987)

Sitting just across North Greenway Hayden Loop to the east of TPC Scottsdale's famed Stadium course, the less famous Champions layout was also built by Tom Weiskopf & Jay Morrish, but it has since undergone a $12 million 2007 renovation at the hands of Randy Heckenkemper. Lengthened by nearly 700 yards, the Champions has been transformed from a kinder and gentler sibling into a full-size, tactically interesting test in its own right, with natural desert terrain now flanking many fairways and a trio of lakes meaningfully affecting four holes. Though the Pima Freeway and lots of corporate development touch the layout's outer reaches (holes 6-8 actually wrap around a pair of new resort hotels) there are a number of engaging holes present, particularly in the form of two highly strategic tests utilizing the native terrain, the 477-yard 5th (a dual-fairway dogleg left offering a shortcut over water) and the adjacent 359-yard dogleg left 15th, which dares a long carry over rough territory. The outward half, which forms a counter-clockwise circle around the property's perimeter, also features the 461-yard straightaway 2nd and the 575-yard 9th, where an arroyo must be carried on the second and a small lake lies short left of the green. The 3,692-yard back nine then offers solid early par 4s at the 474-yard 11th and the 446-yard 12th but is better defined by a strapping close which, following the tempting 15th, includes the 213-yard 16th, the 605-yard straightaway 17th and the 460-yard 18th, where water closely guards much of the left side.

TPC Scottsdale (Stadium) - Scottsdale   ♦♦♦♦

Tom Weiskopf & Jay Morrish   www.tpc.com/scottsdale
17020 North Hayden Rd, Scottsdale, AZ 85255   (480) 585-4334
7,261 yds   Par 71   Rating: 74.7 / 142   (1986)

Entertaining guests from the multiple major resorts built around its edges, the Stadium course at the TPC Scottsdale is seldom rated among the elite courses in Arizona; indeed, at the time of this writing, *Golf Digest* doesn't even rank it among the top 10 course in Scottsdale. Yet upon its opening, it came to near-immediate fame as the permanent home of the PGA Tour's Phoenix Open (under various corporate monikers) beginning in 1987, a run of tournament golf which has endowed the club with numerous memorable moments, and made several of its holes among the most famous in desert golf. Following the then-popular TPC "Stadium Golf" template, designers Tom Weiskopf and Jay Morrish created a spacious track that has an eye on spectator friendliness – a point brought richly into evidence each February when, even allowing for some wild exaggerating of numbers, the Phoenix Open annually draws the largest galleries (easily) in the world of professional golf. But beyond such economic considerations, this is also one of the more engaging layouts in the often-cookie-cutter TPC chain, beginning with a par-35 front nine which stretches over 3,600 yards and opens with a pair of mid-size par 4s followed by the 558-yard 3rd, a straightaway test which makes a late jog rightward to a green angled beyond a dry wash. The 183-yard 4th then backs up against the Scottsdale Princess hotel, a notable point only in that hereafter, the routing ventures away from flanking development almost completely. And this is also where the action begins to pick up, for the front nine's strongest golf lies within a trio of longer par 4s which includes the 470-yard dry wash-crossing 5th, the 475-yard 8th (a gentle dogleg left) and the 453-yard 9th, which is made especially interesting by the centerline pot bunker that fronts its shallow putting surface. Better known, however, is a TV–friendly back nine which opens with the 428-yard 10th, a dogleg right which, as part of a 2014 renovation, had the huge bunker which fills its corner extended further downrange. There follows a pair of well-known water holes in the 472-yard 11th (where a large lake flanks the entirety of the left side) and the 192-yard 12th, which somewhat quirkily features the same hazard guarding the green both long and right. One hole which was substantially affected by the 2014 renovation was the 558-yard 13th, where what was once a very wide fairway divided by a patch of native terrain has been narrowed to normal proportion (removing the site of a controversial 1999 ruling allowing fans to move a boulder for Tiger Woods), and lay-up zone bunkering has been significantly altered. The action then turns for home at the 490-yard par-4 14th (a gentle dogleg left) and the 553-yard 15th, where left-side water squeezes the fairway and the green is set upon an island. The 332-yard 17th has become famous as a driveable pond-side par 4 (whose putting surface includes a dangerous back left quadrant pinched between sand and water) while the 442-yard 18th features left-side water (and a new Church Pew bunker) off the tee. But most celebrated of all – by miles - is the 163-yard 16th, really just a basic par 3 but one made famous/infamous by the rowdy crowds (reportedly 16,000) which fill its surrounding bleachers and skyboxes each February. Despite having decent size and a solid 74.7 rating, this is also a layout which annually yields some very low scores (including Mark Calcavecchia's then-record 256 total in 2001, and Phil Mickelson's lipping out a putt for 59 in 2013) – a good indicator of a well-designed track capable of rewarding skilled play. **(GD**: #22 State)

1	2	3	4	5	6	7	8	9	Out
403	442	558	183	470	432	215	475	453	3631
4	4	5	3	4	4	3	4	4	35
10	11	12	13	14	15	16	17	18	In
428	472	192	558	490	553	163	332	442	3630
4	4	3	5	4	5	3	4	4	36

Viewpoint Golf Resort - Mesa

Michael Rus   www.viewpointgolfresort.com
650 North Hawes Rd, Mesa, AZ 85207   (480) 373-5555

6,324 yds   Par 71   Rating: 69.2 / 117   (1996)

A large RV-oriented facility located just south of the Red Mountain Freeway and the Salt
Gila Aqueduct, the Viewpoint Golf Resort plays over both a short regulation-size 18 and a
nine-hole executive course (page 109), layouts which, beyond both being crossed by
power lines, are somewhat different in character. The 6,324-yard regulation 18 is a
compact affair occupying small enough acreage to be turfed from wall to wall, a major
aesthetic difference from most modern desert courses. Its design, however, is largely
basic, with water usually more decorative than dangerous and quality longer holes at a
premium. A primary exception is the 481-yard par-5 18th where, provided one's drive
manages to avoid the invasive power lines, the temptation will be to go for a shallow
green which extends leftward into a pond. Rather more representative, however, are
shorter par 4s like the 337-yard 2nd (where a left-side creek pinches the driving zone), the
321-yard tightly bunkered 10th and the 340-yard pond-narrowed 13th. Housing being
limited strictly to the perimeter is a positive but overall, this is fairly basic stuff.

We-Ko-Pa Golf Club (Cholla) - Fort McDowell

Scott Miller   www.wekopa.com
18200 E. Toh Vee Circle, Fort McDowell, AZ 85264   (480) 836-9000

7,225 yds   Par 72   Rating: 73.4 / 138   (2001)

One of the Scottsdale area's more outlying facilities, the Yavapai Indian-owned We-Ko-Pa
Golf Club serves an adjacent resort and casino complex and features a pair of strong,
housing-free courses which are quite different in character and style. Scott Miller's older
Cholla layout is longer and flashier, mining playing interest from the surrounding desert
as well as several split fairways and the property's lone significant water hazard. Play
opens with an immediate run of strong holes, led by the strategic 351-yard 1st (where an
optional left-side sand carry leaves an easy pitch), the dry wash-crossed 588-yard 2nd, the
469-yard 4th, and a pair of desert-crossing par 3s, the 178-yard 3rd and the stiff 207-yard
5th. Most noteworthy, however, might be the 350-yard uphill 7th, whose fairway is split
by a large section of rock-and-brush, with the right side offering a better angle into a
tightly bunkered green. The slightly shorter back nine is arguably the more interesting
half and is initially dotted with quirky holes like the 566-yard 10th and the 420-yard 13th
(both marked by dead-center trees in their driving zones) as well as the 327-yard 15th,
which plays to an enormous, driveable putting surface. The closing trio is a muscular
group and includes the 472-yard 16th (a dry wash-crossed dogleg left where longer hitters
may have to lay up), the 578-yard 17th and the 432-yard split-fairway 18th, where a long
drive across left-side sand removes a right-side lake from play on the second. There is
plenty of engaging golf here to be sure, though the more classically inclined may favor
the resort's Coore & Crenshaw-designed alternative. **(GW: #67 Resort)**

We-Ko-Pa Golf Club (Saguaro) - Fort McDowell   ♦♦♦½

Bill Coore & Ben Crenshaw   www.wekopa.com
18200 E. Toh Vee Circle, Fort McDowell, AZ   85264   (480) 836-9000
6,966 yds   Par 71   Rating: 72.0 / 137   (2006)

The We-Ko-Pa Golf Club's Coore & Crenshaw-designed Saguaro course is one of the region's top public-access facilities, for it utilizes the natural roll of the terrain (not to mention the presence of the namesake cacti) and lots of strategic bunkering to create a shorter but highly engaging test – a sort of classic-style test in the midst of an open desert. The layout's overall length is actually misleading as three of its best holes are sub-340-yard par 4s: the 336-yard 2nd, the 331-yard blind (and centerline-bunkered) 7th and the simple but quite engaging 337-yard 10th, which plays to a heavily contoured green horseshoed around a tiny fronting bunker. The equally tiny 137-yard 9th demands similar precision but the remaining front nine standouts are much grander, led by the 469-yard arroyo-hopping 1st, the 631-yard 4th (requiring another blind tee shot) and the 442-yard 6th, a bunkerless dogleg left. The back nine's most obviously tactical hole is the 538-yard split-fairway 14th, where the narrower right-side option shortens the hole considerably. However, the loop is really better characterized by the 197-yard 11th (whose green angles rightward, behind sand), the 255-yard 15th (where the bunkering lies to the left) and the 508-yard par-4 closer, an imposing brute which dares a diagonal drive across dangerous native country. And therein lies the rub: While the 14th hole offers a brief shot of flash, the Saguaro is more about lay-of-the-land, old-fashioned substance that is not immediately apparent on a course map or yardage guide. Thus while it may not rate among Coore & Crenshaw's absolute elite, the Saguaro still stands comfortably among the region's very best. (**GD**: #19 State, #98 USA Public **GW**: #33 Resort)

Whirlwind Golf Club (Devil's Claw) - Chandler   ♦♦½

Gary Panks   www.whirlwindgolf.com
5692 North Loop Rd, Chandler, AZ 85226   (480) 940-1500
7,029 yds   Par 72   Rating: 72.6 / 129   (2000)

A 36 hole complex located within the Gila River Indian Community (where a Sheraton resort and the Wild Horse Pass Casino stand adjacent), Whirlwind's Gary Panks designs are a challenging but relatively understated pair, relying more on strategic bunkering and a set of sturdy par 4s than flash or a dozen artificial water hazards. The older Devil's Claw course lies north of the resort complex and follows a non-returning routing (though the 9th green is within a short par 5 of the clubhouse), and it demonstrates this tactical bent early on at holes like the 424-yard 1st, the 399-yard 2nd, the 593-yard 3rd and the 410-yard 5th, all of which include prominent bunkering on the side of the fairway which offers the best line of approach to the green. The challenge becomes slightly flashier late in the front nine, with the 160-yard 7th playing across a corner of the layout's lone lake, the 317-yard 8th being potentially driveable (but bothered by a well-placed right-side fairway bunker) and the 441-yard 9th offering dual fairways, with the narrower, harder-to-reach left-side option shortening the hole significantly. The inward half is a tad less engaging but includes several more soundly bunkered par 4s as well as a pair of widely varied par 3s, the stiff 222-yard 12th and the 172-yard 14th, whose green angles leftward beyond the course's largest bunker. Among the closers, most memorable is the 551-yard 17th, where a wide swath of native terrain crosses the fairway 75 yards shy of the putting surface.

Whirlwind Golf Club (Cat Tail) - Chandler   ♦♦♦

Gary Panks   www.whirlwindgolf.com
5692 North Loop Rd, Chandler, AZ 85226   (480) 940-1500
         7,334 yds   Par 72   Rating: 73.6 / 133   (2002)

The Whirlwind Golf Club's newer, longer Cat Tail course is rated a full stroke tougher than the Devil's Claw and, beyond matching its sibling's non-returning routing, also boasts a slightly higher degree of playing interest throughout. This is initially evident during a fine opening run which includes the 567-yard 2nd (where a cluster of left-side bunkers define the go-for-it-or-not second), the watery 162-yard 3rd, the 462-yard 4th (a gentle dogleg left and the number one stroke hole) and especially the 337-yard 5th, a driveable test requiring an angled carry across both water and sand. The 180-yard dry wash-crossing 6th and the 599-yard 7th (which jumps open desert en route to a narrow, tightly bunkered green) then carry the ball towards a 3,781-yard back nine which begins with a pair of backbreakers, the 245-yard lake-backed 10th and the 481-yard 11th, a long, bunkerless two-shotter. Though more muscle is required at the 611-yard 12th and the 441-yard 13th, the action soon ratchets down at a pair of shorter entries, the 389-yard 14th (where flirting with right-side sand – including a tiny centerline fairway bunker - helps avoid a full water carry on the second) and the 176-yard 15th, which plays over more native terrain to a shallow, heavily bunkered green. The final run home is then built around two sturdy par 4s, the 428-yard dogleg right 16th (which flanks the hotel and requires ideal drives to cut across a line of four corner bunkers) and the 450-yard 18th, where invasive left-side sand sits precisely where an ideal tee shot would otherwise finish.

Wigwam Golf Resort & Spa (Gold) - Litchfield Park   ♦♦♦

Robert Trent Jones   www.wigwamarizona.com
300 East Wigwam Blvd, Litchfield Park, AZ 85340   (623) 935-3811
         7,430 yds   Par 72   Rating: 74.5 / 135   (1965)

Arizona's first mega-resort, the Wigwam sits in the western Phoenix suburb of Litchfield Park and features 36 original holes by Robert Trent Jones and a third 18 – situated three blocks away, across North Litchfield Road – added by Red Lawrence in 1974. Though a more basic course occupied this site since just after World War I (originally known as the Goodyear Golf & Country Club), the resort's calling card has long been Jones's Gold course, which measured over 7,100 yards in its infancy, and stretches to a robust 7,430 today. Predictably, so big a layout has several holes which might be considered excessive for a resort clientele (e.g., the 272-yard par-3 3rd as well as a pair of par 5s in excess of 650 yards) but lest one assume this to be standard period Trent Jones overkill, there are actually a number of interesting, normal-size entries as well, several affected by the narrow Airline Canal. Going out, these include the 391-yard 2nd (played to a huge lake-fronted green) as well as two very strong late par 4s, the 465-yard canal-fronted 8th and the 452-yard dogleg right 9th, whose green lies far afield. The trip back begins with the 660-yard 10th which, despite its size, is an appealing double-dogleg par 5 played to a pond- and canal-flanked green. The 190-yard boomerang-green 11th and 174-yard 16th are also watery tests, but the loop is better defined by a group of par 4s which includes the 384-yard 12th, the 366-yard 15th and 422-yard lake-guarded 17th, as well as the 440-yard 18th, where the canal closely guards the putting surface. Though not quite the beast it once was, this remains a strong, often engaging period layout.

Wigwam Golf Resort & Spa (Patriot) - Litchfield Park   ◆◆

Robert Trent Jones   www.wigwamarizona.com
300 East Wigwam Blvd, Litchfield Park, AZ 85340   (623) 935-3811
           6,000 yds   Par 70   Rating: 69.0 / 123   (1965)

Originally known as the Blue course, the Wigwam's 6,000-yard Patriot course was Robert Trent Jones's nod to the vacationing resort player, but while it is certainly much shorter and easier than its sister Gold, the occasional strong hole does appear. Mirroring the Gold in having a non-returning routing flanked by well-established desert homes, the Patriot has also morphed a bit from Jones's original design, its finishers being heavily reconfigured in the mid-2000s to accommodate a driving range move/expansion. The first 13 holes remain largely true to early form, however, and are initially led by the 477-yard par-5 3rd (where a pond sits front-left of the green), the 394-yard dogleg left 6th, the 425-yard 8th (a well-bunkered dogleg right) and the 194-yard 9th, which plays to a shallow green fronted by a centerline bunker. A pair of Jones originals kick off the inward half, with the 323-yard 11th playing between sand and water to a tiny, tightly bunkered green, and the 218-yard 13th being routed across a row of fronting bunkers. But everything from the 14th tee onward indeed owes to Forrest Richardson's 2004 renovation and, though stylistically somewhat different, includes the 132-yard 15th (whose narrow island green is not overly forgiving) and the 464-yard 18th, a long, notably tough closer.

Wigwam Golf Resort & Spa (Heritage) - Litchfield Park   ◆◆

Red Lawrence   www.wigwamarizona.com
300 East Wigwam Blvd, Litchfield Park, AZ 85340   (623) 935-3811
           6,852 yds   Par 72   Rating: 72.4 / 126   (1974)

The Wigwam Resort's Heritage course (née the Red) was one of the later designs of Red Lawrence's long career and falls somewhere between the Gold and Patriot layouts in terms of size and challenge, measuring 6,852 yards but possessing little of the Gold's grandeur or playing interest. Situated across Litchfield Road to the west, it, like its sisters, predates Arizona's turf limitation laws and is thus grassed from wall to wall. Toss in the presence of numerous now-mature trees and the Heritage takes on something of a parkland style, with its housing-flanked routing being filled with functional holes whose hazarding (both sand and water) tends to be more visible than truly invasive. The front nine is clearly the less-engaging half, with favorites being largely limited to the 499-yard par-5 4th (a sharp dogleg left around sand) and the 408-yard 9th, where left-side trees and sand menace the tee shot. The back initially continues in a similar vein before the action picks up somewhat at the 382-yard pond-guarded 14th, then at the 414-yard straightaway 15th. The finishers, however, are on an entirely different scale and include the 454-yard 16th (a demanding dogleg left), the 254-yard par-3 17th and especially the 591-yard 18th, which doglegs left between trees and a pair of lakes to a tree-framed putting surface.

Wildfire Golf Club (Palmer) - Phoenix   ♦♦½

Arnold Palmer   www.wildfiregolf.com
5350 East Marriott Dr, Phoenix, AZ 85054   (480) 473-0205
            7,145 yds   Par 72   Rating: 72.7 / 142   (1997)

Sharing its site with Marriott's Desert Ridge Resort & Spa, the Wildfire Golf Club lies in Phoenix's northern reaches, and features 36 holes of modern, rough-edged desert golf flanked on most sides by rows of single-family houses. An LPGA Tour stop since 2011, it initially featured the Palmer course, the longer and slightly tougher of the resort's offerings and a layout which sees the majority of its best holes appear on its front nine. These include the 450-yard dry wash-crossing 2nd, the 605-yard 3rd (which finds the same wash flanking the right side), the demanding 465-yard 7th (a sharp dogleg left with a dauntingly narrow fairway) and the 520-yard 9th, where another arroyo (plus a key centerline bunker in the lay-up zone) greatly affects play. The inward half is slightly shorter and, in the main, less interesting, though a prominent exception is the wild 530-yard 14th, which features dry wash-divided split fairways on the lay up. The rest of the loop is anchored by four longish par 4s, the best of which include the 450-yard 17th (which bends gently right to a water-flanked green) and the 430-yard finisher, whose somewhat shallow putting surface sits behind a prominent centerline bunker. The LPGA utilizes a composite layout which includes nine holes from each course but puzzlingly, it is the Palmer's back nine (played as the front) which gets the tournament call.

Wildfire Golf Club (Faldo) - Phoenix   ♦♦♦

Nick Faldo   www.wildfiregolf.com
5350 East Marriott Dr, Phoenix, AZ 85054   (480) 473-0205
            6,846 yds   Par 71   Rating: 72.3 / 132   (2002)

The Wildfire Golf Club's new millennium Faldo course may carry a lower rating and slope than the older Palmer layout, but it stands as the more tactically engaging track from start to finish. Entirely devoid of water, it instead relies on over 100 bunkers to enliven play, and is shaped in a style which Faldo has likened to the courses of the Australian Sandbelt. While a 72.3 back tee rating isn't likely to strike fear into many hearts, there is plenty of thought-provoking golf here, with the fun starting at a local favorite, the 408-yard 2nd, which plays over a fairway divided by three centerline bunkers. Thereafter, the front nine features a quartet of more interesting holes, including the 164-yard 3rd (where a stonewall-buttressed green sits above a dry wash), the well-bunkered 452-yard dogleg left 4th, the 350-yard 6th (whose putting surface sits beyond a barranca and an enormous fronting bunker) and the 534-yard 9th, where the same barranca forces a go-for-it-or-not decision on the second. Whereas the outward half circumnavigates the resort complex, the back nine extends to the north, where its homeward run is flanked by undeveloped desert. The loop flexes its muscle at the 460-yard 10th and 478-yard 12th, as well as at the 607-yard 15th, a narrow desert-flanked three-shotter. Its best holes, however, are among its shortest: the 360-yard 13th (a dogleg left around a vast waste bunker) and the 314-yard 16th, where copious bunkering offers three distinct options from the tee. It is this nine which the LPGA utilizes during their annual visit, playing it as their inward half.

Falcon Dunes Golf Course - Waddell   ♦♦

Gary Panks   www.lukeservices.com
15100 West Northern Ave, Waddell, AZ 85355   (623) 535-9334
                  6,611 yds   Par 71   Rating: 70.5 / 125   (1998)

Though the nearby Falcon Golf Club actually sits closer to the Luke Air Force Base runways, it is this facility which serves as a primary recreational facility for the sprawling military complex. Built by Gary Panks on a square parcel of flattish, former agricultural land to the north of the tarmac, this is a compact but fairly solid layout which features attractive views of the nearby White Tank Mountains and offers the usual area landscape of native vegetation and dry washes - though for the most part these hazards are not used nearly as invasively as they might have been. The front nine is the less-engaging half but it does include strong tests like the 220-yard 5th, the 408-yard dogleg left 7th and 553-yard 9th, where a crossing arroyo can affect longer hitters off the tee. But much of the better golf falls on the back, beginning at the 430-yard 12th, and extending through the watery 401-yard 14th, the 342-yard drive-and-pitch 15th and the 607-yard 16th, a big three-shotter which dares a large dry wash crossing on the second. As with most military courses there are limited frills here, but it remains a sturdy, reliable layout.

500 Club at Adobe Dam - Glendale

Brian Whitcomb   www.the500club.com
4707 West Pinnacle Peak Rd, Glendale, AZ 85310   (623) 492-9500
              6,867 yds   Par 72   Rating: 72.2 / 122   (1989)

In a region where golf's frequent *raison d'être* is to support surrounding real estate development, there is automatically something to like in a facility which has advertised that "The only house you'll see…is the clubhouse!" Situated at the base of the Hedgpeth Hills in the northern suburb of Glendale, the 500 Club indeed backs this claim up, being a housing-free layout of mid-range size and playing interest. Its longer 3,590-yard front side is perhaps the less-engaging half, though in recent years the addition of a rather unforgiving island green has lifted the 419-yard 4th above the 211-yard bunkerless 5th and the 229-yard 8th as the loop's strongest entry. The more compact back opens with the club's most engaging trio: the 507-yard dry wash-crossed 10th (where an Oakmont-like Church Pew bunker guards the fairway's left side), the 161-yard 11th (whose elevated green sits amidst the foothills) and the 380-yard 12th, which descends to another recently renovated green complex, this one 60% surrounded by water. Following another strong par 3 at the 218-yard 13th, the back-and-forth homestretch is then led by 480-yard 18th, a reachable, pond-fronted par 5. A slightly newer executive nine (page 96) adjoins.

Aguila Golf Club - Laveen

Gary Panks   www.phoenix.gov/golf
8440 South 35th Ave, Laveen, AZ 85339   (602) 262-6011
              7,007 yds   Par 72   Rating: 72.8 / 128   (1999)

Owned and operated by the City of Phoenix, the Aguila Golf Club is a full-size Gary Panks-designed facility which, with an eye towards its daily fee clientele, is somewhat less imposing in its hazarding than it is in size. Indeed, no less than 12 greens are bunkered on only one side, and two more are devoid of sand entirely. The layout's muscle is evident in a collection of long par 4s which, after the 433-yard 1st, include a particularly long quartet composed of the 462-yard 4th, the 441-yard 9th (where a pond lies left of the green), the 460-yard bunkerless 12th (a gentle dogleg left) and the 471-yard 18th, which parallels the 9th and plays to a green along the opposite side of the same pond. Though only marginally invasive, water makes several more strategic appearances, mainly at the 309-yard 8th (where a lake must be carried if one attempts to drive the green), the 531-yard 10th (whose bulkheaded green angles leftward into a pond) and the 321-yard 17th, which curves leftward around another pond and thus tempts the better player into one more aggressive tee ball. A short, lightly bunkered par-3 nine adjoins (page 96).

Ahwatukee Country Club - Phoenix   ♦♦

Johnny Bulla   www.ahwatukeegolf.com
12432 South 48th St, Phoenix, AZ   85044   (480) 893-9772
             6,713 yds   Par 72   Rating: 70.8 / 120   (1973)

Situated on the south side of town, between the Maricopa Freeway and South Mountain
Park, the Ahwatukee Country Club is a well-established Phoenix facility built by former
PGA Tour star (and Arizona golfing legend) Johnny Bulla in 1973. Its site climbing gently
from south to north, the layout forms two narrow loops through some mature residential
neighborhoods, with virtually every hole lined on both side by single-family homes. As
with most of Bulla's design work, this is more functional than tactical golf, thus invariably
making those holes dotted with man-made ponds among the most interesting. Going
out, these include the 184-yard all-carry 4th, the 406-yard 6th (where longer hitters will
have to lay up off the tee) and the 514-yard dogleg left 9th – though the 220-yard 8th
(played to a narrow green angled leftward between bunkers) is arguably the loop's
toughest test. The shorter back nine is slightly less engaging, peaking at the 386-yrd 13th
(where a left-side lake threatens the drive), the 192-yard over-water 14th and the 312-
yard 15th, where aggressive drives must account for some large left-side trees.

Apache Wells Country Club - Mesa   ♦½

Arthur Jack Snyder   www.apachewellscountryclub.com
5601 East Hermosa Vista Dr, Mesa, AZ   85215   (480) 830-4725
             6,038 yds   Par 71   Rating: 67.5 / 110   (1962)

Routed through a large mobile home development, the Apache Wells Country Club lies
adjacent to Falcon Field Airport in Mesa's northern reaches, and was built by Arthur Jack
Snyder way back in 1962, when there was little beyond farmland and desert elsewhere in
the neighborhood. Measuring just over 6,000 yards, Snyder's track was clearly crafted
with the recreational player very much in mind, with only 18 bunkers in play (five greens
are completely hazardless) and water seriously affecting play only once, at the 151-yard
4th. No par 4 reaches 400 yards (though the 392-yard 3rd comes close) and, as the layout
easily predated Arizona's turf limitation law, native desert virtually never affects play.
Certainly a nice form of backyard golf for the community's residences (many such
developments being built around short courses) but not on the serious golfer's radar.

Arizona Traditions Golf Club - Surprise   ♦♦

Dick Bailey   www.arizonatraditionsgolfclub.com
17225 North Citrus Rd, Surprise, AZ   85374   (623) 584-4000
                6,235 yds   Par 70   Rating: 68.7 / 115   (1997)

Situated beyond Sun City West, along the (current) northwestern edge of Phoenix area
civilization, the Arizona Traditions Golf Club is a short, real estate-encircled facility which,
on several occasions, rises above the basic to provide some tactically interesting golf.
The shorter front nine lies northwest of the clubhouse and is mostly rudimentary, save
for a trio of holes in its mid-section: the 426-yard 4th (a challenging dogleg left around a
cluster of trees), the 380-yard dogleg right 5th (where the layout's lone water hazard fills
the corner and flanks the green) and the tightly bunkered 210-yard 7th. Following the
formulaic double green at the 477-yard par-4 12th (shared with the par-3 3rd), the action
picks up again at the 553-yard 13th (a dogleg left around a trio of corner bunkers) and the
375-yard dogleg left 15th, where sand and a centerline tree affect the drive. A pair of
strategically engaging closers then end the round: the 352-yard dogleg left 16th (which
dares a shortcut across desert terrain, to a green fronted by a centerline bunker) and the
590-yard 18th, where a long desert crossing to an alternate fairway defines the second.

ASU Karsten Golf Course - Tempe   ♦♦♦

Pete Dye   www.asukarsten.com
1125 East Rio Salado Pkwy, Tempe, AZ   85281   (480) 921-8070
                7,002 yds   Par 70   Rating: 73.8 / 131   (1989)

Located on the campus of Arizona State University, the Karsten Golf Course is named for
PING founder (and longtime area resident) Karsten Solheim and, though saddled with an
aesthetically challenging site, has long rated among the stronger collegiate courses in the
West. Its par-34 front nine lies south and east of the clubhouse and measures only 3,251
yards, though a bit of strength is required over a trio of longer par 4s: the 420-yard pond-
flanked 4th, the demanding 493-yard 5th and the 446-yard 9th, whose entire right side is
flanked by a large lake. The 3,751-yard inward half lies mostly across East Rio Salado
Parkway and opens with the 498-yard 10th, a seriously demanding two-shotter which
spent much of its early life as a slightly longer par 5. The 209-yard 12th (guarded left by
two deep bunkers) is also worthy of note, but the loop's backbone lies in a trio of large
watery closers: the 457-yard 15th (whose green angles along a right-side lake), the
extremely dangerous 248-yard 16th (ditto) and the 471-yard 18th, which, following Pete
Dye tradition, flanks the same railroad tie-bulkheaded lake (which now lies on the left) as
the 9th. Though strong enough to test the games of Mssrs. Mickelson, Casey and Rahm,
this is clearly not among Dye's most artistic layouts, but the site – stuck among power
lines, modern buildings and petroleum storage tanks – has much to do with that. Note:
At the time of this writing, it appears that a long-rumored closing of the course is now
imminent as the golf teams moves to Papago Park and this land is redeveloped.

Bear Creek Golf Complex - Chandler   ♦♦

Nicklaus Design   www.bearcreekaz.com
500 East Riggs Rd, Chandler, AZ 85249   (480) 883-8200
                6,825 yds   Par 71   Rating: 71.6 / 122   (2000)

Lying just east of Sun Lakes, and a mile north of the Pinal County line, the Bear Creek Golf Complex was built by Nicklaus Design associate Bill O'Leary and features the Bear course, a layout clearly geared a notch or two below championship-level golf. The mostly flat landscape has been shaped into a gently rolling layout with native terrain separating its fairways, but its degree of hazarding and strategy is well beneath the Nicklaus norm. Water, for example, a staple of most every Nicklaus design, only materially affects two holes, the 179-yard 5th (whose green angles rightward, beyond a lake) and the 558-yard pond-guarded 18th. A handful of longer par 4s provide some strenuous moments (notably the 458-yard 9th and two bunkerless tests, the 460-yard 11th and the 458-yard 14th) but more engaging are holes like the 556-yard 7th (played across a split-fairway lay-up zone) and the 437-yard 10th, a sharp dogleg left. Actually, this represents pretty good stuff as affordable public golf goes, but visitors should not arrive expecting the full, tactically heavy Nicklaus experience. Also present is the Cub, a lightly hazarded 18-hole executive layout which occupies the property's southeastern section (page 97).

Cave Creek Municipal Golf Course - Phoenix   ♦½

Unknown   www.phoenix.gov/golf
15202 North 19th Ave, Phoenix, AZ 85023   (602) 866-8076
                6,732 yds   Par 72   Rating: 71.8 / 124   (1984)

Located half a mile southwest of the Turf Paradise Race Track and a quarter-mile east of Interstate 17, Cave Creek Municipal Golf Course is a City of Phoenix facility built on the site of a retired landfill and gravel pit. The eponymous creek bisects the property but scarcely factors into play, leaving a shortish layout (it measures 6,229 yards from the white tees) which seldom offers more than functional municipal golf. Play opens with a wild near-boomerang green at the 363-yard 1st, but the remainder of the front nine is highlighted by its strong closing run, a stretch which includes the tightly bunkered 197-yard 7th, the 437-yard straightaway 8th and the 422-yard 9th, a gentle dogleg left. The 521-yard 11th features a diagonal drive across the creekbed before play ratchets up somewhat in the property's water-dotted southwest corner, where both the 392-yard 14th and the 518-yard 16th slip between fairway-side lakes. Mainstream municipal stuff.

Club West Golf Club - Phoenix   ♦♦

Brian Whitcomb & Ken Kavanaugh   www.clubwestgolf.com
16400 South 14th Ave, Phoenix, AZ 85045   (480) 460-4400
       7,051 yds   Par 72   Rating: 72.7 / 130   (1993)

A residence-lined track lying between South Mountain Park and the northern edge of the Gila River Indian Community, the Club West Golf Club is routed over rolling desert terrain which at times becomes downright hilly. Though not really a sophisticated design from a tactical perspective, it is a scenically enjoyable track offering plenty of size, as well as a bit of variety in the magnitude of its challenge. The slightly shorter front nine opens with several diminutive holes before eventually flexing its muscle at the 543-yard arroyo-crossing 8th and a trio of strong par 4s: the 442-yard uphill 5th, the 458-yard dogleg left 7th and the 470-yard 9th, which plays to one of the layout's more heavily bunkered greens. The back initially features the 592-yard 12th (which crosses some low-lying desert before turning left, around a hillside) but reaches its peak over a closing stretch kicked off by a pair of par 3s routed over tumultuous ground, the 170-yard downhill 15th and the 215-yard 17th, which plunges sharply to a pair of alternate greens. The 440-yard pond-guarded 18th (the layout's lone water hole) then makes for a suitably strong finisher.

Coldwater Golf Club - Avondale   ♦♦

Forrest Richardson   www.coldwatergolfclub.com
100 North Clubhouse Dr, Avondale, AZ 85323   (623) 932-9000
       6,758 yds   Par 72   Rating: 71.5 / 120   (2000)

A housing-oriented facility situated half a mile south of Interstate 10 in Phoenix's western suburbs, the Coldwater Golf Club was built by ex-Arthur Jack Snyder associate Forrest Richardson at the dawn of the new millennium. A shortish, only moderately difficult test, it is heavily enough shaped that, despite no overwhelming variance to the natural terrain, the mounding which frames fairways and greens is often quite significant – though this might be viewed as a necessity given that not less than 11 greens are bunker-free. The 3,177-yard front nine is led by shorter entries like the 325-yard 3rd (where a centerline bunker bothers the drive), the 115-yard pond-fronted 8th and the 412-yard 9th. The 3,581-yard inward half then features a quartet of longer holes: the 562-yard 11th (a dogleg left to a bunkerless plateau green), the 444-yard dry wash-crossed 12th, the 387-yard 15th (whose putting surface is fronted by a large, perfectly circular bunker) and the 495-yard 18th, a reachable par 5 with water flanking the right side.

Copper Canyon Golf Club - Buckeye   ♦♦½

Brian Curley   www.coppercanyongolfclub.com
26577 W Desert Vista Blvd, Buckeye, AZ 85396   (928) 252-6783
                 6,808 yds   Par 72   Rating: 71.7 / 127   (2007)

Anchoring Del Webb's new millennium Sun City Festival development which, for the moment, sits largely by itself in the desert northwest of White Tank Mountain Regional Park, the Copper Canyon Golf Club offers a moderately challenging Brian Curley-designed 18 which winds its way expansively throughout the large, densely packed community. The slightly longer outward half follows a clockwise routing west of the clubhouse and, though effectively bunkered, is really more basic than engaging, with the 457-yard 3rd, the 170-yard 4th, and the 428-yard 6th (which plays to a narrow green angled beyond sand) nosing ahead of a somewhat homogenous field. The back nine is a tad more lively, however, particularly over an early stretch which includes the 163-yard lakeside 11th, the 520-yard 12th (where ponds affect all three shots) and a pair of driveable, smartly bunkered par 4s, the 322-yard 13th and the 338-yard 14th. The 557-yard 18th (where a huge bunker blocks the ideal left-side lay-up zone) is another favorite, though equally noteworthy is the 423-yard 15th, a pond-guarded dogleg right which heads a trio of holes isolated far away on the property's partially developed north side, about halfway to Prescott. By any measure, golf carts are definitely required here.

Coyote Lakes Golf Club - Surprise   ♦♦

Arthur Jack Snyder & Forrest Richardson   www.coyotelakesgolfclub.com
18800 N Coyote Lakes Pkwy, Surprise, AZ 85374   (623) 566-2323
                 6,088 yds   Par 71   Rating: 69.3 / 122   (1993)

The Coyote Lakes Golf Club is one of the region's more interestingly situated golfing facilities, for it is built within the Agua Fria riverbed, the vast dry wash which separates the neighboring Del Webb communities of Sun City and Sun City West. Designed by Arthur Jack Snyder and Forrest Richardson, the course occupies a low-lying north-south ribbon of land whose higher surroundings are housing-covered, with some patches of native terrain and four man-made lakes helping to spice up play. The 3,163-yard front nine runs north of the clubhouse where, following the 373-yard 2nd (whose fairway is awkwardly narrowed by one of the lakes), it is highlighted by the 375-yard 5th (with two small trees dividing its fairway) and the 541-yard arroyo-crossed 6th. The back then proceeds southward, where water affects both of the par 5s (the 486-yard 10th and the 485-yard 13th) as well as the 149-yard 14th, before the stiff 431-yard 18th squeezes its way between a left-side bunker and a sandy hillside to a narrow, bunkerless putting surface.

Desert Canyon Golf Club - Fountain Hills ♦♦

John Allen www.desertcanyongolf.com
10440 Indian Wells Dr, Fountain Hills, AZ 85268 (480) 837-1173
6,489 yds   Par 71   Rating: 69.9 / 125   (1971)

By nearly 25 years the first golf course in this fast growing town northeast of Scottsdale, the Desert Canyon Golf Club lies adjacent to the Yavapai Indian Community, where it dates all the way back to 1971. The scenic layout is often flanked by housing (usually at reasonable distance) and utilizes some particularly rolling terrain, though its design is mostly of the functional style prevalent to its period. Play opens strongly, however, first at the downhill 373-yard 1st (which bends leftward, around a pond), then at the 243-yard 2nd (a powerful, slightly uphill par 3) and the slightly awkward 388-yard 3rd, a 90-degree dogleg left around a hillside and two prominent trees. The longer back nine is built around a closing stretch that includes noteworthy climbs at the 516-yard 14th and the 427-yard 15th, a large descent at the 160-yard 16th (which drops to a very narrow green benched into a hillside) and a bit of both at the 393-yard 18th, which drops off the tee before climbing to a putting surface angled behind a prominent fronting bunker.

Dobson Ranch Golf Course - Mesa ♦♦

Red Lawrence www.dobsonranchgolfcourse.com
2155 South Dobson Rd, Mesa, AZ 85202 (480) 644-2291
6,593 yds   Par 72   Rating: 71.2 / 125   (1974)

Owned and operated by the City of Mesa, the Dobson Ranch Golf Course is a well-established municipal facility, with its short, little-altered Red Lawrence-designed course dating to 1974. A fairly basic test from a strategic perspective, the layout is routed around two interior housing developments and makes only functional use of both sand and several man-made water hazards. Its biggest strength lies in a quintet of shortish par 3s, the most engaging of which are the 154-yard 4th (whose narrow green angles rightward between bunkers), the 149-yard 7th (played to another narrow, angled putting surface) and the heavily bunkered 183-yard 12th. The limited use of water was surely a concession to municipal pace-of-play concerns, leaving only the 417-yard 8th (with a lake and creekbed flanking its right side) and the reachable 490-yard par-5 18th (where a pond must be carried off the tee, and a lake lies well left of both fairway and green) as the sole entries where it materially threatens. Solid (if largely basic) municipal stuff.

Dove Valley Ranch Golf Club - Cave Creek   ◆◆◆

Robert Trent Jones II   www.dovevalleyranch.com
33750 N. Dove Lakes Dr, Cave Creek, AZ 85331   (480) 488-0009
            7,011 yds   Par 72   Rating: 72.7 / 131   (1998)

A housing-bordered Robert Trent Jones II design situated in the northern reaches of the
Phoenix/Scottsdale area, the Dove Valley Ranch Golf Club is a flattish desert design made
reasonably playable by its wide fairways and the limited use of artificial water hazards.
Bobby's work, while aesthetically quite modern, generally carries a strategic orientation,
an attribute quickly apparent at the 447-yard dogleg right 2nd, whose wide fairway begs
the competent ball-striker to try and shortcut a corner lake.   The remainder of the
outward half is less enticing, circumnavigating a residential neighborhood and really only
featuring the 427-yard 7th (with native desert closely flanking the left side) and the 576-
yard 8th. The far-more-engaging back nine lies mostly south of Black Mountain Parkway ,
where holes 11-17 utilize an ancient dry wash to present the best sustained stretch of
golf. Initial favorites here include the 450-yard 11th (a demanding two-shotter played to
a narrow, desert-flanked green), the 364-yard split-fairway 12th and the 365-yard dogleg
left 14th, which twice crosses the dry wash. The real highlights, however, are a pair of
challenging par 5s, the 580-yard 15th (an arroyo-crossing double dogleg) and the 539-yard
17th, which bends leftward, around a line of houses, en route to a triangular green set
beyond the wash. The 401-yard lakeside 18th may be slightly at odds with the rest of the
loop's more natural aesthetic, but it does represent a suitably challenging close.

Encanto Golf Course - Phoenix   ◆◆

William P. Bell   www.phoenix.gov/golf
2775 North 15th Ave, Phoenix, AZ 85007   (602) 534-6823
            6,361 yds   Par 70   Rating: 69.5 / 114   (1935)

Phoenix's oldest public golf course (as well as the former home of legendary hustler
Titanic Thompson), Encanto was built in 1935 by the prolific California designer William P.
Bell in a location far closer to downtown than one could ever utilize today in a major
American city. Though the layout's front side has been slightly reconfigured (in part to
accommodate a driving range), a decent amount of Bell's work remains intact – but it can
fairly be said that this was never quite on par with the elite of his portfolio in the first
place. The front nine lies east of 15th Avenue and is led by more aggressively bunkered
holes like the 319-yard 2nd (which backs up against Encanto Lagoon), the 190-yard 3rd and
the 409-yard dogleg left 4th, where sliced approaches can again find the Lagoon. Though
size is at a premium overall, longer entries do appear at the 550-yard 8th, the 430-yard
9th, the 453-yard 15th and the 417-yard dogleg left 16th. Thus while only decent municipal
golf today, there is enough old-time ambience here to make for a pleasant game. A nine-
hole executive loop built by Bell's son William F. adjoins (page 99).

Golf Club of Estrella - Goodyear

Jack Nicklaus II   www.estrellagolf.com
11800 S. Golf Club Dr, Goodyear, AZ 85338   (623) 386-2600
                7,139 yds   Par 72   Rating: 73.0 / 137   (1999)

Anchoring a real estate development in Phoenix's southwestern suburbs, the Golf Club of Estrella is a Nicklaus organization design whose spacious, housing-oriented routing makes ample use of the rolling desert terrain, as well as some heavily shaped bunkering and the odd artificial water hazard. Featuring fine views of the Sierra Estrella Mountains and utilizing Nicklaus's standard strategically oriented design approach, it initially opens with a pair of enjoyable early tests, the natural 416-yard 2nd (where a narrow arroyo angles before the green) and the manufactured 174-yard 3rd, whose putting surface sits beyond a massive cape-and-bay-filled bunker. A similarly man-made pond tightly guards the green at the 386-yard 5th before the loop saves its best for a closing run that includes the 206-yard 7th (whose shallow green wraps around fronting sand), the dry wash-fronted 557-yard 8th and the 435-yard 9th, where a small bunker and a patch of open desert divide a very wide fairway. The slightly longer back nine quickly offers the 434-yard 11th (whose narrow putting surface angles beyond a massive front-left bunker complex) as well as the straightaway 545-yard 13th, where another arroyo fronts the green complex. Among the closers, favorites include the uphill 605-yard 16th (which plays to one more dry wash-fronted green) and the 437-yard 18th, an alternate fairway test favoring a drive angled across a dividing line of four bunkers. Challenging, reliably engaging stuff.

Falcon Golf Club - Litchfield Park

Brian Curley   www.playfalcongolf.com
15152 W Camelback Rd, Litchfield Park, AZ 85340   (623) 935-7800
                6,733 yds   Par 71   Rating: 70.8 / 126   (1997)

The Falcon Golf Club occupies a narrow rectangular tract situated along the southern boundary of Luke Air Force Base, making for the occasional exciting (if noisy) appearance of F-16 fighter jets as they begin and end their training flights over the Sonoran desert. Given the shape of the site, the course perhaps inevitably includes some back-and-forth sequences within its routing, and though it may never have been intended as a top-flight test, it is hardly a pushover, due largely to the presence of rough native terrain along either side of many fairways. Longer holes like the 584-yard 9th and the 464-yard 16th bulk up the scorecard, but more memorable is a collection of five par 3s led by the 218-yard 6th, the 187-yard 11th (where a single centerline bunker fronts a shallow green) and especially the 225-yard 18th, whose smallish putting surface is closely guarded by right-side water and a trio of bunkers. Among the multi-shot holes, favorites include the 418-yard 4th (where the second crosses a wide swath of native desert), the 423-yard dogleg right 7th and the 537-yard pond-flanked 17th. But the airplanes still steal the show.

Foothills Golf Club - Phoenix   ♦♦½

Tom Weiskopf & Jay Morrish   www.thefoothillsgc.com
2201 East Clubhouse Dr, Phoenix, AZ 85048   (480) 460-4653
          6,968 yds   Par 72   Rating: 72.6 / 128   (1987)

Joining its near neighbor Club West in the narrow swath of land between South Mountain Park and the Gila River Indian Community, the Foothills Golf Club is a housing-lined, moderately challenging Tom Weiskopf and Jay Morrish design dating to 1987. Though a shade less strategically engaging than many a Weiskopf-authored track, there are a predictably high number of solid holes present on a layout which relies relatively little on water, and which includes three bunkerless greens on its inward half. The 3,334-yard front nine opens with the 421-yard 1st (where one of two marginally relevant lakes can catch a pulled approach) and later offers the soundly bunkered 410-yard 3rd and the 510-yard 8th, as well as a pair of noteworthy shorter tests, the 152-yard pinpoint 4th and the driveable 311-yard 6th. The inward half measures exactly 300 yards longer and is proportionally stronger, with stout par 4s like the 437-yard 11th, the 451-yard 15th (where drives angle along the second lake) and the 457-yard 18th forming the backbone – the latter two playing to angled, bunkerless putting surfaces. Also adding interest is the 526-yard 12th, which features a very narrow, tightly bunkered green. Like Club West, the proximity of the mountains makes for some particularly scenic golf.

Glen Lakes Golf Course - Glendale   ♦

Jay Hillhouse   www.glenlakesgolfaz.com
5450 West Northern Ave, Glendale, AZ 85301   (623) 930-1111
          2,486 yds   Par 33   Rating: 31.0 / 98   (1966)

Barely rising above executive course status at 2,486 yards and a par of 33, the Glen Lakes Golf Course is a compact nine holer (nearly 20% of the property's acreage is consumed by the practice range) of generally limited challenge. It opens with a pair of full-size holes (the 394-yard 1st and 365-yard 2nd) but never offers an entry in excess of 306 yards thereafter – though the 206-yard water-flanked 7th is a solid enough one-shotter by any standard. With only five bunkers in play, and three lakes being little more than a tangential presence, this doesn't quite make up in playing interest what it lacks in size. Still, a decent facility for beginners or the less polished.

Grand Canyon University Golf Course - Phoenix   ♦♦½

William F. Bell   www.gcugolf.com
5902 West Indian School Rd, Phoenix, AZ 85033   (623) 846-4022
        7,239 yds   Par 72   Rating: 74.3 / 135   (1961)

This, the former Maryvale Golf Course, was built in 1961 by William F. Bell and operated
by the city of Phoenix as a municipal facility for more than half a century. But in 2016,
nearby Grand Canyon University funded a large John Fought-authored renovation and
now operates the course, keeping it open to the public and splitting profits with the city.
Bell's work fit his period standard, being a mid-range, sporadically bunkered test well
suited to recreational golfers. Fought, however, turned it into something much more,
for while nearly all of Bell's routing was retained, considerable length was added, as well
as more than 40 bunkers and 10 new green complexes. The result is long and strong test
which boasts far greater playing interest, and which opens in huge fashion with the 503-
yard par-4 1st and the 642-yard 3rd. There follows four additional two-shotters in excess
of 460 yards, as well as a trio of par 3s stretching beyond 200. Generally more engaging,
however, are shorter tests like the 352-yard 4th (played to a narrow, bunker-squeezed
green), the 421-yard dogleg left 5th, the 182-yard over-water 13th (the layout's smallest
par 3) and the 342-yard 14th. Notably, most of Fought's bunkers angle along the sides of
fairways and the short 13th represents the sole water carry, allowing this to remain a
reasonably playable layout for the municipal golfer not seeking a U.S. Open challenge.

Grayhawk Golf Club (Talon) - Scottsdale   ♦♦♦

Gary Panks & David Graham   www.grayhawkgolf.com
8620 E. Thompson Peak Pkwy, Scottsdale, AZ 85255   (480) 502-1800
        6,973 yds   Par 72   Rating: 73.3 / 146   (1994)

A significant player in Scottsdale's modern golf boom, the 36-hole Grayhawk Golf Club
grabbed an early place in the limelight by hosting the old Anderson Consulting
Championship (unofficial forerunner to today's WGC Match Play) during the late 1990s,
as well as the PGA Tour's Frys.com Open from 2007-2009. Situated just west of the
McDowell Mountains, and conveniently close to the Pima Freeway, it initially offered the
Gary Panks and David Graham-designed Talon course, a housing-lined 1994 creation built
south of East Thompson Peak Parkway, which served as the original match play host. An
unspectacular design by new millennium standards, the Talon is a lightly bunkered test
that relies mostly on the native terrain and a cadre of longish par 4s for its challenge.
Going out, the best golf is found primarily at the 346-yard dogleg right 2nd (where
aggressive drives flirt with a long stretch of right-side sand), the 153-yard 5th (played
across a large quasi-waste bunker), the 459-yard bunkerless 6th and the 562-yard 9th,
whose green fits snugly within the curvature of another large right-side bunker. More
memorable is an inward half which, beyond several par 4s in the 450-yard range, includes
the 175-yard 11th (known as much for the short suspension bridge that reaches it back
tees as its ravine-crossing tee shot), the 303-yard 13th (a heavily bunkered driveable
dogleg right), the 126-yard island-green 17th (which bears little resemblance to anything
else on the golf course) and the 588-yard pond-guarded finisher.

Grayhawk Golf Club (Raptor) - Scottsdale

Tom Fazio   www.grayhawkgolf.com
8620 E. Thompson Peak Pkwy, Scottsdale, AZ 85255   (480) 502-1800
            7,090 yds   Par 72   Rating: 74.2 / 140   (1995)

The Grayhawk Golf Club's Tom Fazio-designed Raptor course arrived in 1995 and, being the longer and tougher layout, counted Mike Weir among its winners upon hosting the Frys.com Open from 2007-2009. Somewhat less bunkered than the period Fazio norm, its front nine is mostly straight ahead desert golf, with favorites including the 395-yard tightly bunkered 2nd, the 460-yard 3rd (whose huge green angles behind a massive expanse of front-right sand), the attractively bunkered 174-yard 8th and the 464-yard 9th, whose putting surface sits above a front-right swale. The longer back nine represents a more complex story, however, as it has recently witnessed the complete reconstruction of holes 15-17 to make way for further real estate development. The early holes remain intact, however, and include the 390-yard 10th (where ideal drives are actually aimed away from the man-made creek that flanks the right side), the 468-yard 12th (which requires an all-carry approach to a sand-fronted green) and especially the 230-yard uphill 13th, a brutal one-shotter played to an elevated green flanked by a very deep right-side bunker. Unfortunately, the new holes do not appear to match the quirky challenges of the old 15th and 16th, while the new 331-yard 17th lacks the sheer difficulty of its 464-yard predecessor. However, the 521-yard 18th (whose reachable green angles right, along one final water hazard) remains intact as a temptingly reachable par-5 finisher.

Great Eagle Golf Club - Surprise

Ken Kavanaugh / Greg Nash   www.surprisegolfclub.com
17200 West Bell Rd, Surprise, AZ 85374   (623) 584-6000
            6,683 yds   Par 72   Rating: 72.1 / 125   (1986)

Laid out within the confines of the Happy Trails RV Resort (which was originally built by famed Hollywood couple Roy Rogers and Dale Evans), the Great Eagle Golf Club began life with nine holes built by Ken Kavanaugh in 1986 before being expanded to 18 by Greg Nash three years later. The front nine lies on the property's west side where, after a pair of early driveable par 4s (the 326-yard 2nd and the 338-yard 3rd), it is led by two strong closers, the demanding 231-yard 8th (whose green angles leftward, towards a lake) and the solid 429-yard 9th. The back then forms a counter-clockwise circle to the east, with holes frequently flanked down both sides by mobile homes. Though not quite top-shelf stuff, there is some stronger golf here, led first by the 179-yard 11th (whose green is cradled within a vast left-side bunker) and the massive 582-yard 12th. Similarly broadly proportioned is the 234-yard 14th, a very tough one-shotter which heads up a closing stretch highlighted by the 328-yard 16th (where a nest of small bunkers fronts the reachable green), the 510-yard lake-guarded 17th and the long 440-yard finisher.

Hillcrest Golf Club - Sun City West

Greg Nash & Jeff Hardin
20002 N Star Ridge Dr, Sun City West, AZ 85375
7,036 yds   Par 72   Rating: 72.7 / 126   (1978)

www.hillcrestgolfclub.com
(623) 584-1500

An independently operated public course lying within the heart of Del Webb's vast Sun City West development, the Hillcrest Golf Club spent some time on the national stage as host of the LPGA's Safeway International from 1980-1982, then as a Champions Tour stop from 1984-1988. A core design that is ringed by both housing and the Maricopa County Events Center, it is a strong, occasionally interesting test but also one marked by some repetitive touches. To wit: the 582-yard 4th, the 547-yard 7th and the 536-yard 13th are fairly similar dogleg lefts around lakes, while the 168-yard 8th and the tricky 211-yard 14th both play to wide, somewhat shallow greens backed immediately by water. A bit of power is required at longer par 4s like the 430-yard 5th, the 454-yard 9th and the 466-yard 18th, while water affects the middle five holes of the back nine which, in addition to the 13th and 14th, also include the 345-yard 12th (played to a tree-impeded peninsula green complex) and the 432-yard lake-flanked 16th. Not quite as flashy or rustic as some of the region's newer courses, but how many of them have hosted victories by Casper (twice), January and Geiberger, as well as Jan Stephenson and Beth Daniel?

Ken McDonald Golf Course - Tempe

Arthur Jack Snyder
800 East Divot Dr, Tempe, AZ 85283
6,876 yds   Par 72   Rating: 72.3 / 127   (1974)

www.tempe.gov/golf
(480) 350-4607

Owned and operated by the city of Tempe, the Ken McDonald Golf Course was designed by Arthur Jack Snyder in 1974 and is a mid-size, typically flat area layout with holes routed through three different tracts, all of which lie adjacent to the Western Canal. The front nine includes three holes situated west of the canal (following the waterway's 90-degree turn northward) including the 516-yard 4th, which runs parallel to it. The loop's best golf, however, comes at the 184-yard bunker-ringed 5th, the 200-yard 8th and the 401-yard 9th, a dogleg right whose fairway narrows appreciably as it slithers between a pair of water hazards. The back nine begins south of the canal, where it borders a city steam generating plant and opens with the notably strong 553-yard 10th, where a pond flanks the favored right side of the lay-up zone. The finishers are similarly robust, with the 216-yard 13th setting up a run which includes the 541-yard 15th (which dares one to carry a left-side pond on the second), the tough 449-yard dogleg left 16th and, back across the canal, the 462-yard straightaway 18th. Solid stuff for a 1970s muni.

Kokopelli Golf Club - Gilbert   ♦♦

Bill Phillips   www.kokopelligc.com
1800 West Guadalupe Rd, Gilbert, AZ   85233   (480) 926-3589
          6,716 yds   Par 72   Rating: 72.1 / 135   (1992)

Occupying a nearly rectangular, housing-permeated tract which straddles Guadalupe Road, the Kokopelli Golf Club is a narrow and frequently quite challenging layout despite only measuring a shade over 6,700 yards. The front nine includes three holes on the north side of the road (numbers 1, 2 and 9) with the remaining six circumnavigating a residential neighborhood to the south, where favorites include the 346-yard 3rd (whose green juts forward into a pond), the 352-yard 7th and the 563-yard 8th. The back opens with a long forced water carry at the 369-yard 10th followed by the tough 426-yard 12th, but ultimately features a pair of watery par 5s, the 531-yard 15th (where a left-side lake can affect both drives and seconds) and the 574-yard 18th, a gentle dogleg left where a left-side lake this time threatens the second and third. While the golf is playable enough, the corporate and commercial development which flanks the property's western and southern sides does little to enhance the overall ambience.

Las Colinas Golf Course - Queen Creek   ♦½

Mike Asmundson   www.lascolinasgolfclub.com
21515 N Village Loop Rd, Queen Creek, AZ   85242   (480) 987-3633
          6,655 yds   Par 71   Rating: 69.5 / 120   (1984)

Dating to 1984, the Las Colinas Golf Course is a short and relatively basic layout routed through a now-well-established residential development one mile from the Pinal County line. As a 120 slope suggests, this is not the most demanding of courses; indeed, water only affects the 444-yard dogleg left 4th, the 426-yard 10th and the 169-yard 17th (and never invasively) while bunkering is sporadic enough that fully seven greens are entirely hazardless. Relatively few holes, then, can be considered standouts, though the 4th, the 10th (which bends gently right, past a pond) and the 420-yard 18th (where a dead-center tree threatens indiscriminately aimed tee shots) are decent, full-size tests.

Las Sendas Golf Club - Mesa

Robert Trent Jones II   www.lassendas.com
7555 East Eagle Crest Dr, Mesa, AZ 85207   (480) 396-4000
            6,925 yds   Par 71   Rating: 73.1 / 144   (1996)

Built among the foothills of the Usery Mountains, in northeastern Mesa, the Las Sendas Golf Club features a Robert Trent Jones II-designed 18 which bears the usual fairway-side housing throughout, but also includes one significant ripple: five holes routed along the base of a rocky mountainside lying within the property's center. The earlier of Bobby's two Phoenix area projects (see Dove Valley Ranch, page 61), Las Sendas opens with two of its most demanding entries, the 458-yard 1st (a dangerous dogleg right around water) and the 564-yard 2nd, where a row of centerline bunkers threatens both the second and third. The mountainside is first encountered at the dry wash-crossed 430-yard 4th (where it closely backs the elevated green), the uphill 194-yard 5th (whose putting surface is benched into its slopes) and the 523-yard 6th, a quirky dogleg right which dares a long second skirting its rock-strewn base in order to leave a wide-open pitch. Following the difficult 467-yard 10th, the back nine then visits the eastern side of the peak at the uphill (and semi-blind) 135-yard 11th, and more invasively at the 440-yard dogleg left 12th, where the rocky slope abuts the entire right side. The closers, though mountain-free, are a similarly strong bunch, led by the 581-yard 15th (which is flanked and crossed by native desert), the tightly bunkered 183-yard 16th and the 576-yard 18th, a downhill double dogleg requiring two long water carries for those opting for the aggressive approach.

Legend at Arrowhead - Glendale

Arnold Palmer   www.legendatarrowhead.com
21027 North 67th Ave, Glendale, AZ 85308   (623) 561-1902
            7,005 yds   Par 72   Rating: 73.0 / 129   (1986)

Routed through a densely packed residential development situated between the Agua Fria Freeway and the hills of Thunderbird Park, the Legend at Arrowhead is an Arnold Palmer-designed course whose nines follow expansive routings among the usual rows of single-family homes. Bunkering is of a smaller (and aesthetically more pleasing) scale than on many a Palmer work, though this is initially belied at the 511-yard 2nd and the 429-yard 3rd, whose fairways are both flanked by large expanses of sand. Water then becomes the primary hazard at a trio of strong outward holes: the 431-yard dogleg right 5th (whose fairway is pinched by sand, water and a lone right-side tree), the 529-yard 6th (which dares a long, all-carry second) and the 413-yard dogleg left 9th. The longer back nine is somewhat the less-engaging half, finding much of its challenge in longer par 4s like the 441-yard bunkerless 13th, the 441-yard 15th (a gentle dogleg right) and the soundly bunkered 407-yard 17th. The 169-yard 16th (played to a shallow target perched above right-side sand) is an engaging short hole before play closes with the 530-yard 18th, a lake-flanked dogleg right. Despite its size, a fairly payable track for the less skilled.

Legend Trail Golf Club - Scottsdale

Rees Jones   www.legendtrailgc.com
9462 East Legendary Lane, Scottsdale, AZ 85262   (480) 488-7434
              6,845 yds   Par 72   Rating: 71.8 / 138   (1995)

Anchoring a secluded residential development in Scottsdale's northeastern reaches, the Legend Trail Golf Club offers one of Rees Jones's more restrained designs, a moderately proportioned track which shows little of the oversized, wall-to-wall bunkering that defines much of his new millennium work. On a front nine which fans out north of the clubhouse, play starts out quietly over several nondescript par 4s, with the action really only picking up at the 335-yard 6th (potentially driveable across a diagonal dry wash) and the 495-yard 7th, a reachable par 5 whose green juts into the facility's lone water hazard. But the back is very much a different story, lying mostly across Legend Trail Parkway, measuring 3,515 yards and featuring a range of more interesting holes. Among the most engaging is the 435-yard 11th, a sharp dogleg left where a sliver of alternate fairway might, under ideal conditions, tempt the better player to try to carry a vast swath of desert (not to mention a neighboring home) off the tee. The 235-yard 12th and 365-yard dry wash-fronted 14th also rate highly, as do a pair of back-to-back par 5s which might be considered the layout's two best entries: the 530-yard 16th (where a narrow dry wash cuts across the fairway before returning to guard an angled green) and the 510-yard 17th, where a wider section of the same arroyo cuts across the fairway and flanks the right side. Solid stuff – and not at all what many familiar with Jones' stylings might expect.

Lone Tree Golf Course - Chandler

Darryl Wilson   www.lonetreegolf18.com
6262 South Mountain Blvd, Chandler, AZ 85249   (480) 219-0831
              6,984 yds   Par 71   Rating: 71.2 / 123   (2001)

A residence-oriented facility built along the Pinal County line, the Lone Tree Golf Course was a new millennium addition designed by one Darryl Wilson and follows an expansive routing through a typical regional backdrop of single-family homes. For the most part this is functional (if good-sized) golf which provides little in the way of heavy tactical questions; indeed, the backbone of the layout is a quartet of long but fairly basic par 4s composed of the 460-yard 7th, the 481-yard 13th, the 470-yard 15th and the heavily bunkered 449-yard 17th. More engaging, however, is a group of par 3s which includes the 198-yard 8th (played to a sand-free, S-shaped green perched above a deep centerline depression), the unforgiving 181-yard island-green 12th (hardly an original but highly testing) and the 156-yard 14th, where an angled, table-top putting surface sits above a wide, front-left hillside. Also notable is a pair of watery par-5 finishers, the 551-yard 9th (where aggressive seconds must carry a left-side lake) and the 572-yard 18th, which is bothered by right-side water off the tee and a left-side lake thereafter.

Longbow Golf Club - Mesa

Ken Kavanaugh   www.longbowgolf.com
5601 East Longbow Pkwy, Mesa, AZ 85215   (480) 807-5400
                7,050 yds   Par 71   Rating: 72.9 / 140   (2003)

A flattish, heavily landscaped layout built by Ken Kavanaugh just northeast of Falcon Field Airport, the Longbow Golf Club is a well-thought-of, housing-free Phoenix-area test that relies primarily upon native terrain, plus a heavy dose of strategic bunkering for its challenge. Currently an annual stop on the LPGA's developmental Symetra Tour (from 6,400-yard tees), it kicks off with the 626-yard 1st, a robust opener whose shallow green bends around a small centerline bunker. Thereafter, the front nine's best stuff lies in a collection of strong and varied par 4s, initially led by the dangerous 429-yard 4th (which curls leftward around a lake to a very narrow green wedged between sand and water), the 416-yard 5th (where ideal drives carry a large right-side bunker) and the 420-yard 6th, whose putting surface is flanked left both by water and a massive bunker. The loop also closes notably with a Mutt-and-Jeff pair composed of the driveable, smartly bunkered 338-yard 8th and the strenuous 474-yard 9th. The inward half also opens strongly, as the 451-yard 10th is a tough dogleg left with the desert scraping its edges. Thereafter, play is led by a pair of longish, tightly bunkered par 3s (the 193-yard 11th and the 224-yard 16th) as well as two engaging par 5s, the 554-yard 15th (whose second is impeded by a prominent left-center bunker) and the 556-yard dogleg right 18th, which first jumps a small arroyo, then features a small centerline bunker in the heart of the lay-up zone.

McDowell Mountain Golf Club - Scottsdale

Randy Heckenkemper   www.mcdowellmountaingc.com
10690 East Sheena Dr, Scottsdale, AZ 85255   (480) 502-8200
                7,072 yds   Par 71   Rating: 73.3 / 137   (1999)

Owned by a group that includes five-time Major champion Phil Mickelson, the McDowell Mountain Golf Club (née the Sanctuary at Westworld) was renovated in 2011 by original designer Randy Heckenkemper, with length, wider fairways and several waste bunkers being added. Built along the foothills of the McDowell Mountains, it occupies a T-shaped property, with the clubhouse sitting on higher ground and the majority of both nines filling lower-lying land running parallel to the Central Arizona Project Canal. The outward half extends southward where, if holes like the 225-yard dry wash-flanked 3rd, the stiff 432-yard 7th or the 191-yard arroyo-fronted 8th fail to appeal, one can instead catch a glimpse of Frank Lloyd Wright's famed Scottsdale home, Taliesin West, which lies a quarter-mile up an adjacent hillside. Following the 542-yard 9th (a tactically engaging uphill dogleg left), the back nine runs out to the north, where the 448-yard centerline-bunkered 11th leads the charge early. The 161-yard desert-crossing 14th marks the turn for home, with the closing run then being highlighted by the 474-yard 15th and the 234-yard 17th, a long lake-fronted par 3 and the layout's only real water hole. Most testing of all, however, is the 508-yard 18th, a brutal, uphill par 4 which curls rightward along a narrow arroyo. Given his success designing Whisper Rock's well-thought-of Lower course, one wonders why Mickelson didn't again team up with Gary Stephenson to perform this renovation himself, but this is a much-improved facility regardless.

Ocotillo Golf Resort - Chandler

Ted Robinson   www.ocotillogolf.com
3751 South Clubhouse Dr, Chandler, AZ 85248   (480) 917-6660
        Gold/Blue: 7,016 yds   Par 72   Rating: 72.7 / 134   (1986)
        White: 3,285 yds   Par 35   Rating: 35.6 / 128   (1986)

Situated in Phoenix's southern suburbs, the Ocotillo Golf Resort dates to the mid-1980s and features 27 Ted Robinson-designed holes that are both housing- and water-oriented; indeed, Robinson's man-made network of lakes affects play on some 20 holes - though often only peripherally. The highest-rated combination pairs the Gold and Blue nines, with the former being the club's longest but also its least engaging. Still, there is plenty of challenge present, initially at a pair of waterside par 3s (the 212-yard 5th and the 177-yard 8th), then especially at the 468-yard 9th, a hole whose strength lies more in its size than its pair of fairly manageable lake carries. The Blue then opens with a 590-yard water-fronted monster before fanning out to the north, where the most dangerous entries include the 197-yard 4th, the 170-yard 7th, and a pair of very watery closers, the 415-yard 8th (a gentle dogleg right requiring a forced-carry second) and the 383-yard lake-fronted 9th. On the somewhat shorter White nine, an awkward test is encountered early at the 532-yard dogleg left 2nd, where water can force longer hitters to lay up off the tee. But better holes follow, led by the 162-yard 3rd (featuring a forgiving island green), the 340-yard 4th (played over a hugely wide fairway to a water-fronted putting surface) and the genuinely demanding 479-yard 9th, the club's longest two-shotter and one which may force lesser players to lay up shy of a long water carry on the approach.

Painted Mountain Golf Resort - Mesa

Frank Boxburger   www.paintedmountaingolf.com
6210 East McKellips Rd, Mesa, AZ 85215   (480) 832-0156
        6,021 yds   Par 70   Rating: 66.6 / 111   (1969)

A modest facility with housing-lined golf holes built on either side of East Hermosa Drive, the Painted Mountain Golf Resort offers a short, basic layout that barely exceeds 6,000 yards, is lightly bunkered and features seven entirely hazardless greens. Notable holes, then, are somewhat scarce, though the par-33 back nine does include the 168-yard 12th (where water might grab a ball missed significantly right), the 375-yard pond-fronted 13th and the 395-yard 18th, where another small water hazard sits short-right of the putting surface. Utterly incongruous, then, is the 605-yard 1st, a huge dogleg right that includes a lake guarding the corner and more than 25% of the course's bunkers. Toss in the 225-yard par-3 2nd and, if nothing else, you've got a challenging start. Go figure.

PalmBrook Country Club - Sun City   ◆½

Jeff Hardin   www.palmbrookgolf.com
9350 West Greenway Rd, Sun City, AZ 85351   (623) 977-8333
              6,853 yds   Par 72   Rating: 71.5 / 125   (1972)

One of the Sun City area's older golf facilities, the PalmBrook Country Club was built by Jeff Hardin in 1972 on a narrow, oddly shaped tract just east of the initial Sun City development, where it offers a moderately challenging track hemmed in on all sides by housing. Its front nine sits north of the clubhouse and is little more than short, basic golf, with nearly all of its holes moving, largely unimpeded, to greens mechanically bunkered left and right. The back then runs out to the south and is noticeably better, enlivened by an interconnected set of water hazards that manage to become somewhat invasive at the 349-yard 10th, then more so at the 185-yard 11th (an all-carry test angled across a pond) and the 403-yard 12th, where another small pond flanks the angled green's right side. The hazard also marks the right side of the 475-yard 16th (easily the layout's toughest par 4) as well as the 558-yard 17th and the 398-yard 18th. Hardly among the region's elite, but the inward half in particular represents pleasant backyard golf.

Palm Valley Golf Club (Palms) - Goodyear   ◆◆½

Arthur Hills   www.palmvalleygolf.com
2211 North Litchfield Rd, Goodyear, AZ 85338   (623) 935-2500
              7,015 yds   Par 72   Rating: 73.3 / 131   (1993)

Located one mile north of Interstate 10 and 13 miles west of downtown Phoenix, the Palm Valley Golf Club is another densely packed residential development, but one boasting a pair of widely divergent 18-hole courses, the regulation-size Palm course and a deluxe executive track, the Lakes (page 101). The older Palms was built in 1993 by Arthur Hills and, though occasionally squeezed somewhat by housing, is a strong, aesthetically restrained desert track which makes frequent use of the native sandy terrain. Smartly, its nines have been reversed in recent years, for the current outward half is somewhat the less interesting, offering the 195-yard 3rd (whose green angles above native sand and rocks) and strong par 4s at the 455-yard 6th and the 445-yard 9th as favorites The back steps up the pace with the 515-yard dry wash-pinched 11th, as well as a pair of long, desert-crossing par 3s at the stiff 225-yard 13th and the 205-yard 17th. Several solid par 4s are also present (notably the 430-yard 12th and the 425-yard 16th) before play closes with one of the region's most imposing par 5s, the 545-yard 18th, where the club's lone water hazard menaces the left side on both second shot and approach.

Papago Golf Course - Phoenix

William F. Bell   www.papagogolfcourse.net
5595 East Moreland St, Phoenix, AZ 85008   (602) 275-8428
              7,333 yds   Par 72   Rating: 75.0 / 130   (1963)

A City of Phoenix municipal mainstay since opening in 1963, Papago Golf Course also managed – despite William F. Bell's largely basic stylings – to gain some national acclaim upon hosting the U.S. Amateur Public Links in 1971. More recently, the course has undergone an underfinanced/highly expensive renovation at the hands of a subsidiary of the Arizona Golf Association, with William Fuller's longer, heavily bunkered redesign drawing considerably fewer players than before, even after entertaining the LPGA in 2009. One reason for this, perhaps, is that length is now overwhelming here, with six par 4s extending beyond 440 yards and three par 3s ranging between 233-253. There is not, however, a comparably imposing degree of playing interest among these holes, leaving the 561-yard pond-guarded 1st, the 187-yard 11th (all-carry over the same water) and the driveable (but well-bunkered) 322-yard 12th to hold the most appeal for many. Still, several of the long par 4s are engaging driving tests (e.g., the 442-yard 6th, where left-side bunkers mandate some thought) and holes like the 383-yard 5th, the 454-yard dogleg left 7th and the 542-yard pond-flanked 9th certainly rise above the mundane. And then there is a set of closers which, at least in terms of size, are championship-ready: the 442-yard dogleg right 16th (where two more bunkers severely squeeze the corner), the 243-yard 17th and the 464-yard uphill 18th. Arizona State University has recently agreed to manage the facility long-term, with its golf teams moving into a new practice facility to be designed here by one of the school's more prominent alums, Phil Mickelson.

PebbleCreek (Eagle's Nest) - Goodyear

Keith Foster   www.robson.com
3645 Clubhouse Dr, Goodyear, AZ 85395   (623) 935-6750
              6,790 yds   Par 72   Rating: 72.1 / 129   (1993)

A 45-hole housing-lined complex built just north of Interstate 10, some 15 miles west of downtown Phoenix, PebbleCreek first played golf over its older Keith Foster-designed Eagle's Nest course in 1993. Though a shortish track by modern standards, there is a fair amount of interesting golf present, with Foster's routing utilizing seven man-made lakes (all lateral hazards angled along/against green complexes) as well as the Bullard dry wash, which curves through the heart of the layout. The front nine opens and closes with solid par 5s (the 515-yard arroyo-crossing 1st and the 510-yard lake-guarded 9th), with additional favorites including a pair of holes whose green complexes angle rightward, into lakes, the 170-yard 4th and the 405-yard 7th. The back continues the prominent (if only marginally invasive) use of water at the 190-yard 12th, the pond-guarded 510-yard 13th and the 340-yard 15th. Perhaps more engaging, however, are a pair of entries which incorporate the dry wash, the 325-yard 11th (driveable, but with bunkers right and dry wash left) and the 440-yard 18th, a difficult driving hole which doglegs left across the hazard. For most one day visitors, this will be the club's layout of choice.

PebbleCreek (Tuscany Falls) - Goodyear   ♦♦

Dick Bailey   www.robson.com
3645 Clubhouse Dr, Goodyear, AZ   85395   (623) 935-6750
    Falls/Palms: 6,640 yds   Par 72   Rating: 70.8 / 123   (1999)
    Lakes: 3,345 yds   Par 72   Rating: 35.5 / 130   (2006)

In 1999, PebbleCreek opened the first 18 holes of what would become a 27-hole sister facility to Eagle's Nest, the Dick Bailey-designed Tuscany Falls. Playing out of a separate clubhouse on the south side of Pebble Creek Parkway, this somewhat less demanding layout began with today's Falls and Palms, each of which follows an expansive clockwise routing through densely packed housing. The Falls is the club's least-engaging loop and largely offers basic, functional golf before the action picks up a bit at the 322-yard 7th (potentially driveable but with water left) and the 525-yard 9th, whose green is tucked beyond a front-right pond. The Palms is noticeably stronger from the start, opening with a solid 426-yard par 4 whose green is flanked left by water. Thereafter, favorites include a pair of pond-guarded par 3s (the 185-yard 4th and the 171-yard 8th) as well as the 403-yard 7th, a soundly bunkered dogleg right. Opening seven years after its siblings, the Lakes nine runs out to the west, through a section of the property whose real estate was not completely built out at the time of this writing. Much of its best golf comes among a quartet of early holes: the 510-yard lake-flanked 1st, the quirky 340-yard 2nd (played to a very shallow green fronted by sand and backed by water), the 210-yard 3rd (whose putting surface angles left, beyond sand) and the 355-yard pond-guarded 5th. This is not quite on par with Eagle's Nest overall, but it's not a bad option for variety's sake.

Pueblo El Mirage Country Club - El Mirage   ♦½

Ken Killian & Fuzzy Zoeller   www.pemgolf.com
11201 North El Mirage Rd, El Mirage, AZ   85335 (623) 583-0425
    6,596 yds   Par 72   Rating: 71.1 / 125   (1985)

An RV resort located across the dry Agua Fria riverbed from Sun City, the Pueblo El Mirage Country Club dates to 1985, when it was built by Chicago architect Ken Killian with input from two-time Major champion Fuzzy Zoeller. Routed among rows of mobile homes and RV sites, it is a shortish, moderately interesting layout that clearly tried to balance the needs of a 55-and-over recreational clientele with presenting some degree of challenge. Water provides the primary points of interest here, affecting seven holes – though on the outward half, it will only concern the capable ball striker at the 535-yard 8th, where a pond is separated from the green's left edge only by a terribly positioned cart path. Coming home, ponds are a primary consideration at the 378-yard 10th, the 503-yard 11th (where a right-side hazard can test aggressive seconds) and especially the 421-yard 15th, a genuinely tough par 4 where another pond muscles in front-left of the putting surface. Mid-range stuff in the bigger picture, but well-suited to its clientele.

Quintero Golf & Country Club - Peoria

Rees Jones
16752 West State Rte 74, Peoria, AZ   85383
7,249 yds   Par 72   Rating: 75.3 / 148   (2000)

www.quinterogolf.com
(928) 501-1500

Isolated in the foothills of the Hieroglyphic Mountains, the Quintero Golf & Country Club is a scenic, occasionally hilly Rees Jones design which, after beginning life as a private club, has rated among the state's elite public access facilities since being converted by the recession in 2011. Jones's enormously scaled bunkering inevitably dominates the scene here, but on this occasion it is less aesthetically invasive than usual, and can often prevent stray shots from careening into the more dangerous open desert – no small thing on a course with a local rule allowing a 15th "rock club" to be carried. On balance, the layout's better half is the front nine, where the 406-yard 3rd offers a better approach angle to drives cozied up to a left-side lake, the 586-yard 8th is an dry wash crossing dogleg right par 5 (and potentially dangerous as its fairway is a viable alternative driving target for the par-5 2nd), and both the downhill 219-yard 6th and 212-yard pond-guarded 9th are strong, memorable one-shotters. The inward half, though slightly shorter and less imposing, features a strong run at the 212-yard pond-guarded 13th, the 552-yard 14th (which runs downhill between lines of bunkers), the 379-yard 15th (an attractive two-shotter played to an elevated green) and the 225-yard 16th, whose putting surface lies between sand and a left-side dry wash. Though palpably challenging (as a 75.3 rating clearly suggests), there is also enough playing interest to stand this among Jones's better period works. A planned Greg Norman-designed second layout now appears ever lost due to the recession. **(GD: #15 State, #86 USA Public   GW: #181 Modern)**

Rancho Mañana Golf Club - Cave Creek

William Johnston
5734 E Rancho Mañana Blvd, Cave Creek, AZ   85331
6,016 yds   Par 70   Rating: 66.7 / 128   (1988)

www.ranchomanana.com
(480) 488-0398

A short, quirky and occasionally quite interesting layout built in scenic, hilly country north of Scottsdale, the Rancho Mañana Golf Club is partially routed amidst housing, but also along/across a pair of dry washes, and onto the lower slopes of Go John Mountain. The front nine visits the most volatile terrain, with holes like the 374-yard 3rd and the 168-yard 5th benched into the mountainside, the 195-yard 7th and the 192-yard 9th plunging directly down it, and the 379-yard dogleg right 4th climbing sharply (and a bit awkwardly) up its slopes. The longer and more housing-flanked back nine offers a pair of holes incorporating the Galloway dry wash, the 401-yard 12th (where it fronts the green) and the 508-yard dogleg right 16th, which plays across and along it. A prominent lake affects three more inward holes (the 148-yard 14th and 377-yard 15th most directly) while right-side ponds and a small angled dry wash guard the green at the 556-yard finisher. In spite of its diminutive statistics, there is plenty of worthwhile golf here – though unfortunately, what it lacks in playing yardage, it easily makes up for in massive cart rides.

Raven Golf Club - Phoenix   ♦♦½

Gary Panks & David Graham   www.ravenphx.com
3636 East Baseline Rd, Phoenix, AZ 85042   (602) 243-3636
        7,078 yds   Par 72   Rating: 73.2 / 132   (1995)

Taking a cue from Las Vegas's famed Shadow Creek, designers Gary Panks and David
Graham moved mountains of earth and imported more than 6,000 pine trees in attempts
at creating something unique at this, the former Raven at South Mountain – though very
much unlike Shadow Creek, they had to deal with housing pinching into the property's
east and west flanks. The result was a layout aesthetically different from most in its
market and a fairly solid test, particularly over a four-hole front nine run that includes the
324-yard heavily bunkered 5th (which offers at least three distinct tee shot options), the
428-yard 6th, the 221-yard 7th (played diagonally across a lake and a long buffering
bunker) and the 421-yard 8th, which doglegs right, around a water hazard whose angle
will likely prevent all but the very longest of hitters from trying to cut the corner. The
inward half is, on the whole, less engaging, but closes strongly with a trio of somewhat
varied par 4s: the 366-yard 15th (where a prominent right-side fairway bunker greatly
affects the drive), the stiff 453-yard 16th and the 428-yard 18th, whose bunkerless green
extends rightward, into a trio of waterfall-connected ponds.

Scottsdale Silverado Golf Club - Scottsdale   ♦½

Ross Graves & Jack Gilmore   www.scottsdalesilveradogolfclub.com
7605 East Indian Bend Rd, Scottsdale, AZ 85250   (480) 778-0100
        6,313 yds   Par 70   Rating: 67.8 / 114   (2000)

Built along a turn in the Arizona Canal, Scottsdale Silverado occupies one of the region's
less favorable sites, its V-shaped property actually becoming so narrow that several back
nine holes are arranged single file – alternating outbound, then inbound, and requiring
some staggeringly long cart rides – simply to fit. The front nine (which at least manages
to run two-wide) is built mostly around functionally strong entries like the 441-yard 3rd,
the 420-yard 4th and a pair of 201-yard par 3s, the tightly guarded 6th and the 8th. Despite
its bizarre routing, the back does manage to offer the occasional interesting test, led by
the 528-yard dry wash-crossed 11th, the 430-yard straightaway 17th and – following a
450-yard cart ride – the 157-yard 18th, which plays to a well-bunkered green complex
which extends leftward, into a lake. The golf itself rises somewhat above the mundane,
but the logistics of the site are among the most bizarre one will ever encounter.

Shalimar Country Club - Tempe ♦½

Unknown   www.shalimarcountryclub.com
2032 East Golf Ave, Tempe, AZ 85282   (480) 838-0488
           2,406 yds   Par 33   Rating: 31.2 / 109   (1961)

A borderline executive nine built two miles southeast of the Arizona State University campus, the Shalimar Country Club is a certainly a layout well-suited to collegians whose skills may not be up to the rigors of Pete Dye's soon-to-be-extinct ASU Karsten course. Fairly simple in its design, the majority of holes feature small, lightly protected greens, though two entries manage to stand well above the rest: the 155-yard 5th (where sand lies left and water short and right) and the 300-yard 9th, whose green is nearly ringed by both a creek and a buffering collection of bunkers. As these two have more combined bunkers than the other seven holes combined, this can certainly be defined as basic golf.

Southern Ridge Golf Club - Laveen ♦½

Dan Pohl   www.southernridgegc.com
5740 West Baseline Rd, Laveen, AZ 85339   (602) 237-4567
           6,751 yds   Par 72   Rating: 71.5 / 121   (1993)

Originally built as a 27-hole facility before sacrificing nine interior holes to make way for residential development, this, the former Bougainvillea golf club, was designed by ex-PGA Tour player Dan Pohl on a typically flat site on Phoenix's southwest side. It would seem that the reconfiguration (more than any planned quirk) is responsible for the presence of six par 5s and six par 3s (as well as back-to-back one-shotters at the 4th and 5th), but on the whole this is fairly standard golf which makes little use of either man-made water hazards or the native desert. The shorter front nine bobs and weaves among the housing, and is led by the 530-yard 2nd (whose green opens up to second shots played close to right-side out-of-bounds), the 200-yard 4th (played to a shallow, well-bunkered putting surface), the 218-yard 8th and the 520-yard 18th, whose lay-up zone and green are flanked left by the course's lone water hazard. The back then runs along the property's western side and provides muscular moments at the 448-yard 15th and the 425-yard 18th.

Starfire Golf Club - Scottsdale   ♦½

Arnold Palmer   www.starfiregolfclub.com
11500 North Hayden, Scottsdale, AZ 85260   (480) 948-6000
        Squire/Hawk: 5,622 yds   Par 68   Rating: 68.9 / 124   (1953)
        King·   3,258 yds   Par 36   Rating: 37.2 / 141   (1983)

A housing-permeated 27-hole facility, the Starfire Golf Club (née the Scottsdale Country Club) is a short, relatively tight layout which for 30 years was composed of 18 holes built in the early postwar years by Lawrence Hughes. That original 18 was actually of a standard proportion but became quite compact when it was redesigned (around copious new housing) by Arnold Palmer's company in 1983. Today known as the Hawk and Squire nines, they both measure well below 3,000 yards, carry pars of 34 and feature functional, occasionally awkward holes wedged in tightly amidst the housing. Though the shorter half, the Squire includes longer entries like the 403-yard dogleg right 4th and, most notably, the 232-yard 9th, an incongruously long, tightly bunkered par 3. The Hawk is longer overall but less engaging, offering little that is memorable beyond a pair of basic water holes, the 369-yard 16th (a forced-lay-up dogleg left) and the 153-yard all-carry 17th. On an entirely different plane, however, is the King nine, which Palmer added in 1983 on the east side of North Hayden Road. Following a somewhat attenuated routing amidst still more rows of houses, it is a tough modern loop driven by a quartet of water holes: the 421-yard 3rd, the 146-yard 4th (played to a near-island green), the 203-yard 8th (which angles across a lake) and the 504-yard pond-guarded 9th.

Stonecreek Golf Club - Phoenix   ♦♦½

Arthur Hills   www.stonecreekgc.com
4434 E. Paradise Village Pkwy, Phoenix, AZ 85032   (602) 953-9111
        6,871 yds   Par 71   Rating: 72.8 / 131   (1988)

Originally built (as the Anasazi Golf Club) during the early 1980s by Pete Dye's less-celebrated brother Roy, the Stonecreek Golf Club was renovated into its present form by Arthur Hills in 1988. Hills largely retained Dye's original routing within a housing-flanked dry wash but reshaped things to better fit his own style, also planting hundreds of trees and expanding a meandering hazard (occasionally widened into a lake) which materially affects play on more than half of the holes. The much shorter front nine lies west of the clubhouse and includes a pair of shorter, pond-guarded par 4s (the 364-yard 1st and the 389-yard 6th) as well as the 181-yard 3rd (whose green angles along a large waste bunker) and the 410-yard dogleg left 9th. The inward half then moves across North Tatum Boulevard to the east where the central water hazard is the primary factor on a quintet of holes, the best of which include the watery 197-yard 12th, the 378-yard 14th (a dogleg right, around a lake) and the 609-yard 16th, whose dry wash-pinched fairway leads to a narrow green angled behind a pond. It also crosses the 436-yard 18th as well as the 350-yard 10th, which shares a somewhat gimmicky double green with the par-4 17th.

Sun City (North) - Sun City

Milton Coggins   www.sunaz.com
12650 N. 107th Ave, Sun City, AZ 85351   (623) 876-3010
                6,423 yds   Par 72   Rating: 69.7 / 115   (1960)

The first planned development ever built by the Del Webb Company, Sun City broke ground in 1960 and eventually grew to include the eight courses run by Recreation Centers of Sun City as well as several additional facilities which are today operated independently. The pioneering layout was the Milton Coggins-designed North course, a short, user-friendly track which set a period standard for being routed through endless neighborhoods of small, single-family homes. A predictably basic design, it underwent a 2014 renovation which involved a rebuilding of greens and a significant reshaping and repositioning of bunkers – but it is still best suited to a leisure-oriented clientele. The front nine is the less-engaging half, though the 435-yard bunkerless 2nd and the 210-yard 7th are solid enough. The back (which lies across 107th Avenue to the east) raises the ante somewhat at the 165-yard over-water 12th, the 530-yard 13th, the driveable 315-yard 16th and especially the 580-yard 18th, a long, sweeping dogleg left.

Sun City (South) - Sun City

Milton Coggins   www.sunaz.com
11000 N. 103rd Ave, Sun City, AZ 85351   (623) 876-3015
                6,811 yds   Par 72   Rating: 71.8 / 119   (1962)

Dating to 1962, the South course was Sun City's second golfing facility chronologically, yet it remains the communitiy's longest layout from the championship tees. Also built by Del Webb's apparent designer of choice, Milt Coggins, the South spent most of its existence as a basic, functional track before undergoing a 2010 renovation by Tripp Davis, a project which focused on the repositioning of bunkers with a far greater tactical bent. These changes are apparent at holes like the 305-yard 2nd (where four hazards affect the aggressive drive), the 342-yard 4th (where two bunkers now protect the favored left side of the fairway), the 359-yard centerline-bunkered 8th and the 546-yard 13th, where another centerline hazard requires thought for longer hitters off the tee. There are also several longer par 4s present (notably the 437-yard 1st, the 456-yard soundly bunkered 3rd and the 441-yard bunkerless 16th) as well a pair of over-water par 3s (the 189-yard 5th and the 164-yard 17th), though these one-shotters are not overly demanding.

Sun City (Lakes West) - Sun City

Milton Coggins   www.sunaz.com
10433 W. Talisman Rd, Sun City, AZ 85351   (623) 876-3020
        6,195 yds   Par 72   Rating: 69.1 / 118   (1968)

The last Sun City course to be designed by Milton Coggins, the Lakes West dates to 1968 and is a somewhat distinctive facility in that its narrow routing forms nearly a perfect circle around a large residential area. It is also, however, the lowest-rated of Sun City's regulation offerings and, even after a 2008 rebunkering by Tripp Davis, still provides mostly short, functional golf. Aside from the over-water 162-yard 2nd, the front nine includes little that is memorable save for the 487-yard 9th, where two prominent trees and a crossing creek affect the second, and the green is flanked right by a pond. The back then includes a trio of shorter, water-affected holes which rate among the layout's most engaging: the 383-yard pond-guarded 10th, the 336-yard 17th (where a right-side lake flanks both fairway and an L-shaped green) and the 316-yard 18th, whose tee shot is complicated by both a creek crossing at the 270-yard mark and a left-side pond.

Sun City (Riverview) - Sun City

Jeff Hardin   www.sunaz.com
16401 N. Del Webb Blvd, Sun City, AZ 85351   (623) 876-3025
        6,336 yds   Par 72   Rating: 69.8 / 119   (1972)

Locate immediately north of Sun City's Lakes West golf course, the Riverview was added in 1972 by Jeff Hardin and is named for the nearby Agua Fria riverbed, an occasionally massive (and partially developed) dry wash which separates Sun City from its sister Del Webb community Sun City West. Another short and relatively basic test, it too occupies a curiously shaped, housing-enclosed site, with the T-shaped front nine circumnavigating a small neighborhood and featuring the 321-yard 3rd (whose green partially boomerangs around a bunker), the 369-yard 4th (where a pond aggressively pinches the right side of the fairway) and the 407-yard 6th, a sharp dogleg right which makes a slightly early turn. The back then follows a more basic out-and-back routing to the east where it is lead by a pair of fairly engaging par 5s (the nicely bunkered 478-yard 11th and the 526-yard dogleg left 14th) as well as the 389-yard pond-guarded 14th and the 376-yard 17th, which plays over a creek-flanked fairway to a heart-shaped green with sand left and water right.

Sun City (Willowcreek) - Sun City

George Fazio   www.sunaz.com
10600 W. Boswell Blvd, Sun City, AZ   85373   (623) 876-3030
            6,357 yds   Par 72   Rating: 69.7 / 122   (1974)

The Willowcreek course at Sun City bears the distinction of having had something of a marquee designer, as it was built by George Fazio (with the usual period assist from nephew Tom) in 1974. It is, however, somewhat tamer than many entries in the 1950 U.S. Open runner-up's portfolio, especially within its bunkering, which shows little of the tight greenside hazarding he frequently employed. The layout is built on a north-south axis, with the front nine crossing West Union Hills drive to the north, where its best holes are also its longest, including the 540-yard 3rd, the 202-yard 8th and the 431-yard 9th. The shorter inward half offers a bit more, however, particularly within shorter par 4s like the 300-yard 12th (where a bunker and several trees narrow the route) and the 327-yard 14th (the driveability of which is tempered right-side water), as well as the 413-yard 18th, a gentle dogleg left enlivened by a corner bunker and several right-side trees. An 18-hole Fazio-designed executive course plays out of this same clubhouse (page 105).

Sun City Country Club - Sun City

Milton Coggins   www.suncitycountryclub.org
9433 North 107th Ave, Sun City, AZ   85351   (623) 933-1353
            6,275 yds   Par 72   Rating: 68.8 / 120   (1967)

Originally built as the first private golf facility created by the Del Webb Company, the Sun City Country Club was, perhaps predictably, laid out by the firm's initial designer of choice Milton Coggins along the southern edge of the sprawling community. Hemmed in by housing from nearly the beginning, Coggins' work has changed very little over half a century, leaving it short (only one par 5 reaches 500 yards) and relatively easy by modern standards. Little more than functional in its architecture, its most memorable test, by miles, is the 153-yard 7th, which plays to a not-altogether-forgiving near-island green – a much bolder concept in 1967 than it might be today. Additional favorites include the 525-yard 3rd (whose lay-up zone is narrowed by mature trees) as well as back nine entries like the 305-yard 13th (where some extremely invasive trees narrow the approach), the 153-yard 17th (played to a green fronted by four bunkers) and the 425-yard 18th, easily the club's longest par 4 and a fairly narrow one (by both sand and trees) to boot.

Sun City Grand (Desert Springs) - Surprise ◆◆

Greg Nash   www.grandinfo.com
19900 N. Remington Dr, Surprise, AZ 85374   (623) 546-7401
                7,006 yds   Par 72   Rating: 71.9 / 123   (1996)

A sprawling Del Webb Company 55-and-over community located just across Highway 60 from Sun City West, Sun City Grand offers a quartet of modern courses built by Greg Nash, with occasional help from his Hall-of-Fame partner Billy Casper. The oldest (and longest) layout is Desert Springs, a Nash-designed entry which, like its sister courses, features two nines routed in wide loops to provide maximum real estate frontage – though the housing is generally well buffered by wide swaths of desert sand. Among Desert Springs' better holes are its par 5s, a somewhat diverse quartet which includes the 509-yard 7th (with green pinched between left-side sand and right-side water), the 592-yard 11th (whose narrow putting surface is flanked left, right and long by both sand and water) and the 529-yard 18th, where a large right-side bunker impedes both aggressive and laid-up seconds. The front nine also features the 425-yard 5th (a narrow, heavily bunkered test rated the number one stroke hole) while the back offers additional strong closers at the 439-yard straightaway 15th, the 435-yard similarly straight 16th and the 206-yard 17th, a genuinely tough par 3 whose green curls rightward around a pond.

Sun City Grand (Granite North) - Surprise ◆◆

Greg Nash & Billy Casper   www.grandinfo.com
15949 W. Clearview Blvd, Surprise, AZ 85374   (623) 546-7580
                6,720 yds   Par 72   Rating: 71.4 / 122   (1997)

The second segment of Sun City Grand's 72 holes to be built was the 36-hole Greg Nash & Billy Casper-designed Granite Falls facility, whose North course sits a short cart ride from the clubhouse on the north side of West Clearview Boulevard. Though housing-lined throughout, the North is somewhat more creative in its use of the native desert terrain, particularly on shortish front nine par 4s like the 365-yard 2nd and the 370-yard 7th. The outward half also offers the 190-yard 3rd (played to an extremely narrow target) and the 525-yard 4th, a demanding enough test to be rated the number one stroke hole. The 560-yard 10th features more native terrain pushing in along its right side and kicks off a 3,405-yard back nine which quickly offers two notable smaller entries at the 400-yard pond-menaced 11th and the 155-yard tree-and sand-guarded 12th. The scale of things picks up towards the close, however, first at the 430-yard bunker-narrowed 14th, then at the 215-yard 15th and the 440-yard 16th, whose fairway is guarded both right and left by sand. The 505-yard 18th, though obvious not backbreaking, then makes for an interesting closers as its reachable, stonewall-buttressed green is nearly surrounded by water.

Sun City Grand (Granite South) - Surprise   ♦♦

Greg Nash & Billy Casper   www.grandinfo.com
15949 W. Clearview Blvd, Surprise, AZ 85374   (623) 546-7580
                 6,839 yds   Par 72   Rating: 71.2 / 120   (1997)

The South course at Sun City Grand's Granite Falls facility was, like its sister North, designed by both Greg Nash and Billy Casper, and despite being some 119 yards longer, rates as the slightly easier layout. There is, however, frequently a tactical bent to play, a point brought quickly into evidence at the 362-yard 1st (where drives carrying a huge left-side bunker yield a simple, wide-open pitch) and the 411-yard 2nd, where tee shots played close to more left-side sand are similarly favored. The remainder of the front nine is led by a pair of mid-size par 5s, the 543-yard lake-guarded 3rd and the 531-yard 6th, as well as the 375-yard 9th, which dares an aggressive drive angled across two right-side bunkers. Save for the obviously stout 226-yard 13th, the inward half starts quietly but is relatively backloaded, eventually closing with a varied quartet composed of the 315-yard 15th (where a narrow spit of land might allow the ultra-aggressive to run a driver onto a peninsula green), the 426-yard sand-squeezed 16th, the demanding 220-yard 17th and the 540-yard finisher, which plays to another water-defended green complex.

Sun City Grand (Cimarron) - Surprise   ♦♦½

Greg Nash   www.grandinfo.com
17100 W. Clearview Blvd, Surprise, AZ 85374   (623) 975-5654
                 6,809 yds   Par 72   Rating: 71.6 / 127   (2003)

The last of Sun City Grand's four courses arrived in the new millennium, with the Greg Nash-designed Cimarron layout being constructed along the (current) northwestern edge of Phoenix-area civilization in the community's northwestern corner. Arguably both the toughest and most engaging of the club's layouts, it can still be classified as a track whose bark is rather worse than its bite, with much sand and water in view, but seldom placed to threaten the competent ball-striker in an oppressive manner. After opening with a pair of pleasant drive-and-pitches, the shorter front nine features solid par 3s at the 166-yard 4th (with green angled rightward above a lake) and the 199-yard semi-island green 7th, as well as its two par 5s, the 516-yard 3rd (whose reachable putting surface angles leftward beyond a hollow and a prominent tree) and the 574-yard 6th (the number one stroke hole). The back leads with the watery 406-yard 11th and the effectively bunkered 531-yard 13th before eventually closing big via the 221-yard bunkerless 17th and the 548-yard 18th, an interesting three-shotter upon which a narrow green is wedged between a pair of lakes and a large right-side bunker threatens the ideal lay-up zone.

Sun Lakes (Cottonwood) - Sun Lakes   ♦½

Greg Nash   www.sunlakesofarizona.com
25630 Brentwood Dr, Sun Lakes, AZ 85248   (480) 895-9449
            6,565 yds   Par 72   Rating: 71.3 / 125   (1983)

Another of the region's sprawling multi-course residential developments, Sun Lakes lies six miles due south of Chandler and offers a mix of regulation and executive courses, adding up to 99 holes in total. The club's oldest regulation layout is the Greg Nash-designed Cottonwood course, which occupies a narrow, oddly shaped tract within the geometrically arranged property's south-central section. A shortish test of moderate challenge, it presents mostly functional, lightly bunkered desert golf broken up by the occasional more engaging water hole. Favorites in this regard include the 370-yard dogleg right 4th and 209-yard 5th (set upon opposite sides of the same lake) and, later, the 212-yard 13th, where water lurks both right and long. Less engaging are the 400-yard 9th (whose fairway twists awkwardly between lakes) and the 367-yard 18th, each of which includes water hazards that will force many a longer hitter to lay up off the tee.

Sun Lakes (Oakwood) - Sun Lakes   ♦½

Gary Panks   www.ironoaksaz.com
24218 South Oakwood Blvd, Sun Lakes, AZ 85248   (480) 895-7275
      Sonoran/Lakes: 6,577 yds   Par 72   Rating: 71.5 / 125   (1985)
      Palms: 3,249 yds   Par 36   Rating: 37.3 / 133   (1985)

Immediately north of Sun Lakes' Cottonwood course is the development's newer 27-hole Oakwood facility, all three nines of which were designed by Greg Nash in 1985. Though all three of its loops are similarly proportioned (and housing-lined), the highest-rated combination pairs the Sonoran and Lakes nines which, like at Oakwood, rely on the regular infusion of water to spice up otherwise basic tests. The Sonoran follows a clockwise routing to the northeast of the clubhouse and finds its best entries within a trio of later holes: the 286-yard 6th (a driveable par 4 with water down its right side), the 388-yard lake-flanked 7th and the 559-yard 9th, which bends leftward to another pond-side green. The Lakes forms a counterclockwise circle to the west where, though shorter, it offers a pair of water-flanked par 5s (the 510-yard 1st and the 544-yard 7th) as well as diminutive tests like the 133-yard over-water 2nd and the 395-yard 9th, whose green complex extends leftward, into a pond. The Palms nine, though similar on the scorecard, is a tad less engaging, with only its 188-yard lake-crossing 7th and 394-yard 8th (a gentle dogleg left to a tightly bunkered green) really lingering in the memory. Still, these interchangeable nines will, for many, rate at least the equal of the Cottonwood course.

Sun Lakes (Ironwood) - Sun Lakes   ♦♦½

Gary Panks   www.ironoaksaz.com
550 West Champagne Dr, Chandler, AZ 85248   (480) 895-0614
              5,163 yds   Par 67   Rating: 63.5 / 105   (1993)

The Ironwood course lies along the property's eastern side and is a short, compact test which, at 5,163 yards and a par of 67, barely reaches regulation status. Routed against the standard backdrop of single-family homes, it opens and closes with par 5s of just over 500 yards, but is populated in between by seven par 3s and a collection of par 4s which includes only one (the 392-yard 12th) that exceeds 360. While the 296-yard 7th and the 333-yard lake- and sand-guarded 9th tempt a drive towards the green, the most reliably good golf is found among the one-shotters, particularly the 145-yard 6th (played across native sand) and a pair of pond-guarded tests, the 151-yard 10th and the 178-yard 16th.

Sundance Golf Club - Buckeye   ♦♦♦½

Greg Nash   www.sundancegolfaz.com
900 South Sundance Pkwy, Buckeye, AZ 85326   (623) 328-0400
              6,944 yds   Par 72   Rating: 72.0 / 127   (2003)

Situated off the south side of Interstate 10, some 25 miles west of downtown Phoenix, the Greg Nash-designed Sundance Golf Club is a housing-lined new millennium facility which often makes more aggressive use of native terrain than many public layouts in the region. This is apparent early at the 412-yard 2nd (where a centerline tree and a swath of crossing desert affect the drive), the 565-yard 4th (a dogleg right with the desert creeping along its left side and an angled line of small bunkers crossing the lay-up zone) and the 371-yard 5th, a split-fairway test daring a long right-side carry across some rough country. The 175-yard 6th plays over the club's lone water hazard, a uniqueness soon forgotten on a back nine led by a trio of shorter, tactically exciting par 4s: the 333-yard 11th (which slithers between patches of desert), the 418-yard split-fairway 12th and the 347-yard 15th, which plays across another dry wash-divided fairway, daring another long right-side carry. Factor in stout back nine par 4s like the 445-yard 14th and the 490-yard downhill 17th, as well as the 601-yard 18th and there is a decent amount of muscle required as well. As an added plus, nearly all of the bunkering is small of size, giving things a more restrained feel than most new millennium layouts in the region.

SunRidge Canyon Golf Club - Fountain Hills   ◆◆◆

Keith Foster   www.sunridgegolf.com
13100 North SunRidge Dr, Fountain Hills, AZ 85268   (480) 837-5100
            6,823 yds   Par 71   Rating: 72.0 / 138   (1995)

The SunRidge Canyon Golf Club lies within the McDowell Mountain foothills that separate Fountain Hills from Scottsdale, where its engaging Keith Foster-designed layout follows a non-returning routing amidst rows of single-family homes. A former Arthur Hills associate, Foster has a built a résumé full of tactically engaging courses and SunRidge is no exception, though creating something workable over this often narrow site was no simple task. Play mostly descends on a less-exciting outward half which, following the soundly bunkered 318-yard 1st, features the downhill 463-yard 5th, the 202-yard 6th (which angles across a deep arroyo) and the 551-yard 9th, a downhill par 5 twice crossed by native desert. The par-35 back nine, though nearly 250 yards shorter, ascends up the eastern side of the canyon and is the more engaging half, particularly among a trio of par 3s that includes the 169-yard 12th (which angles across a dry wash), the 181-yard downhill 14th (whose rock-buttressed green sits above a pond) and the 209-yard 17th, where varied tees greatly alter the angles of play to a narrow boomerang green. The predictably tempting 308-yard 10th (with centerline bunker affecting the tee ball) is an appealing entry, while longer incoming favorites include the 533-yard 16th as well as a pair of very solid par 4s, the 457-yard 15th and uphill 432-yard dogleg left finisher. Somewhat off the national radar, but one of the region's stronger public stops.

Superstition Springs Golf Club - Mesa   ◆◆½

Greg Nash   www.superstitionspringsgc.com
6542 East Baseline Rd, Mesa, AZ 85206   (480) 985-5622
            7,005 yds   Par 72   Rating: 73.1 / 128   (1986)

Once rated among the top public facilities in the region, the Greg Nash-designed Superstition Springs Golf Club is a flashy modern layout whose front nine, in particular, is somewhat challenged ambience-wise; it surrounds a city water reclamation plant, flanks multiple corporate parks and car dealerships and crosses beneath the Superstition Freeway en route to several outlying holes. Perhaps not surprisingly then, its most memorable entries are a pair with enough flash to overshadow their surroundings, the 610-yard 6th (which doglegs right, around a pond, then plays to a narrow, snake-like green whose back third is ringed by sand) and the 425-yard Cape-like 9th, which curls along both a lake and three wildly shaped bunkers bulkheaded above the waterline. The back nine (which lies to the south, across East Baseline Road) offers several more attention-grabbers, including the 360-yard 10th (whose green juts rightward, into a lake), the watery 401-yard 14th (where 10 bunkers flank the putting surface) and the 231-yard 15th, whose own seven greenside bunkers seem paltry by comparison. Play then concludes with the 537-yard bunkerless (but quite watery) 17th and the awkward 455-yard 18th, where longer hitters must lay-up shy of a man-made creek. Contrived stuff certainly, but also a layout which well represents high-end public golf of its period.

Toka Sticks Golf Club - Mesa

Unknown www.tokasticksgolf.com
6910 East Williams Field Rd, Mesa, AZ 85212 (840) 988-9405
6,870 yds   Par 72   Rating: 72.5 / 123   (1951)

Originally built as a recreational amenity for the former Williams Air Force Base (closed in 1993 and converted to today's Gateway Airport), the Toka Sticks Golf Club began with nine holes in 1951 before being expanded to 18 by Air Force personnel during the mid-1980s. Built upon an oddly shaped site wedged between former base housing and the Roosevelt Canal, it is, like many military courses, far more functional than strategic in its design, and yet a number of interesting holes do appear. On the front nine, this is evidenced by a trio of strong par 5s: the 500-yard dogleg right 2nd (where the second shot it complicated by a drainage ditch and a centerline tree), the 525-yard 4th (which makes a late left turn around a lake) and the 541-yard 9th, a tough, tree-narrowed dogleg left which for years served as the 18th before the nines were reversed in the new millennium. The 3,529-yard inward half includes the 446-yard 11th (which also crosses the drainage ditch) and the 420-yard straightaway 18th, as well as a trio of successive water holes: the 219-yard bunkerless 13th, the 324-yard dogleg right 14th (at least theoretically driveable, but over water and trees) and the 198-yard 15th.

Tonto Verde (Peaks) - Rio Verde

Gary Panks & David Graham www.tontoverde.org
18401 El Circulo Dr, Rio Verde, AZ 85263 (480) 471-2710
6,733 yds   Par 72   Rating: 71.6 / 129   (1994)

Situated immediately adjacent to the private, 36 hole Rio Verde Country Club, Tonto Verde represents the expansive development's public side – a slightly puzzling choice as its pair of Gary Panks and David Graham-designed courses represent, by any measure, the facility's better half. Opened in 1994, the older Peaks course is a shortish track routed amidst medium-density housing, but its utilization of both native terrain and simple, tactically sound bunkering still make for a reasonably engaging round. On the outward half, favorites include the 572-yard uphill 4th (crossed by a narrow arroyo, and smartly – if simply – bunkered), the 351-yard 5th (which dares a left-side drive over water and plays to a pondside green), the 420-yard downhill 6th (the number one stroke hole) and the similarly descending 402-yard 9th. Coming home, the 518-yard 11th and the 305-yard dry wash-fronted 13th lead the way early, while the homeward run is highlighted by the 420-yard 14th (a dry wash-crossed dogleg right) and the 397-yard 18th, a straightaway test played to a green flanked left by both water and sand.

Tonto Verde (Ranch) - Rio Verde   ♦♦½

Gary Panks   www.tontoverde.org
18401 El Circulo Dr, Rio Verde, AZ 85263   (480) 471-2710
              7,004 yds   Par 72   Rating: 72.8 / 134   (1999)

Tonto Verde's Ranch course shares a clubhouse with the older Peaks layout, and was built five years later by Gary Panks (sans David Graham) on similarly housing-dotted desert terrain immediately to the east. Nearly 300 yards longer (and rated more than a stroke tougher), it utilizes a non-returning routing (although the 5th green comes close) and begins in relatively staid fashion, with the front nine's best coming at the 418-yard 6th (the number one stroke hole), the 569-yard arroyo-crossing 8th and the 412-yard 9th, a gentle dogleg left. After opening with the 362-yard 10th (where some tight fairway bunkering requires a moment's thought), the back nine is a rather more muscular loop, save for the 314-yard 14th, a driveable test with a small bunker sitting some 40 yards shy of the green, precisely where one would like to aim their drive. On the brawnier side, the 578-yard 13th is enlivened by a dry wash crossing 40 yards shy of its putting surface, the 430-yard 16th plays to a small, bunkerless green, and the 437-yard 18th is made difficult off the tee by one more centerline bunker. Most memorable, however, is the 531-yard 17th, an option-filled hole which first offers alternate fairways off the tee, then the opportunity to get home via a long desert carry on an aggressive second.

Tres Rios Golf Course - Goodyear   ♦½

Red Lawrence   www.estrella-golf.com
15205 West Vineyard Ave, Goodyear, AZ 85338   (623) 932-3714
              6,846 yds   Par 71   Rating: 70.9 / 118   (1962)

Previously known as Sierra Estrella and the Estrella Mountain Golf Course, Tres Rios lies beneath the northern foothills of Estrella Mountain and offers a Red Lawrence-designed layout which is notable both for its age and a complete lack of residential development. Like much of Lawrence's work, the design is more solid than tactically superb, and it can be argued that its two most interesting holes jump up almost before one is fully warmed up: the 544-yard downhill 1st (where a centerline tree can require some thought) and the 401-yard 3rd, a sharp dogleg right to a lake-guarded green. But if Tres Rios lacks for flash, it does provide as a backbone a collection of strong, occasionally tree-narrowed par 4s to test the golfer's mettle. This is particularly true on a 3,554-yard back nine which includes the 471-yard dogleg left 13th, the 430-yard 16th and the 435-yard out-of-bounds-flanked 17th. Hardly the area's most thought-provoking test, but a pleasantly mature entry.

Trilogy Golf Club at Power Ranch – Gilbert   ◆◆½

Dick Bailey   www.bluestargolf.com/powerranch
4415 East Village Pkwy, Gilbert, AZ   85297   (480) 988-0004
                  6,932 yds   Par 71   Rating: 71.5 / 126   (1999)

Though measuring 6,932 yards on the scorecard, the Trilogy Golf Club at Power Ranch actually plays much shorter, as its four par 5s – which average 585 yards – consume more than one-third of the total yardage by themselves. This is especially true on a front nine which includes the 605-yard 3rd and the 620-yard 7th, though here at least, such brutes are somewhat offset by the presence of three par 3s, the nest of which is the 210-yard pond-flanked 8th. There is far more interesting golf on the back, which runs counter-clockwise around a large residential neighborhood and sees a wide dry wash invasively affect a run of four holes along its northern boundary. This hazard is driven across at the 557-yard 13th (where it then flanks the entire left side) before being crossed at both the 430-yard dogleg left 14th and the 195-yard bunkerless 15th. The wash is perhaps most invasive at the 450-yard 16th (where it guards the left side of the fairway, then angles before the green) before play turns for home at the 558-yard dogleg left 17th and the 413-yard 18th, a dogleg right to a green angled beyond front-right water.

Trilogy Golf Club at Vistancia – Peoria   ◆◆◆

Gary Panks   www.trilogygolfclub.com/vistancia
12575 West Golf Club Dr, Peoria, AZ   85383   (623) 328-5100
                  7,291 yds   Par 72   Rating: 73.6 / 135   (2004)

Built within a residential community in what presently constitutes the Phoenix area's northwestern reaches, the Trilogy Golf Club at Vistancia is a long, modern Gary Panks-designed test routed primarily among the houses. Its front nine occupies the property's northern half and, after the 203-yard pond- and bunker-flanked 2nd, picks up the pace at the dry wash-crossed 416-yard 3rd (the number one stroke hole), the 608-yard soundly bunkered 5th and the 211-yard 7th, whose heavily contoured green falls away to the left. There follows a strong six-hole mid-section (numbers 8-13) which, in addition to the 509-yard 9th (a reachable par 5 crossed by a swath of native terrain), includes several stout par 4s led by the 446-yard tightly bunkered 11th and the 487-yard 13th, where more sand guards the favored right side of the fairway.   The finishing stretch is initially led by the 564-yard 14th (whose well-bunkered green is backed by water) and the 348-yard 15th, where angled centerline bunkers require some decision-making off the tee. Water is a visible (but mostly tangential) presence at the 163-yard 17th (where it affects only a single front-right pin) and the 560-yard 18th, whose entire right side is flanked by a twisting hazard which, save for just off the putting surface, will mostly catch only a highly proficient slice. Overall, this is effective (if a bit formulaic) development golf.

Troon North Golf Club (Monument) - Scottsdale   ♦♦♦

Tom Weiskopf & Jay Morrish   www.troonnorthgolf.com
10320 East Dynamite Blvd, Scottsdale, AZ 85262   (480) 585-7700
         7,070 yds   Par 72   Rating: 72.9 / 147   (1990)

Playing off the 1986 success of their nearby (private) Troon Golf Club, Tom Weiskopf and Jay Morrish returned to built the Monument course at Troon North just a mile up the road in 1990 and, at least initially, met with similarly popular results. Indeed, what was then simply known as "Troon North" cracked *Golf Digest*'s national top 100 in 1993 (at an impressive 65th), then proceeded to hang around the ranking for most of the decade. And while its colors don't fly quite as high today (the same publication places it on the edges of the state's top 25), it certainly remains among the Scottsdale area's stronger public tests. A rolling, neatly landscaped track routed among all manner of lower-density housing, its front nine sits north of East Dynamite Boulevard and features a mid-section highlighted by the 564-yard 3rd (a sharp dogleg right with a giant boulder dividing the fairway) and a pair of predictable-yet-effective tests, the tumbling 464-yard 5th (the obligatory bunkerless par 4) and the well-bunkered 306-yard 6th (the equally obligatory driveable one). The back lies across the street to the south and opens with a pair of ascending entries (the 396-yard 10th and 512-yard 11th) as well as the 222-yard pond-flanked 13th. The run home then presents a diverse stretch of golf led by the driveable 299-yard 15th (with narrow green backed against a rocky hillside), the downhill 244-yard 16th, and the similarly descending 495-yard par-4 17th.   (**GD**: #25 State **GW**: #81 Resort)

Troon North Golf Club (Pinnacle) - Scottsdale   ♦♦♦

Tom Weiskopf & Jay Morrish   www.troonnorthgolf.com
10320 East Dynamite Blvd, Scottsdale, AZ   85262   (480) 585-7700
         7,025 yds   Par 71   Rating: 73.0 / 147   (1996)

Tom Weiskopf had become a solo act by the time the Troon North Golf Club added its Pinnacle course in 1996, but he created a layout of similar scale and character to the older Monument layout, this time over more undulating terrain on the property's north side. Whereas the Monument had allowances built in (e.g., larger greens with plentiful chipping areas) to accommodate the daily-fee golfer, the similarly proportioned Pinnacle made few such compromises, its bunkers being built deeper, its corridors of play drawn somewhat narrower. Marked by numerous par 4s with swaths of desert crossing beyond their driving zones (but well shy of their greens), it scores its biggest points with a pair engaging dry wash-crossed par 5s, the 541-yard 5th (where the arroyo divides the lay-up zone) and the 539-yard 11th, a reachable dogleg right with the same wash slashing across the fairway, then flanking the right side of a very narrow green. Among the par 4s, favorites include the 456-yard dogleg right 7th (which rolls past native rocks to a green tucked behind a high-lipped bunker), the 416-yard dry wash-bothered 12th, the 441-yard 17th (played downhill, past a centerline bunker) and the 447-yard 18th, a well-bunkered (and desert-crossed) dogleg left. Though perhaps not Weiskopf's most strategically detailed work, the Pinnacle is tough and scenic enough to hold the interest of better players, and certainly stands up nicely with its older sister layout.   (**GW**: #82 Resort)

Union Hills Country Club - Sun City

Greg Nash   www.unionhillscc.com
9860 Lindgren Ave, Sun City, AZ 85373   (623) 974-5888
6,970 yds   Par 72   Rating: 72.8 / 128   (1974)

An original golfing anchor of the Del Webb Company's pioneering Sun City development, the Union Hills Country Club was long ago sold to its members and today operates as a freestanding semi-private club on a typically narrow, housing-lined site. A largely basic layout which, if nothing else, has grown rather longer than most in Sun City family, it begins with a front nine which moves northward, across Union Hills Drive and, as the lesser half, boasts only its par 3s (the 215-yard 5th and the 205-yard 7th) as offering much in the way of resonance. The longer back nine then forms a narrow semi-circle to the southeast and is noticeably better, first offering a pair of water holes at the 150-yard 12th and the 399-yard dogleg right 14th, then closing with a good-size run which includes the 220-yard 15th, the 555-yard 16th (a gentle dogleg left with water right of the putting surface) and the recently lengthened 495-yard 18, a surprisingly stiff par-4 closer.

Verde River Golf & Social Club - Rio Verde

Ken Kavanaugh   www.verderivergolf.com
29005 North Verde River Way, Rio Verde, AZ 85263   (480) 471-3232
7,058 yds   Par 72   Rating: 72.7 / 138   (2006)

Originally built as a part of the adjacent Rio Verde/Tonto Verde development, the Verde River Golf & Social Club was originally known as the Vista Verde Golf Club – but more than just its name has changed since its 2006 opening. For the layout was recently remodeled by Tom Lehman and while it still retains virtually all of Ken Kavanaugh's original routing, it has been shortened (from 7,219 yards), slightly resequenced and had nearly 30 bunkers removed, making it more playable for the average greens fee-paying golfer. With most of its planned housing still unbuilt at the time of this writing, this remains a tactically interesting track and, not surprisingly, one which utilizes native dry washes to regular effect. These arroyos affect nearly half of the holes, with the strongest entries including the potentially driveable 348-yard 8th (where a dry wash angles 20 yards shy of the green), the 549-yard 12th (whose centerline lay-up zone bunker has been removed), the 335-yard 15th (offering multiple targets across its wash-divided fairways) and endless, uphill test whose sliver of a green angles beyond another parched creekbed. Also noteworthy is the 396-yard 17th (originally the 18th), which plays to one more very narrow putting surface, this one angled along the layout's lone true water hazard. This is, by leaps and bounds, the strongest of the five Verdes courses, but it is debatable as to whether the revised version is better or simply easier.

Verrado Golf Club (Founders) - Buckeye

John Fought & Tom Lehman   www.verradogolfclub.com
4242 North Golf Dr, Buckeye, AZ 85396   (623) 388-3008
           7,258 yds   Par 72   Rating: 73.9 / 139   (2004)

Expansively routed through multiple residential developments near the White Tank Mountains, some 25 miles west of Phoenix, the John Fought and Tom Lehman-designed Raven at Verrado is a long but manageable layout which makes only limited use of water and boasts bunkering more strategically sound than flashy. The front nine follows a long course to the southeast where its backbone lies in muscular tests like the 478-yard bunker-narrowed 4th, the 588-yard 5th and the 477-yard 8th – though more engaging are a pair of shorter holes which utilize somewhat elevated terrain, the 397-yard 2nd (whose green is buttonhooked beyond an unmaintained front-left ravine) and the downhill 222-yard 3rd. The back also makes an early ascent into some nearby foothills, climbing at the 442-yard centerline-bunkered 12th and the bunkerless 310-yard 13th (where a false front repels timid approaches back into the fairway), then descending sharply at the 184-yard 14th. The layout's only water appears close to the clubhouse, first flanking the green of the 382-yard 9th, then defending the putting surfaces of the 154-yard 17th and the 494-yard par-4 18th, the latter a demanding downhill finisher which passes bunkers and native terrain en route to a large lakeside green. Though housing is present on a number of holes, several more appear destined to stay undeveloped for the foreseeable future.

Verrado Golf Club (Victory) - Buckeye

Tom Lehman   www.verradogolfclub.com
20855 W. Tiger Mountain Dr, Buckeye, AZ 85396   (623) 388-3008
           7,258 yds   Par 72   Rating: - / -   (2017)

One of the first major golf projects to be completed in the region in the aftermath of the recession, the Verrado Golf Club's Tom Lehman-designed Victory course was too new at the time of this writing to have yet been rated by the Arizona Golf Association. Playing out of a separate clubhouse built nearly a mile to the north, it bears the odd distinction of measuring 7,258 yards – exactly the same length as the older Founders course. It is, however somewhat different in its stylings, particularly over a front nine that stretches northward and appears several years (at least) away from being flanked by anything but open desert. Making good use of the rolling native terrain, this is a layout which starts somewhat tamely but picks up noticeably towards the close of the front nine, led by the 335-yard 7th (driveable, but with a centerline bunker clogging the route), the tumbling 632-yard 8th (whose platform green borders a sharp left-side fallaway) and the 492-yard 9th, a huge par 4 played to another elevated target, this one sitting above a vast right-side bunker. The 3,665-yard inward half also mixes some very large and very small holes, with favorites including the 474-yard 13th (where a prominent left-side ridge cuts impedingly into the fairway), the driveable 309-yard 14th (where another sharp left-side fallaway borders a very narrow green) and the 590-yard dogleg right 18th, which plays across both a lake and a heavily rolling fairway. Challenging (and still often rustic) stuff.

Villa de Paz Golf Course - Phoenix   ♦♦

Greg Nash & Jeff Hardin   www.villadepazgolf.com
4220 North 103rd Ave, Phoenix, AZ 85037   (623) 877-1172
                6,641 yds   Par 72   Rating: 70.1 / 123   (1977)

An early entry in the portfolio of courses jointly produced by Greg Nash and Jeff Hardin, Villa de Paz occupies a typically flat northwest Phoenix site, where it is spaciously routed through a mature residential neighborhood. Though neither long nor crushingly difficult, it is a well above average public layout which relies upon six greenside ponds to regularly enliven play. Some of these hazards are fairly basic in their placement (e.g., at forced-carry par 3s like the 160-yard 2nd and the 172-yard 11th) but others are more tactically situated, such as at the 450-yard 4th (a sharp dogleg right par 5), the potentially driveable 343-yard 8th and the 523-yard 10th. The overall shortness of the par 4s holds the layout back challenge-wise, but at least two more are temptingly driveable for longer hitters (the 341-yard 7th and the 329-yard 15th). And lastly there is the powerhouse 18th, a 470-yard par 4 which doglegs significantly right en route to a green angled behind one final pond. The stylings are fairly basic, but this represents better-than-average public golf.

Westbrook Village Golf Club (Lakes) - Peoria   ♦½

Ted Robinson   www.westbrookvillagegolf.com
19260 North Westbrook Parkway, Peoria, AZ 85382   (623) 566-4548
                6,412 yds   Par 71   Rating: 70.1 / 122   (1982)

A member-owned, 36-hole facility which also allows public access, Westbrook Village Golf Club first played over its Ted Robinson-designed Lakes course, a short, basic layout which bears few of the skinny cape-and-bay bunkers and waterfall-laden water hazards that would eventually become the Robinson signature. Tactically things are limited here, with the opening 16 holes offering only two really engaging tests, the 337-yard 6th (whose green complex extends leftward into a lake) and the 413-yard 10th, a sweeping dogleg right. But the closing pair are another story, with the 185-yard 17th playing across a large pond and the 530-yard 18th bending around a long, narrow lake, which also fronts the green. Though obviously never intended to be much more than functional golf, the Lakes did have its aesthetic improved significantly during 2015 when large, water-consuming sections of rough were removed and replaced by open desert sand.

Westbrook Village Golf Club (Vistas) - Peoria   ♦½

Ken Kavanaugh   www.westbrookvillagegolf.com
19260 North Westbrook Parkway, Peoria, AZ 85382   (623) 566-4548
            6,432 yds   Par 72   Rating: 69.9 / 119   (1990)

The Westbrook Village Golf Club's newer Ken Kavanaugh-designed Vistas course lies across North 91st Avenue to the east of the older Lakes course, and plays out of a separate clubhouse. Though a hair longer, it is rated and sloped slightly easier than its more established sibling, but its overall design is for the most part more engaging. The 3,306-yard front nine manages to provide a little muscle via a pair of bunkerless par 4s (the 411-yard 3rd and the incongruously long 467-yard 6th) but is otherwise led by two shorter tests, the 487-yard dogleg right 5th (where water can snare a hooked second or third) and the more aggressively bunkered 347-yard 9th. The back provides a bit more interest, first at the 147-yard 11th (played across a large expanse of sand), then at the 469-yard 14th (a pond-guarded par 5) and the 296-yard 15th, which is driveable but across a trio of large right-side bunkers. The 347-yard soundly bunkered 18th is an obviously small finisher, but it plays to a very shallow green angled behind front-right sand.

Western Skies Golf Club - Gilbert   ♦♦

Brad Whitcombe   www.westernskiesgolf.com
1245 East Warner Rd, Gilbert, AZ 85296   (480) 545-8542
            6,744 yds   Par 72   Rating: 70.6 / 123   (1992)

A shortish layout routed among housing and lots of native, sandy terrain, the Western Skies Golf Club is a slightly offbeat design which relies less on man-made water hazards than many area layouts but also lacks a touch of the luster generally provided by a more established course architect. Despite its modest frame, many of its stronger holes are of the longer variety, including the 441-yard dogleg left 8th (the number one stroke hole) the 435-yard 9th, the 220-yard bunkerless 12th and the 545-yard 16th, a straightaway test which slips between two goalpost-like trees en route to a narrow, S-shaped green. And while water is indeed used sparingly, its presence does enhance the memorability of holes like the 201-yard 4th and the 353-yard 18th (both featuring large bunkers buffering their greens from otherwise adjacent lakes), as well as the 353-yard pond-side 17th. But with fairway bunkers bothering drives on only two holes, and its par 4s averaging only 382 yards, this remains a layout well-suited to an average golfing clientele.

Wickenburg Country Club - Wickenburg   ◆◆

William P. & William F. Bell / Terry Woodland   www.wickenburgcountry.club
1420 North Country Club Dr, Wickenburg, AZ 85390   (928) 684-2011
6,320 yds   Par 71   Rating: 70.5 / 128   (1949)

Golf at the Wickenburg Country Club began in 1949 when two generations of Billy Bells built a short, compact and notably sandy nine, the remains of which can still be seen at the present holes 1, 8, 10, 12 and 18. But in 2006 the club hired one Terry Woodland to renovate the existing loop and add nine more holes, with the resulting 18 showing something of a dichotomy between some tricked-up newer entries and many of the more natural older ones. Among the former fall the 454-yard par-5 2nd (a sharp dogleg left whose green is guarded by a man-made pond) and the 373-yard 4th, which is menaced by a similarly manufactured right-side creekbed. More organic-feeling tests include the 422-yard uphill 13th and the 513-yard 18th (a downhill dry wash-crossing closer), as well as a trio of desert-surrounded par 3s which appear within a four-hole stretch: the 235-yard 14th, the 161-yard 16th and the 229-yard 17th. A slow-to-develop real estate subdivision is in the process of surrounding several of the new outlying holes, a concession to the economic realities of modern golf – and the source of several mammoth cart rides.

Wickenburg Ranch (Big Wick) - Wickenburg   ◆◆◆

William Brownlee & Wendell Pickett   www.wickenburgranch.com
3312 Maverick Dr, Wickenburg, AZ 85390   (928) 668-5535
7,059 yds   Par 71   Rating: 72.4 / 139   (2014)

A new real estate-oriented facility located just off Route 93, five miles northwest of town, Wickenburg Ranch features a strong, challenging 18 which drew a fair bit of regional publicity upon opening – an unintended benefit of being one of the Southwest's earliest new post-recession layouts. Presently open for public play prior to a planned conversion to private status down the road, this is modern, bells-and-whistles desert golf, with four man-made lakes and 70 bunkers enlivening play – though such stylings often do feel a tad incongruous upon the desert landscape. Though there is plenty of interesting golf present, things occasionally touch on formulaic, the most obvious example being a trio of longer par 5s with dry washes crossing +/- 30 yards shy of their greens: the 622-yard 5th, the 562-yard 7th and the 614-yard 18th. Conversely, the layout's collection of six par 3s includes some notable entries, led by the 209-yard uphill 2nd (whose tiny green sits beyond six front-left bunkers), the 183-yard pond-fronted 4th, the 246-yard 13th (played significantly downhill, but to a lakeside green) and the 212-yard 17th, another downhill test played across two fronting bunkers. The two-shotters may be the course's least distinguished subset, but among their best are the 438-yard downhill 3rd (a sharp dogleg left around a hillside) and the 343-yard 6th, a dogleg right which dares a long carry across a corner pond. A nine-hole par-3 course adjoins (page 109).   **(GD: #21 State)**

500 Club at Adobe Dam (Futures) - Glendale   ♦½

Brian Whitcomb   www.the500club.com
4707 West Pinnacle Peak Rd, Glendale, AZ 85310   (623) 492-9500
               1,464 yds   Par 28   Rating: 26.5 / 74   (2004)

A new millennium addition to the then-15-year-old regulation course at the 500 Club at Adobe Dam, the par-28 Futures layout fills a patch of sandy acreage between the big 18 and West Pinnacle Peak Road, and is a well-above-average facility of this type. After opening with a 282-yard straightaway par 4, it plays over eight one-shotters measuring between 73-182 yards, all of which feature relevant bunkering, little of which can be considered invasive. The strongest entry (on size alone) is the 182-yard 2nd, but the 157-yard 4th and the 164-yard 5th weigh in relatively close behind.

Adobe Dam Family Golf Center - Glendale   ♦

Pete Jelsrud   www.adobedamfamilygolfcenter.com
3847 West Pinnacle Peak Rd, Glendale, AZ 85310   (623) 581-2800
               1,783 yds   Par 31   Rating: 29.1 / 87   (1993)

Situated within the Adobe Dam Recreation Area, less than a mile east of the 500 Club course, the Adobe Dam Family Golf Center is a short executive nine which differs from many such user-friendly layouts by leaving native desert to flank nearly all of its fairways. The holes themselves are mostly basic, however, with only six bunkers affecting play and water being a threat only at the 142-yard 9th. The 475-yard 2nd (a dogleg left to the rare tree-guarded green) is easily the longest and most imposing entry.

Aguila Golf Club (Par 3) - Laveen   ♦

Gary Panks   www.phoenix.gov/golf
8440 South 35th Ave, Laveen, AZ 85339   (602) 237-9601
               1,081 yds   Par 27   Rating: 28.7 / 81   (1999)

Squeezed in between this municipal facility's main 18-hole layout and the adjacent Cesar Chavez Park, the Aguila Golf Club's Par 3 course is clearly well-suited to beginners and the less skilled. Its holes range in length from 66-183 yards, and with only four bunkers and zero water in play, there is little here to get in the way of forward progress. The 66-yard 4th, though obviously tiny, does pose the question of how to stop so short a pitch quickly, as one of the four bunkers fronts the great majority of the putting surface.

Augusta Ranch Golf Club - Mesa

Bill Phillips   www.augustaranchgolf.com
2401 S. Lansing, Mesa, AZ 85209   (480) 354-1234
                 3,788 yds   Par 61   Rating: 59.2 / 88   (1999)

An occasionally ambitious executive facility located in the Phoenix area's far eastern reaches, the Augusta Ranch Golf Club weaves its way through neighborhoods of single-family homes over two nines which vary significantly in challenge. The front is basic short course fare, with only the 145-yard 8th (played across a large fronting bunker) and the 144-yard over-water 9th standing out. The back, on the other hand, offers a quartet of engaging par 4s: the 299-yard lake-fronted 10th, the 293-yard 12th (driveable between bunkers and out-of-bounds), the 300-yard ditch-fronted 15th and especially the 316-yard 18th, where left-side water flanks the fairway and edges in before the green.

Bear Creek Golf Complex (Cub) - Chandler

Nicklaus Design   www.bearcreekaz.com
500 East Riggs Rd, Chandler, AZ 85249   (480) 883-8200
                 3,501 yds   Par 59   Rating: 57.3 / 83   (2001)

Situated adjacent to a regulation-size Nicklaus-designed municipal facility known as the Bear course, the Bear Creek Golf Complex's Cub course is an 18-hole executive track which begins with six compact par 3s just south of the clubhouse before ranging out (and expanding) to the northeast. But with only a single bunker in play (at the 286-yard 17th) and plenty of maintained turf buffering its fairways from the rough native terrain, this is both a less challenging and less engaging layout than one might anticipate under the Nicklaus masthead. Still, it surely serves its purpose of catering to the less-skilled, and the 129-yard 18th sharing a water hazard with the main course's closer is a nice touch.

Bellair Golf Course - Glendale ♦½

Red Lawrence, Greg Nash & Jeff Hardin   www.bellairgolf.com
17233 North 45th Ave, Glendale, AZ 85308   (602) 978-0330
                 3,943 yds   Par 59   Rating: 56.2 / 90   (1972)

Built by veteran desert designer Red Lawrence with help from then-youngsters Greg Nash and Jeff Hardin, the Bellair Golf Course is a frequently challenging executive layout which relies far more on Lawrence's large greenside bunkers than a profligate use of water for playing interest. This is readily visible at tightly bunkered holes like the 123-yard 5th, the 104-yard 11th and the 184-yard 12th, as well as the 286-yard 17th, where two centerline bunkers enliven play. Longer entries include the 217-yard 4th, the 203-yard 8th (whose green angles around front-right sand) and the 354-yard 9th. Solid of this type.

Continental Golf Course - Scottsdale   ◆

Greg Nash   www.continentalgc.com
7920 East Osborn Rd, Scottsdale, AZ 85251   (480) 941-1585
                3,766 yds   Par 60   Rating: 58.4 / 85   (1978)

A Greg Nash-designed executive layout with its nines sitting on either side of East Osborn Road, the Continental Golf Course provides a mostly rudimentary test, with only five bunkers appearing (none terribly invasively) and water popping up in the form of two lakes and a mostly decorative creek. While the 141-yard 4th requires a partial carry across one of the water hazards, the real story lies at the 340-yard 18th, a dogleg right which bends around the second and offers several lines of play, including a full water carry towards the green. The rest, however, is mostly basic.

Coronado Golf Course - Scottsdale   ◆

Milton Coggins, Greg Nash & Jeff Hardin   www.coronadogolfscottsdale.com
2829 North Miller Rd, Scottsdale, AZ 85257   (480) 947-8364
                1,850 yds   Par 31   Rating: 28.4 / 80   (1961)

The Continental Golf Course's immediate neighbor to the south, Coronado is a similarly basic facility, whose executive-size nine is wedged into an oddly shaped site, and around a driving range. Sand is once again scarce and while three lakes dot the landscape, none factor very seriously into play – unless one snaphooks the tee ball at the 278-yard 6th . Well-suited to the less skilled, but not on the serious golfer's radar.

Desert Mirage Golf Course - Glendale   ◆

Bill Phillips   www.golfdm.com
8710 West Maryland Ave, Glendale, AZ 85305   (623) 772-0110
                2,046 yds   Par 31   Rating: 29.6 / 89   (1999)

A good-size executive loop situated on a residence-encircled site half a mile east of University of Phoenix Stadium, the Desert Mirage Golf Course is another facility which offers mostly rudimentary golf before culminating in an engaging finisher – in this case the 322-yard 9th, whose green is buttonhooked beyond a left-side lake. The first eight holes are divided on either side of the driving range and are led by the 353-yard straightaway opener, the 327-yard 4th (which curves rightward, between the driving range and left-side out-of-bounds) and the 170-yard 8th.

Desert Sands Golf Course - Mesa   ◆

Arthur Jack Snyder   www.desertsandsgc.com
1922 South 74th St, Mesa, AZ 85208   (480) 832-0210
            4,029 yds   Par 65   Rating: 59.8 / 88   (1969)

Lying just south of the Superstition Freeway, the Desert Sands Golf Course is an Arthur Jack Snyder-designed executive layout that began life as a private club for the residential development through which it winds. Operating as a public facility today, it is a good-size but completely basic track, with nary a bunker to be seen and ponds only materially affecting play at the 151-yard 8th (right of the green) and the 137-yard 10th (front-left). Another area facility well-suited to the lesser skilled or the beginner.

Encanto Golf Course (Executive) - Phoenix   ◆

William F. Bell   www.phoenix.gov/golf
2775 North 15th Ave, Phoenix, AZ 85007   (602) 253-3963
            1,710 yds   Par 30   Rating: - / -   (1952)

Playing out of a separate clubhouse around the corner on West Encanto Boulevard, the Encanto Golf Course's executive nine borders the facility's venerable regulation layout, a 1935 Billy Bell design. The executive course, which was laid out by Bell's son William F. , is a simple, nearly hazard-free loop – the "nearly" being required due to the presence of a single left-side fairway bunker (likely to steer tee shots away from adjacent homes) at the 312-yard 9th hole. Three par 4s are included, though two of them (the 267-yard 1st and the 245-yard 5th) will regularly be reached by most capable ball strikers today.

Fiesta Lakes Golf Course - Mesa   ◆

Unknown
1415 South Westwood, Mesa, AZ 85210   (480) 969-0377
            1,503 yds   Par 29   Rating: 35.0 / 113   (1978)

Built just east of the Fiesta Mall, along the northern side of the Superstition Freeway, the Fiesta Lakes Golf Course is a short, nearly bunker-free par-3 layout with a pair of short par 4s slipped in for variety. The first of these, the 274-yard 4th, is one of three holes to incorporate a central lake, with the 155-yard 5th and 117-yard 6th both playing across corners of the hazard. The remaining six holes are essentially basic, though overall the layout boasts one huge plus: with numerous mature trees lining its fairways, there is an uncommon amount of shade here for summer play.

Fountain of the Sun Country Club - Mesa   ♦½

Red Lawrence   www.foscc-az.com
500 South 80th St, Mesa, AZ 85208   (480) 986-3128
          4,254 yds   Par 63   Rating: 60.1 / 94   (1972)

A short Red Lawrence-designed 18 built in 1972 on the site of a former cotton farm, the
Fountain of the Sun Country Club winds its way through rows of condominiums and
single-family homes and is, for the most part, purely a functional executive test. Sand is
relatively rare (10 greens are bunkerless) and water is present only at the 153-yard 18th.
However, moments of length are provided by the 400-yard tree-bothered 1st and the
516-yard dogleg right 10th – a twosome which bear the highly dubious distinction of
having cart paths routed directly down the middle of their fairways.

Greenfield Lakes Golf Course - Gilbert   ♦½

Ray Pacioni   www.greenfieldlakesgolfcourse.com
2484 East Warner Rd, Gilbert, AZ 85296   (480) 503-0500
          4,107 yds   Par 62   Rating: 58.6 / 88   (1997)

Its two nines lying on opposite sides of East Warner Road, the Greenfield Lakes Golf
Course is a notable executive layout in that it includes a pair of regulation-size par 5s, the
475-yard straightaway 12th and the 530-yard 18th, whose final 150 yards bend gently
along a lake. Bunkers are nonexistent but water is a frequent hazard, affecting six holes
in addition to the finisher, with the strongest being the 180-yard 3rd (water right), the
151-yard 4th (ditto), the 351-yard 9th (whose green angles rightward, beyond a pond) and
the 157-yard 13th. Hardly strategically inclined, but solid of this type.

Leisure World Country Club (Heron Lakes) - Mesa   ♦½

Johnny Bulla   www.leisureworldgolfarizona.com
908 South Power Rd, Mesa, AZ 85206   (480) 664-0762
          4,024 yds   Par 62   Rating: 61.5 / 100   (1978)

Though later joined by the regulation-size Coyote Run course seven years after its birth,
Leisure World's first golf facility was actually Heron Lakes, an above-the-median
executive track designed in 1978 by the iconic Johnny Bulla. While the longer front nine
includes a short par 5 (the 467-yard 4th) as well as the 364-yard 7th, the 1,833-yard back is
the story here, with a central lake allowing both the 162-yard 11th and the 179-yard 16th
to play as genuinely challenging water holes, and the 181-yard, well-bunkered 15th being
a strong dry test. The rest is mostly basic, occasionally well-bunkered short-course golf.

Moon Valley Country Club (Moonwalk) - Phoenix   ♦

Unknown   www.moonvalleycc.com
151 West Moon Valley Dr, Phoenix, AZ 85023   (602) 942-0000
1,687 yds   Par 54   Rating: - / -   (1990)

The creatively named Moonwalk course was a distinctly modern addition to the Moon Valley Country Club, with its 18 pitch-and-putt-length holes being squeezed into what used to be the club's 1st and 2nd fairways during a circa-1990 reconfiguration. An obviously nice amenity for the club's less-skilled, this is very basic golf, with holes averaging only 94 yards and no bunkers or water hazards present – though several patches of native desert have reappeared in recent years. Still, a pleasant luxury to have.

Palo Verde Golf Course - Phoenix   ♦

Unknown   www.phoenix.gov/golf
6215 North 15th Ave, Phoenix, AZ 85015   (602) 249-9930
1,752 yds   Par 30   Rating: 28.7 / 81   (1962)

Nestled into a residential neighborhood just a short drive north of downtown, the Palo Verde Golf Course is a no-frills executive nine routed around both a small lake and the facility's driving range. Though bunkerless throughout, the opening three holes follow a clockwise path around the lake – but only shots missed significantly right stand a chance of ending up wet. Two par 4s (the 1st and the 9th) measure at least 300 yards but on the whole, this is strictly basic neighborhood fare – and a good place to learn.

Palm Valley Golf Club (Lakes) - Goodyear   ♦♦

Hale Irwin   www.palmvalleygolf.com
2211 North Litchfield Rd, Goodyear, AZ 85338   (623) 935-2500
4,745 yds   Par 62   Rating: 61.8 / 95   (1999)

Sitting across North Litchfield Road from the Palm Valley Golf Club's regulation Palms course, the newer Lakes layout is an executive facility designed by Hall-of-Famer Hale Irwin – but one offering far more size and challenge than one expects of a "short" facility. Indeed, this may be the only executive track in the country boasting six par 4s in excess of 400 yards, with the 410-yard 2nd, the 403-yard 11th and the 409-yard 16th all playing to waterside greens, and the 430-yard 18th culminating in a narrow putting surface angled behind front-right sand. The par 3s range in length from 139-192 yards and are generally well-bunkered, making for one of the strongest short courses one is likely to encounter.

Paradise Peak West - Phoenix

Gary Grandstaff   www.theparadisepeakwest.com
3901 East Pinnacle Peak Rd, Phoenix, AZ 85050   (480) 515-2043
                    1,437 yards   Par 29 Rating: - / -   (1988)

Anchoring a 55-and-over community located in quieter country north of Scottsdale,
Paradise Peak West is a short private facility which provides no rating or slope
information. Though wedged into a rectangular housing-surrounded site, the course is a
notch above the norm for its type, mostly due to the extensive use of native terrain,
which affects play (often meaningfully) on eight holes. Despite homes pinching in closely
on a couple of occasions, this is certainly one of the region's better undersized entries.

Paradise Valley Park Golf Course - Phoenix

Milton Coggins / Greg Nash & Jeff Hardin   www.paradisevalleygc.com
3505 East Union Hills Dr, Phoenix, AZ 85050   (602) 992-7190
                    4,145 yds   Par 61   Rating: 59.2 / 88   (1972)

Bordered on its western flank by Paradise Valley Community College and the Piestewa
Freeway to the east, Paradise Valley Park began as a Milton Coggins-designed nine in
1972 before being expanded by local favorites Greg Nash and Jeff Hardin during the
1980s. Mostly basic in its design, the layout features large greens, sporadic bunkering
and water (in the form of one central lake) affecting only the left sides of the 150-yard
16th and the 327-yard 18th. The 475-yard 9th is the course's lone par 5, while more testing
muscle appears at the 202-yard 2nd and the 212-yard 16th.

Peoria Pines - Peoria

Greg Nash   www.peoriapines.com
8411 North 107th Ave, Peoria, AZ 85345   (623) 972-1364
                    4,412 yds   Par 63   Rating: 61.1 / 100   (1978)

Long known as the Country Meadows Golf Club, Peoria Pines lies just south of Sun City
and bills itself as a "Power Executive" course – this due presumably to the presence of
two full-size par 5s, as opposed to the electrical lines which slice across the course's mid-
section. The front nine fills a triangular tract on the east side of North 107th Avenue and,
in addition to the pond-guarded 527-yard 9th, is led by the 200-yard 4th and the 262-yard
7th, where a ditch and a cart path combine to divide the fairway into four sections. The
back then lies across the road to the west and is less engaging, its strongest entries being
the imposing 225-yard 13th and the 510-yard 18th, a gentle dogleg left.

Rolling Hills Golf Course - Tempe   ♦½

Gary Panks   www.tempe.gov/golf
1415 North Mill Ave, Tempe, AZ 85281   (480) 350-5275
             3,828 yds   Par 62   Rating: 58.9 / 93   (1987)

Situated within Papago Park, a mile southeast of the park's well-known regulation 18 and just south of the Phoenix Zoo, Rolling Hills is actually owned and operated by the City of Tempe, and is a short, lightly bunkered facility laid out by Gary Panks in 1987. Though often rudimentary, the layout does include a strong mid-section, led by the 151-yard 7th (played across lower ground to a shallow green) and a trio of driveable par 4s: the 282-yard 9th, the 268-yard 10th and the 301-yard 11th. Easily the layout's longest par 4, the 401-yard well-bunkered 18th doglegs gently left and provides a big finish.

Royal Palms Golf Course - Mesa   ♦

David Gill   www.royalpalmsgolfcourse.com
1415 East McKellips Rd, Mesa, AZ 85203   (480) 964-1709
             1,543 yds   Par 30   Rating: 26.1 / 97   (1976)

Built by Illinois-based architect David Gill during the mid-1970s, the Royal Palms Golf Course is a very short executive nine which only rises above par-3 status by having the 241-yard 1st, the 254-yard lakeside 3rd and the 225-yard 5th (which flanks the same water hazard) play as tiny par 4s. Wedged into a narrow sliver of land (and surrounded by housing), its remaining holes are basic, lightly bunkered par 3s ranging in length from 98-159 yards, making for a pleasant but not overly demanding round.

Scottsdale National Golf Club (Bad Little 9) - Scottsdale   N/A

Tim Jackson & David Kahn   www.sngc.com
28490 North 122nd St, Scottsdale, AZ 85262   (480) 443-8868

In addition to building a brand-new regulation facility of note at the Scottsdale National Golf Club (page 29), former GoDaddy.com boss Bob Parsons had architects Tim Jackson and David Kahn also build this, one of the world's quirkiest par-3 courses. Though no hole yardages are published, the nine wild entries average 108 yards and feature an off-the-wall range of green complexes, with some putting surfaces being huge and multi-level and others being far smaller – including the absolutely tiny 999-square foot 9th. Given the ability to set pins above some very deep bunkers, behind center-of-the-green boulders (at the 5th) or on some extraordinarily narrow fingers of putting surface (at the 6th), the loop can be set up to play very tough – particularly on Fridays, when Parsons reportedly offers a $1,000 for anyone who can break par. This sort of thing may not appeal to everyone, but dull or unoriginal this most certainly is not.

The Short Course - Paradise Valley

Forrest Richardson   www.mountainshadowsgolfclub.com
5445 East Lincoln Dr, Paradise Valley, AZ 85253   (480) 905-8999
                2,310 yds   Par 54   Rating: - / -   (2016)

A recreational centerpiece of the venerable Mountain Shadows resort, The Short Course is a brand-new par-3 layout built on the site of an old, very well-known Arthur Jack Snyder-designed executive course. Forrest Richardson's new version retains portions of Snyder's routing but little more, and weighs in as an elite facility of this type, lying among spacious single-family homes in a scenic desert setting and providing plenty of variety within its challenge. Holes range in length from 75-193 yards and tend to be strategically bunkered, while water affects only a trio of entries in the layout's center. Among these are the 75-yard 7th (whose greens juts dangerously forward into a pond), with other favorites including the 166-yard creek-guarded 11th and the 180-yard centerline-bunkered 15th. A nice replacement for a famed layout, and quite strong of this type.

Springfield Golf Resort - Chandler

Fore Golf   www.springfieldgolfresort.com
1200 East St Andrews Blvd, Chandler, AZ 85249   (480) 895-5759
                4,232 yds   Par 61   Rating: 60.9 / 99   (1996)

A residence-encircled facility situated just over a mile east of the huge Sun Lakes development, directly upon the Pinal County line, the Springfield Golf Resort is a stronger executive layout whose size and bunkering rate it favorably among the region's short courses. The front nine lies north of St Andrews Boulevard and is led by a pair of regulation-size par 4s, the 346-yard lake-flanked 3rd and the 386-yard 9th. The back's best action comes during an early trio of holes: the 348-yard 10th (where a lake lurks behind the green), the 145-yard 12th (which flanks the same hazard) and the 301-yard 13th, a narrow, out-of-bounds-lined test. Seldom flashy, but strong of this type.

Sun City (Lakes East) - Sun City

Jeff Hardin   www.sunaz.com
10433 West Talisman Rd, Sun City, AZ 85351   (623) 876-3024
                3,310 yds   Par 60   Rating: 56.8 / 84   (1970)

Sun City's first executive course, the Jeff Hardin-designed Lakes East, shares a clubhouse with the regulation Lakes West layout, as well as a near-semi-circular routing around a parallel residential neighborhood. Tripp Davis performed a 2006 renovation here, , opening up large areas of native sand and re-shaping some bunkering, but it remains a short, water-free track that is rated the massive development's easiest. Most notable are a trio of regulation-size par 3s: the 161-yard 8th, the 195-yard 9th and the 187-yard 17th.

Sun City (Willowbrook) - Sun City   ♦½

George Fazio   www.sunaz.com
10600 West Boswell Blvd, Sun City, AZ 85373   (623) 561-4600
            3,800 yds   Par 60   Rating: 58.7 / 89   (1974)

While building Sun City's regulation-size Willowcreek course (whose clubhouse it shares), George Fazio also laid out the executive Willowbrook, whose front side is actually one of the more engaging nines (of any size) in Sun City. Following the 297-yard 1st (which had a huge carry bunker removed during a 2013 renovation), the 184-yard 3rd and the 225-yard 4th would be at home on most regulation facilities, while both the 306-yard 5th and 112-yard 6th feature water prominently. The back nine, however, is far more basic – but this remains, comfortably Sun City's most engaging executive entry.

Sun City (Quail Run) - Sun City   ♦

Greg Nash & Jeff Hardin   www.sunaz.com
9774 W. Alabama Ave, Sun City, AZ 85351   (623) 876-3035
            2,029 yds   Par 31   Rating: 29.6 / 88   (1977)

The Sun City development's last executive layout to be built, the nine-hole Quail Run course was added by Greg Nash and Jeff Hardin in 1977, parallel to the Agua Fria Freeway on the community's eastern side. Strictly rudimentary, beginner-friendly stuff, this loop follows a clockwise routing around a large neighborhood but offers little which truly stands out, with only the pond-guarded 136-yard 5th breaking from the basic. The 484-yard 2nd and the 189-yard 3rd do, however, provide some element of size.

Sun City West (Stardust) - Sun City West   ♦½

Greg Nash   www.rcscw.com
12702 West Stardust Blvd, Sun City West, AZ 85375   (623) 544-6012
            4,267 yds   Par 60   Rating: 60.6 / 96   (1980)

The oldest of the Sun City West development's three executive 18s, the Stardust course is a 1980 Greg Nash design which features a fair number of holes that rise above the mundane. Early on, well-bunkered par 3s like the 147-yard 2nd and the 140-yard 5th carry the ball, while the finishers include the water-oriented 160-yard 16th and 202-yard 17th. Most challenging, however are robust par 3s like the 201-yard 3rd, the 225-yard 6th and the 210-yard 12th, as well as a trio of full-size par 4s: the 325-yard bunker-narrowed 9th, the 389-yard 10th and the 385-yard 18th. Well above average executive fare.

Sun City West (Echo Mesa) - Sun City West   ◆◆

Greg Nash   www.rcscw.com
20349 North Echo Mesa Dr, Sun City West, AZ 85375   (623) 544-6014
4,157 yds   Par 60   Rating: 60.6 / 96   (1987)

The Echo Mesa course was Sun City West's second executive layout and, for many, may rate even better than the Stardust, this due mostly to a number of oddly shaped green complexes offering some creative pin positions, notably at the 168-yard over-water 6th, the 141-yard bunker-squeezed 7th and the 390-yard 9th. Several more demanding water-oriented par 3s also appear, including the 108-yard 2nd (played to a dangerous peninsula green), the similarly challenging 215-yard 13th (where water flanks the right side) and the stiff 235-yard 17th, which could hold its own on most any regulation-size layout. Not every hole carries a high level of playing interest, but this strong executive stuff overall.

Sun City West (Desert Trails) - Sun City West   ◆½

Greg Nash & Billy Casper   www.rcscw.com
22525 N. Executive Way, Sun City West, AZ 85375   (623) 544-6017
4,027 yds   Par 61   Rating: 59.6 / 89   (1995)

Sun City West's final executive layout, 1995's Desert Trails, is both the lowest-rated and, arguably, the least engaging of the executive tracks, but there is still enough here to rate it an above-average short course entry. Comparatively little of this quality appears on the front side, though the 214-yard 7th (with green angled beyond front-ride sand) is certainly strong enough. The 351-yard 10th then kicks of an inward half highlighted by the 370-yard 15th and the 121-yard 16th (a pair of more challenging holes situated on either side of a large pond), as well as the 150-yard well-bunkered 17th.

Sun Lakes (Sun Lakes) - Chandler   ◆½

Unknown   www.sunlakesofarizona.com
25425 N. Sunlakes Blvd, Chandler, AZ 85248   (480) 895-9274
3,874 yds   Par 60   Rating: 59.3 / 102   (1974)

Among the Sun Lakes development's 99 holes of golf, the executive Sun Lakes course is the community's oldest, dating to 1974, when it stood virtually alone upon the vast, as-yet-undeveloped south Maricopa County landscape. Measuring 3,874 yards, it occupies a narrow tract whose odd semi-circular shape fits nicely into the geometric platting of the surrounding neighborhood. Golf-wise, it is a mid-range executive track which remains mostly staid in its design, its playing interest briefly rising at over-water par 3s like the 175-yard 2nd, the 127-yard 6th, the 158-yard 16th and the 131-yard 17th.

Sun Lakes (Palo Verde) - Sun Lakes

Unknown   www.sunlakesofarizona.com
10801 E. San Tan Blvd, Sun Lakes, AZ   85248   (480) 895-0300
4,108 yds   Par 62   Rating: 59.7 / 96   (1985)

The Sun Lakes development's second executive course, the Palo Verde, dates to 1985 and is situated at the property's eastern edge where, despite being a somewhat longer executive track, its golf is a touch less engaging than Sun Lakes. Divided by East San Tan Boulevard, its nines form a pair of strikingly similar clockwise loops, with every hole flanked on both sides by housing. What water there is scarcely affects play and the bunkering is largely rudimentary, but there is, at least, a bit of solid size present at the 399-yard 10th, the 369-yard tightly bunkered 13th and the 483-yard par-5 closer.

Sun Village Golf Course - Surprise

Unknown   www.sunvillage.org
17300 N. Sun Village Pkwy, Surprise, AZ   85374   (623) 584-5774
2,000 yds   Par 54   Rating: 50.4 / 64   (1987)

A well-thought-of par-3 layout located just south of Sun City West, the Sun Village Golf Course follows a circuitous routing through a large 55-and-over residential development and is really a layout in two halves. The front nine occupies the property's northern side and features a series of simple, functional holes with large greens, generally bunkered on either side. The back brings water at somewhat into play on its final eight holes, with the most engaging being the 111-yard 15th and the 141-yard 17th. The water never gets too close to any putting surfaces, but it does serve to enliven an otherwise basic track.

SunBird Golf Course - Chandler   ◆½

Gary Panks   www.sunbirdhoa.com
6250 Sunbird Blvd, Chandler, AZ   85249   (480) 802-4901
4,457 yds   Par 66   Rating: 61.3 / 95   (1987)

An uncommonly long and challenging executive facility, the Sun Bird Golf Course anchors a 55-and-over residential community and sits next door to the Springfield Golf Resort, where it was laid out by Gary Panks in 1987. Its 2,614-yard front nine is enormous by short course standards, and includes full-size entries like the 414-yard 2nd, the 220-yard 3rd, the narrow 380-yard 4th and the 478-yard 7th, which slips between two ponds en route to a heavily bunkered green. Only on the 1,843-yard back do things settle back to standard executive size, with stronger entries including a pair of short par-4 finishers, the 284-yard pond-narrowed 16th and the 301-yard 18th, a driveable dogleg left around sand.

Sunland Springs Golf Course - Mesa   ♦½

Unknown   www.sunlandsprings.com
2233 South Springwood Blvd, Mesa, AZ 85209   (480) 984-4999
    Superstition/San Tan:4,732 yds   Par 65   Rating: 61.4 / 96   (1997)
    Four Peaks: 2,165 yds   Par 31   Rating: 29.9 / 90   (1997)

A 27-hole facility lying half a mile south of the Superstition Freeway, along the Pinal County line, the executive Sunland Springs Golf Course provides mostly basic, lightly hazarded golf over three nines routed through rows of single-family homes. The strongest combination (narrowly) pairs the Superstition and San Tan nines, though the former is a sporadically bunkered loop (five greens are hazardless) whose most notable entry is the 519-yard 4th, a dogleg left par 5. The San Tan also includes a full-size three-shotter (the 504-yard 8th) but is highlighted by the 309-yard pond-guarded 2nd. Though comfortably the club's shortest and easiest loop, the Four Peaks nine includes a pair of shorter water holes, the 317-yard 2nd and the 144-yard all-carry 3rd.

Sunland Village Golf Club - Mesa   ♦

Milton Coggins, Greg Nash & Jeff Hardin   www.sunlandvillagegolfcourse.com
725 South Rochester, Mesa, AZ 85205   (480) 832-3691
    3,623 yds   Par 62   Rating: 58.1 / 87   (1975)

A residence-surrounded facility occupying four separate road-divided tracts, the Sunland Village Golf Club sits just west of Leisure World and offers a mostly functional, lightly bunkered layout upon which several lakes provide the occasional dose of heightened playing interest. On the back nine these hazards lie near the property's southern tip where they particularly affect the 242-yard par-4 14th and the 112-yard 15th. A pair of front nine ponds are mostly decorative, however, leaving the 325-yard 8th (which twists past the maintenance yard and between bunkers) as the loop's most engaging entry.

Sunland Village East Golf Course - Mesa   ♦

Milton Coggins   www.svegolf.com
2250 South Buttercup, Mesa, AZ 85208   (480) 986-4079
    3,621 yds   Par 62   Rating: 58.7 / 89   (1987)

Sunland Village East lies three miles southeast of the older Sunland Village Golf Club, where its L-shaped routing – in a concession to real estate sales – includes rows of homes running down the center of each nine in addition to standing along the perimeter. The front is mostly basic stuff (all nine greens are bunkerless) but perks up briefly at the pond-guarded 285-yard 4th and 109-yard 5th. The back is completely dry but does feature some greenside bunkering – though usually in a fashion more decorative than dangerous.

Viewpoint Golf Resort - Mesa   ♦

Michael Rus   www.viewpointgolfresort.com
650 North Hawes Rd, Mesa, AZ   85207   (480) 373-5555
2,162 yds   Par 33   Rating: 30.4 / 94   (1986)

Playing second fiddle to the club's fairly basic primary 18, the Viewpoint Golf Resort's older executive course lies immediately to the east, where it is routed in a perfect rectangle through a sea of RV sites. With every hole thus being dead straight, its design is pretty basic, with only the decently bunkered 216-yard par-4 9th rising much further. Notably, power lines cut across two sections of the routing, running directly over top of the 292-yard 3rd hole and very closely flanking both the 190-yard 7th and the 159-yard 8th.

Wickenburg Ranch (Li'l Wick) - Wickenburg   ♦½

William Brownlee & Wendell Pickett   www.wickenburgranch.com
3312 Maverick Dr, Wickenburg, AZ   85390   (928) 668-5535
1,240 yds   Par 27   Rating: - / -   (2016)

Occupying land that once housed the club's driving range, Wickenburg Ranch's Li'l Wick course is a nine-hole par-3 affair that is designed more for socializing and fun that serious golf. That's not to suggest that it lacks for playing interest, however as water significantly affects three holes and bunkering is plentiful (including some hazards placed adjacent to tees, allowing the rare opportunity to practice long bunker shots). But with the music from the site's central restaurant/hangout deliberately broadcast across the course, lounge chairs (and even a hammock) adorning most tees and four holes lit for night play, this is much closer to Top Golf than, say, the par-3 course at Augusta National.

PINAL
COUNTY

Encanterra Country Club - Queen Creek   ♦♦♦

Tom Lehman   www.encanterragolf.com
36460 N Encanterra Dr, Queen Creek, AZ 85140   (480) 677-8148
        7,176 yds   Par 72   Rating: 73.9 / 130   (2008)

A high-end real estate development built in agricultural country just outside of Maricopa County, the Encanterra Country Club is anchored by a modern Tom Lehman-designed golf course which, despite the contrived nature of its lake-filled desert landscape, offers more playing interest than many of the region's similarly water-heavy facilities. There is often a real strategic bent present; indeed, while water significantly affects the majority of holes, its invasiveness can often be minimized with intelligent shotmaking. On the front nine, this is evident at the 582-yard 3rd (where a lake flanks the right side) and the 458-yard 5th (where drives challenging a huge right-side bunker lessen the impact of left-side water on the second) and especially at the 342-yard 7th, where a long right-side lake carry off the tee leaves a wide-open pitch. The back nine's best entries include another short, watery two-shotter (the driveable 322-yard 12th) as well as a pair of holes whose greens are tucked behind man-made creeks, the 555-yard 13th and the 449-yard 16th. Doses of over-the-top length are also present in juiced-up par 4s like the 504-yard lake-flanked 6th and the 498-yard 15th (the Phoenix Open, after all, is unlikely to be held this far out of town) but regardless, Encanterra is strong enough to stand – for the present – behind only Superstition Mountain as Pinal County's best.

Superstition Mountain (Prospector) - Apache Junction   ♦♦♦

Jack Nicklaus & Gary Nicklaus   www.superstitionmountain.com
8000 E Club Village Dr, Apache Junction, AZ 85218   (480) 983-3200
        7,225 yds   Par 72   Rating: 73.4 / 135   (1998)

Located at the far eastern edge of the metropolitan Phoenix area, in the shadows of the famous peak for which it's named, Superstition Mountain is a real estate development sporting a pair of brawny, typically interesting Jack Nicklaus-designed courses which, in the face of limited competition, each rate among Pinal County's very best. The older Prospector course cut its teeth by hosting the Champions Tour's Tradition in 2002 (won by Jim Thorpe), then later was an LPGA Tour stop (at 6,662 yards) from 2004-2008, counting Lorena Ochoa (twice), Anneka Sorenstam (twice) and Juli Inkster among its champions. Routed amidst mostly low-density housing, the Prospector lies entirely north of the clubhouse, where its outward half kicks off with the 418-yard smartly bunkered 1st, before featuring the 487-yard par-4 3rd (played along a shallow dry wash), the 579-yard dry wash-fronted 7th and the strong 236-yard 8th. The back opens with the 369-yard 10th (where a centerline bunker sits precisely where the ideal drive might finish), then offers another in-fairway hazard of the tee at the 589-yard dogleg left 13th, and a fairly strong two-shotter at the 446-yard barranca-crossed 16th. Refreshingly, a man-made water hazard appears only once, along the left side of the 533-yard finisher, a nearly straight par 5 whose green is tucked beyond the end of the long, narrow lake. Strong enough overall but as a 73.4 rating suggests, not backbreakingly difficult stuff.

Superstition Mountain (Lost Gold) - Apache Junction   ◆◆◆

Jack Nicklaus & Jack Nicklaus II   www.superstitionmountain.com
8000 E Club Village Dr, Apache Junction, AZ 85218   (480) 983-3200
7,351 yds   Par 72   Rating: 74.0 / 140   (1999)

Though it was already open at the time of their visits, neither the Champions nor the LPGA Tour utilized Superstition Mountain's Lost Gold course, and with good reason: Though rating less than a stroke tougher on paper, this is a strong enough golf course that it might not have proven itself the best vehicle for marketing their product. Laid out primarily to the south of its older sibling, Lost Gold includes five par 4s in excess of 445 yards and makes rather more invasive use of the desert, which fronts, or closely flanks, a fair number of greens. This is quickly apparent at the 558-yard 2nd, a tactically engaging dry wash-fronted par 5 which joins the 455-yard 1st in creating a strapping getaway. The remainder of the front nine includes a pair of muscular par 3s at the 208-yard 4th (whose narrow green angles leftward behind a large bunker) and the 219-yard 8th, as well as the 409-yard 9th, whose green is angled across another dry wash. Among the back nine's best are its two par 5s, the 589-yard 10th (which shares the seemingly obligatory double green with the par-3 17th) and the 531-yard 14th, a sharp dogleg right to still another dry wash-fronted putting surface. As on the adjacent Prospector course, the layout's lone water hazard is a single lake which affects play at the last, in this case a dangerous 467-yard par 4 played to a green tucked flush to the hazard. Notably, the club has added forward tees on both courses which allow each to be configured as short courses (one a par 3, one an executive) to widen its playing options for less-skilled golfers.

Francisco Grande Golf Resort - Casa Grande

Ralph Plummer   www.franciscogrande.com
2684 West Gila Bend Hwy, Casa Grande, AZ 85293   (520) 836-6444
            7,545 yds   Par 72   Rating: 75.3 / 130   (1963)

There is a long and very interesting sporting history at the Francisco Grande Resort, for it
was built by former San Francisco Giants owner Horace Stoneham and long served as the
team's annual spring training home. The Baseball fields which once bordered the first
fairway have been replaced by soccer pitches now (though novelties like a bat-shaped
swimming pool drop the occasional historical hint) but Ralph Plummer's 1963 golf course
remains in play – albeit in much larger form than the sub-7,000-yard size of its early
years. Little has changed in terms of design, however, for this is vintage postwar desert
golf: a flat, green, palm-dotted oasis spiced up by the periodic use of water. Strategic
interest is largely absent, but stronger tests include the 420-yard 1st (with water left of
the green), the 183-yard 8th (nearly all carry over a lake) and the 182-yard 16th (ditto).
Even more notable, however, are six very long par 4s, four of which anchor a back nine
which weighs in at a scary 3,859 yards, including 473 and 474-yard finishers. Challenging
(if limited) golf, but there is plenty of neat ambience and history here.

Gold Canyon Golf Resort (Sidewinder) - Gold Canyon

Greg Nash / Ken Kavanaugh   www.gcgr.com
6100 S. Kings Ranch Rd, Gold Canyon, AZ 85219   (480) 982-9449
            6,533 yds   Par 71   Rating: 71.4 / 133   (1982/1998)

Situated in mountain-flanked, golf-rich territory (Superstition Mountain borders it to the
north while the public Mountain Brook abuts its western flank), Gold Canyon is a scenic
facility whose golfing life began in 1982 with nine Greg Nash-designed holes which today
form the back nine of the Sidewinder course. Ken Kavanaugh (and club superintendent
Stuart Penge) added the quirkily routed front nine in 1998, creating what is today the
lesser of the resort's two layouts. The outward half plays around the far side of a large
mountain ridge, where it opens with the loop's lone water hole, a 487-yard pond-flanked
par 5. Thereafter, play is led by the stout 251-yard par-3 2nd, the 400-yard arroyo-fronted
3rd and the 523-yard 6th, a strong par 5 whose left-side dry wash eventually cuts in before
the green. The back is a more real estate-oriented nine which, early on, descends gently
to the west. Its best golf comes late, however, during a four-hole closing stretch which
includes the watery 418-yard 15th, the 447-yard dry wash-crossed 16th, the quirky 319-
yard 17th (where multiple driving options are offered) and the 505-yard 18th, which jumps
one final dry wash en route to a shallow, tightly bunkered green.

Gold Canyon Golf Resort (Dinosaur Mt.) - Gold Canyon   ♦♦♦

Ken Kavanaugh   www.gcgr.com
6100 S. Kings Ranch Rd, Gold Canyon, AZ   85219   (480) 982-9449
              6,652 yds   Par 70   Rating: 71.5 / 144   (1986/1997)

Gold Canyon's newer Ken Kavanaugh-designed Dinosaur Mountain course arrived on the
scene in two parts, with holes 1-4 and 14-18 constructed in 1986, and all that lie in
between added in 1997.   Climbing significantly into the foothills, it is an undulating,
scenically grand design which perhaps draws less national attention than any comparably
memorable course in the state. Some of the strongest action comes early, first at the
uphill 514-yard 3rd (which climbs through a canyon to a very narrow elevated green) and
a pair of long downhill tests, the 467-yard dogleg left 4th (with its scenic view of
Superstition Mountain) and the panoramic 236-yard 5th. Play takes on a bit of housing-
lined conventionality over the next five holes (though the 542-yard pond-flanked 9th is a
solid enough entry) before returning to more adventurous terrain from the 11th tee on
through the close. Highlights on this southbound homeward run include the sharply
downhill 226-yard 14th, the 378-yard 15th (a tempting entry played over an arroyo-divided
split-fairway), the 535-yard 16th (whose elevated green buttonhooks left behind sand)
and the nicely bunkered – but relatively easy - 366-yard 18th. With housing usually being
confined to the course's perimeters, Dinosaur Mountain enjoys enough aesthetic appeal
to rate among Arizona's more highly regarded resort tracks. (**GW**: #180 Resort)

Southern Dunes Golf Club - Maricopa   ♦♦♦

Lee Schmidt, Brian Curley & Fred Couples   www.akchinsoutherndunes.com
40456 West Hwy 238, Maricopa, AZ 85239   (480) 367-8949
              7,546 yds   Par 72   Rating: 76.4 / 142   (2002)

Drawing a fair amount of attention upon its 2002 opening, Southern Dunes began life as
a private, men-only golf club which, after several subsequent incarnations, is today
owned by the nearby Ak-Chin Hotel & Casino. The golf course lies adjacent to the Gila
River Indian Community 25 miles south of Phoenix, and is a sprawling test whose heavy
shaping manages, in its better moments, to resemble a sort of Royal Melbourne in the
desert. Like most courses built by the prolific Scottsdale-based firm of Lee Schmidt and
Brian Curley, there is a clear strategic element present, particularly at holes like the well-
bunkered 451-yard 5th, the 468-yard 12th (which favors drives flirting with left-side sand),
the 323-yard option-laden 14th, and throughout a collection of heavily bunkered par 5s
which average 585 yards in length. The odd nod to finesse also appears, notably at the
14th, as well as the 370-yard dogleg right 2nd and the attractively bunkered 165-yard 4th.
But in the end, a 7,546-yard layout is ultimately about muscle – a point driven home late
in each nine by powerhouse par 4s like the 484-yard 8th, the 483-yard 9th, the 496-yard
dogleg left 15th and the 463-yard 18th, a predictably demanding closer played to a
narrow, water-guarded green. Though clearly geared towards tournament golf, Southern
Dunes still manages to provide ample room for the less skilled to get around relatively
unscathed. Particularly within its bunker shaping, this is a distinctive layout within the
region – and one of the top casino courses in the country. (**GW**: #88 Resort)

Apache Creek Golf Course - Apache Junction   ♦♦

Joe Alsip   www.apachecreekgolfclub.com
3401 S Ironwood Dr, Apache Junction, AZ 85120   (480) 982-2677
6,785 yds   Par 71   Rating: 71.3 / 123   (1994)

Sitting just off the south side of the Superstition Freeway, barely a mile into Pinal County, the Apache Creek Golf Course is a rarity in the Phoenix area: a housing-free layout upon which native terrain runs rampant, with nearly every hole being surrounded by open desert. Though not terribly long and a tad unpolished, there is plenty of solid golf here, especially on the front nine, a 3,338-yard loop whose feature hole is the 145-yard 6th, a diminutive test but one played to a none-too-generous island green. The rest of the loop is best represented by a trio of strong par 4s: the 435-yard 2nd (a sharp dogleg right), the twisting 436-yard 5th (a very tricky driving hole with water down the right side) and the 414-yard 8th, whose green complex is a large grass island within the sand. The back is noticeably less interesting but does include two more short-but-enjoyable water holes (the 153-yard 12th and the 389-yard pond-fronted 17th) as well as a truly gigantic closer, the 490-yard 18th, a sweeping dogleg left and by miles the club's longest par 4.

Apache Sun Golf Club - Queen Creek   ♦

Leo Johnson
919 East Pima Rd, Queen Creek, AZ 85140   (480) 987-9065
2,550 yds   Par 34   Rating: 30.8 / 96   (1985)

Another course situated little more than a mile into Pinal County, the Apache Sun Golf Club is a compact, rudimentary, mostly flat nine-holer best suited to beginners or the less skilled. Hazards are limited (three bunkers in total, and a single, mostly decorative lake) as is the overall level of playing interest, though the 170-yard 7th and the 121-yard well-bunkered 9th are reasonably engaging. But on the whole, very basic stuff.

Arizona City Golf Course - Arizona City

Arthur Jack Snyder   www.myazcitygolf.com
13939 S Cleator Rd, Arizona City, AZ   85223   (520) 466-5327
                  6,742 yds   Par 72   Rating: 72.0 / 116   (1963)

The lone golf facility in this desert town of 10,500, the Arizona City Golf Course dates to 1963 when Arthur Jack Snyder routed it through several residential neighborhoods which, to this day, are not entirely built out. Though saddled with the bland design stylings of its period, this was comparatively solid stuff in its day, particularly down the stretch of each nine. Going out, play concludes with the 420-yard straightaway 7th, the 141-yard pond-fronted 8th and the 430-yard 9th, where the drive must carry a lake and the approach a fronting creek. Coming home water plays an even bigger role, first at the 395-yard 16th (where it guards the green left), then at the 162-yard all-carry 17th, and especially at the 555-yard 18th, a double dogleg which culminates in a green perched above a front-right lake. Given the priority that was clearly given to real estate concerns in Snyder's routing, there are several imposing cart rides required.

Dave White Municipal Golf Course - Casa Grande

Arthur Jack Snyder   www.casagrandeaz.gov
2121 North Thornton Rd, Casa Grande, AZ   85122   (520) 836-9216
                  6,651 yds   Par 72   Rating: 71.4 / 122   (1979)

Owned and operated by the City of Casa Grande, the Dave White Municipal Golf Course dates to 1979, when it was built along sections of the Santa Cruz riverbed by Arthur Jack Snyder. Though borderline-bland in spots (the entire 18 includes only five bunkers), there is more interesting golf here than one might anticipate, with Snyder utilizing a trio of man-made lakes and the riverbed to some advantage. The most relevant lake lies upon the front nine and mostly affects a pair of par 3s, the 171-yard 3rd (where it guards the green short-left) and the 162-yard all-carry 6th. The back opens with the 322-yard dry wash-crossing 10th and later offers the water-flanked 389-yard 13th before coming home with the 540-yard dogleg left 15th as well as a pair of solid par 4s, the 400-yard 17th (a sharp dogleg left and a particularly challenging driving hole) and the 400-yard 18th, which doglegs right to a green fronted by more dry wash. Not quite exciting or tactically rich, but with a bit more character to the greens than one might guess, solid municipal stuff.

The Duke at Rancho Eldorado - Maricopa   ♦♦½

David Druzisky   www.thedukegolf.com
42660 W Rancho El Dorado Pkwy, Maricopa, AZ 85239   (480) 844-1100
            6,998 yds   Par 72   Rating: 72.7 / 128   (2003)

Situated just east of the John Wayne Parkway (surprise!), the Duke at Rancho El Dorado is a 2003 David Druzisky design which is somewhat conflicted in its aesthetics, the golf holes being reasonably natural in appearance while the surrounding rows of housing are rather less so. The Santa Rosa dry wash angles across the front nine but, save for crossing the fairway at the 528-yard 1st, is not utilized as a strategic hazard. With the wash's impact thus being limited, the loop's best entries include the 559-yard centerline-bunkered 4th, the 177-yard 5th (an obviously contrived - though quite challenging – entry with water short and long of the green) and the 436-yard 9th, where drives flirting with (or crossing) left-side desert open the ideal angle of approach. The back nine then opens with a pair of strong two-shotters: the 442-yard rolling 10th and the 417-yard 11th, whose elevated green favors drives played close to a right-side fairway bunker. The scale ratchets down a bit at the smartly bunkered 375-yard 12th and the 399-yard 15th (a gentle dogleg right) before picking up again at the demanding 456-yard 17th (which plays to a bunkerless, slightly elevated putting surface) and the 523-yard 18th, where left-side water significantly affects both lay-up zone and green complex.

Golf Club at Johnson Ranch - Queen Creek   ♦♦

Kenny Watkins   www.johnsonranchgc.com
30761 Golf Club Dr, Queen Creek, AZ 85143   (480) 987-9800
            7,162 yds   Par 72   Rating: 72.7 / 130   (1997)

Designed in 1997 by greenkeeper-turned-architect Kenny Watkins, the Golf Club at Johnson Ranch is a long and reasonably challenging facility whose nines offer a bit of variance in their characters. The flattish outward half is the epitome of housing-oriented golf (every hole is lined down both sides by single-family homes) and mostly about muscle, with the 212-yard pond-fronted 3rd leading a group that includes long (but not overly engaging) tests like the 606-yard 1st, the 460-yard 5th (played over a surprisingly narrow fairway) and the 476-yard 8th. The much shorter back is hardly free of housing but it does ascend briefly into the San Tan Mountain foothills where, following several significantly downhill tests, it features a strong four-hole close. This run includes the 372-yard 15th (which climbs to a bunker-fronted green), the sharply descending 382-yard 16th, the well-bunkered 200-yard 17th and the 558-yard 18th, a long dogleg left upon which a left-side lake cuts invasively into the lay-up zone and also fronts the putting surface.

Kearny Golf Course - Kearny   ♦

Unknown
301 Airport Rd, Kearny, AZ 85237   (520) 363-7441
         3,295 yds   Par 35   Rating: 34.6 / 110   (1961)

Situated in a quiet ex-mining company town between the Tortilla and Mescal Mountains (and bordering the town's modest airstrip), the Kearny Golf Course is a basic nine whose short, bunker-free design exists mostly off the serious golfer's radar. It does, however, provide moments of greater challenge at the 413-yard dogleg left 3rd, a pair of straight tests routed parallel to the tracks of the Southern Pacific Railway (the 525-yard 5th and the 444-yard 6th) and the slightly awkward 357-yard 9th, a tree-lined, early turning dogleg right. Alternate tees provide some occasion yardage variance for 18-hole play.

Mission Royale Golf Course - Casa Grande   ♦♦

Greg Nash   www.missionroyalegolfclub.com
11 South Mission Pkwy, Casa Grande, AZ 85222   (520) 876-5335
         6,700 yds   Par 72   Rating: 71.1 / 122   (2004)

Routed within an 825-acre residential development along the eastern flank of Interstate 10, the Mission Royale Golf Course is a mid-size, moderately challenging Greg Nash design which mixes a long menu of functional holes with a handful of more engaging entries. The highlight, comfortably, is the 310-yard 8th, an option-laden test which offers a several lay-up options within a narrow fairway flanked by sand or an all-out blast across a lake towards the putting surface. Going out, second-tier favorites include the 602-yard 3rd (where a cluster of three bunkers squeeze the lay-up zone), the 517-yard 6th (where a centerline bunker impedes the second) and the 205-yard lake-flanked 7th. The back nine offers another influential centerline bunker at the 355-yard 11th as well as a trio of consecutive long holes played to bunkerless greens: the 442-yard 14th, the 211-yard 15th and the 565-yard 16th. Though several back nine holes presently remain housing-free, virtually none will remain so when the community reaches build-out.

Mountain Brook Golf Course - Gold Canyon   ♦♦

Brian Whitcomb   www.mountainbrookgolf.com
5783 S Mountainbrook Dr, Gold Canyon, AZ 85218   (480) 671-1000
                    6,636 yds   Par 71   Rating: 69.7 / 119   (1996)

A mid-range, residence-lined layout situated between Highway 60 and the 36-hole Gold Canyon Resort, the Mountain Brook Golf Course dates to 1996 and provides a mix of functional golf with a fair number of holes of greater interest. For most, the 3,220-yard front nine will be the less memorable half, its centerpieces being the awkward 375-yard 6th (a forced lay-up dogleg left with a centerline waste area) and a trio of more heavily bunkered tests at the 210-yard 7th, the 412-yard 8th and the 578-yard straightaway 9th. But the back is considerably longer (3,416 yards) and far more engaging, initially offering three holes dominated by a pair of man-made lakes: the 378-yard 11th (which bends gently right, to a waterside green), the 180-yard 12th and especially the 360-yard 13th, a sharp dogleg left daring a long carry over water. Also notable are the 195-yard dry wash-crossing 14th as well as a pair of strong par 4s, the 454-yard 15th and the 425-yard 18th, where a patch of native desert pinches the fairway's left side.

Oasis Golf Course - Florence   ♦♦½

Kenny Watkins   www.clubatoasis.com
5764 East Hunt Hwy, Florence, AZ 85232   (480) 888-8890
                    3,577 yds   Par 36   Rating: 37.0 / 136   (1999)

Borrowing a page from Desert Mountain, the Oasis Golf Course is a nine-hole layout which, instead of providing alternate tees for 18-hole play, offers either alternate greens (in eight cases) or a single long, narrow putting surface (at hole number two) that is large enough to create separate, widely differing pin placements. Routed through housing on either side of East Hunt Highway, the loop initially is led by a pair of broad-shouldered test, the 474-yard par-4 2nd (whose putting surface lies perpendicular to the line of play) and the 595-yard 3rd, where a fronting tree helps separate the targets. Though the standard of design does vary a bit, additional favorites include the 372-yard pond-guarded 5th (where a centerline tree and plenty of flanking desert affect play) and the 392-yard 9th, which utilizes a pair of greens angled beyond more water. As the combined nines add up to a 7,242-yard 18, there is clearly no shortage of challenge present. Thus this manages to succeed in being both derivative and novel stuff.

Poston Butte Golf Course - Florence ♦♦½

Gary Panks www.postonbutte.com
6100 W Merrill Ranch Pkwy, Florence, AZ 85232   (520) 723-1880
7,282 yds   Par 72   Rating: 74.8 / 127   (2007)

The Oasis Golf Course's near neighbor (two miles) to the south, Poston Butte features a long, housing-flanked Gary Panks-designed layout which, as a 127 slope suggests, is actually fairly playable for the less skilled. This owes to the fact that water is almost nonexistent (it affects only two holes) and bunkering is often limited to one side of the green or fairway, allowing the novice to easily chart a safer alternate course. With serious tactical questions a relative rarity, the front nine is led by its par 3s, the 235-yard 4th (played to a long, narrow green) and the 166-yard 7th which, from the back tees, is an all-carry test whose putting surface is angled beyond a huge right-side waste bunker. Beyond the tough 466-yard 10th (where a decorative pond flanks the fairway's left side), the back's most engaging entry is the 352-yard tightly bunkered 15th – though the 169-yard 17th (an unabashed copy of the famed island green 17th at TPC Sawgrass) will certainly get some heart rates up with its unforgiving nature. Notably, very little of the front nine's surrounding housing had yet broken ground at the time of this writing.

Links at Queen Creek - San Tan Valley ♦½

Sam Wese & John Woodhall www.linksqueencreekgolfclub.com
445 East Ocotillo Rd, Queen Creek, AZ 85242   (480) 987-1910
5,787 yds   Par 70   Rating: 67.0 / 110   (1994)

A short, rudimentary facility located just north of the Encanterra Country Club, the Links at Queen Creek has contracted in recent years as a significant chunk of its northwestern acreage was sold off for commercial development. Thus a bit more tightly routed than it once was (and no longer offering a practice range), this is, for the most part, short, basic golf, with bunkers being entirely absent and water making only the occasional significant appearance. But beyond the odd awkward moment (e.g., the 318-yard dogleg right 6th turning before the 200-yard mark), there are some better moments, with the front nine including the 478-yard par-5 3rd (where left-side water affects the drive), the 202-yard 6th, the 374-yard creek-crossed 7th and the 492-yard dogleg right 9th, a tricky driving hole. The back nine offers a real dose of size at the 505-yard 10th and the 238-yard 11th before settling into simple, mostly back-and-forth golf thereafter.

Queen Valley Golf Course - Queen Valley   ♦½

Unknown   www.queenvalleygolfcourse.com
600 North Fairway Dr, Queen Valley, AZ 85219   (520) 463-2214
                4,499 yds   Par 66   Rating: 62.2 / 103   (1963)

Located in higher country (2000+ feet of altitude), the Queen Valley Golf Course teeters on the edge of executive status, only managing a par of 66 by classifying as par 5s the uphill 426-yard 12th and the 377-yard 16th (!) - so full-size golf this most definitely is not. The front nine is a compact, fully-turfed loop situated south of East Silver King Road, and offers only basic, bunker-free golf, its highlight being the 285-yard pond-fronted 3rd. The back then ventures out to the north where it circumnavigates a residential neighborhood situated on higher, more rugged ground, giving it more character. Though the golf is equally rudimentary, holes like the 352-yard 15th and the narrow 16th are routed along the base of the hillside, providing a tad more playing interest. Straight drivers of the ball may *really* find this layout short as many holes have cart paths cut right up the middle of fairways, creating plentiful chances for turbo-charged bounces.

Robson Ranch Golf Course - Eloy   ♦♦

Brad Bartell   www.robson.com
5750 North Robson Blvd, Eloy, AZ 85131   (520) 426-3333
                6,845 yds   Par 72   Rating: 72.0 / 120   (2005)

Anchoring a new millennium residential development located two miles east of where Interstates 10 and 8 divide for their parallel runs across the desert to the Pacific, Robson Ranch is a relatively basic modern layout notable for some larger putting surfaces and the limited use of water. The Brad Bartell design poses relatively few tactical questions, though several of the par 3s are tightly enough bunkered to require precision with one's irons (particularly the 214-yard 17th), and the single entry to encounter water, the 532-yard dogleg right 9th, offers an aggressive second-shot option. Also notable are the 542-yard 5th (which requires a substantial desert crossing on the second), the 546-yard 12th (similarly arranged, but less dangerously) and the 350-yard 8th, where drives carrying a left-side fairway bunker can get close to the putting surface. But far more frequent are basic holes of moderate size, the longest/toughest being the 451-yard straightaway 4th.

Tierra Grande Golf Course - Casa Grande   ♦

Arthur Jack Snyder   www.tierragrandeaz.com
813 West Calle Rosa, Casa Grande, AZ   85194   (520) 723-9717
                    4,433 yds   Par 67   Rating: 64.0 / 98   (1992)

Originally a regulation-size nine laid out by Arthur Jack Snyder in 1992, the Tierra Grande
Golf Course was reconfigured (though not very much expanded) into 18 in 2009, with the
result being a sometimes cramped, strangely routed track which sees both its 9th and 18th
greens located about 300 yards northwest of the clubhouse. To be fair to Snyder's legacy,
very little of his creation still exists, so the design credit is, at this point, more than a bit
attenuated. And the golf itself is palpably limited, with no bunkers in play, only one lake
present (at the 126-yard 7th) and the most prominent hazard likely being the tree which
stands, rather bizarrely, directly in front of the green at the 333-yard 8th.

Gold Canyon RV & Golf Resort - Gold Canyon   ♦

Unknown   www.robertsresorts.com
7151 East US Hwy 60, Gold Canyon, AZ 85218   (480) 982-5800
936 yds   Par 27   Rating: - / -   (1985)

An RV facility situated just south of the Mountain Brook Golf Course, the Gold Canyon RV and Golf Resort is a short par-3 layout which follows a circular counter-clockwise routing around a central clubhouse. For the most part, these are basic holes flanked by mobile homes, with moderate bunkering, and water appearing three times. The last of these, at the 72-yard 9th, is the toughest, playing over a pond to a green nearly encircled by sand.

Palm Creek Golf & RV Resort - Casa Grande   ♦

Unknown   www.palmcreekgolf.com
1110 North Henness Rd, Casa Grande, AZ 85222   (520) 421-7000
2,506 yds   Par 54   Rating: - / -   (1999)

The anchor of an RV resort and residential community situated in agricultural country just west of Interstate 10, Palm Creek is a good-size par-3 course which begins slowly before gaining playing interest mid-stream. The opening eight holes, in fact, are a nondescript bunch before the 174-yard pond-flanked 9th gives a taste of things to come. The back is then built around a man-made creek which touches all nine holes – though seldom invasively enough to be anything more than decorative for the competent ball-striker.

Roadhaven Golf Course - Apache Junction   ♦

Greg Nash   www.roadhaven.com
1000 South Idaho Rd, Apache Junction, AZ 85219   (480) 982-4653
970 yds   Par 27   Rating: 22.0 / 62   (1984)

A short par-3 course which anchors a 55-and-over RV development 35 miles east of Phoenix, the Roadhaven Golf Course was designed by Greg Nash, who reportedly managed to secure some input from Hall-of-Famer Lee Trevino. The result is a loop squeezed tightly among the mobile homes, with just enough bunkering and water to rise above the basic. The 110-yard 4th and the 135-yard 9th (both pond-flanked) rate among the most engaging entries on a layout that adds up to above-average backyard golf.

GILA COUNTY

Golf Club at Chaparral Pines - Payson   ♦♦♦½

Gary Panks & David Graham   www.chaparralpines.com
504 North Club Dr, Payson, AZ 85541   (928) 472-1420
        7,019 yds   Par 72   Rating: 73.2 / 138   (1997)

Located in wooded, mountainous country 80 miles north of Phoenix, Chaparral Pines is a highly regarded Gary Panks and David Graham collaboration whose primary attribute is the naturalness with which it is routed; indeed, native slopes, rock outcroppings and trees all affect play to a notably high degree. The first example of this is the rock formation that occupies the center of the fairway at the short par-5 2nd, mandating a 260-yard carry that might suggest the consideration of alternate routes. More famous, however, is the par-5 7th, a 624-yard double dogleg guarded both left and before the green by a small creekbed. Set against a scenic mountain backdrop, the putting surface is potentially reachable because of the near-5000-foot altitude – a factor also relevant at holes like the panoramic 234-yard 8th, the 488-yard par-4 9th and the 233-yard 13th, which would all be borderline-brutal otherwise. Additional favorites on a deep menu include the 429-yard 1st (played to a plateau green perched above a deep right-side bunker), the potentially driveable 341-yard 3rd and a trio of closers crossed by the overgrown Goat Camp Wash: the 190-yard 16th (where the wash passes left of the narrow green), the 551-yard 17th (a twisting double dogleg which jumps the hazard twice) and the scenic 450-yard 18th. Though man-made lakes appear at the 151-yard 4th and the 438-yard 10th, and the quarry that menaces the 164-yard 6th was excavated during construction, Chaparral Pines is one of the more natural (and scenic) big ticket layouts built during the 1990s – and well worth the drive up from Phoenix. **(GD: #20 State)**

The Rim Golf Club - Payson   ♦♦♦½

Tom Weiskopf & Jay Morrish   www.therimgolfclub.com
300 South Clubhouse Rd, Payson, AZ 85541   (928) 472-1480
        7,193 yds   Par 71   Rating: 72.9 / 140   (1999)

Built just across Highway 260 from Chaparral Pines, The Rim Golf Club is laid out amidst some of America's more impressive stands of Ponderosa pines, but takes its name from the splendid views it offers of the massive Mogollon Rim escarpment. As the final course completed by the team of Tom Weiskopf and Jay Morrish, it serves as a suitable parting shot, featuring impressive scenery to complement a high level of design variety and the effective use of native rock and water hazards. The high altitude makes yardages rather deceptive, but there is plenty of backbone in the form of five par 4s of 450+ yards, all of which rely on more than just length to make them compelling. The layout's most famous hole is the 581-yard 13th, a reachable three-shotter whose photogenic green is backed by a remarkable 80-foot stand of boulders. Other standouts are plentiful, however, and initially include the 476-yard 2nd, the 225-yard 8th (whose large green angles along left-side water) and the 533-yard 9th, a particularly panoramic entry. The back nine, though shorter, flexes its muscles at the 13th, but also on challenging par 4s like the 435-yard 14th (a pond-guarded dogleg right) and the 454-yard 18th, a straightaway test to another green flanked by right-side water. Yet for all of this brawn, the layout's most interesting challenges lie at the 346-yard 5th (driveable, but with several prominent trees defining multiple lines of play) and the 145-yard 12th, whose nasty front bunker draws inspiration from the famed 10th at Pine Valley. Notably, Weiskopf has cited holes 7-18 as the best 12-hole run that he and Morrish ever designed. **(GD: #12 State GW: #66 Modern)**

Apache Stronghold Golf Club - San Carlos   ♦♦♦½

Tom Doak   www.apache-gold-casino-.com/golf
Hwy 70, San Carlos, AZ 85550   (928) 475-7664
7,519 yds   Par 72   Rating: 74.5 / 146   (1999)

The recreational centerpiece of the Apache Gold Casino Resort, the Apache Stronghold
Golf Club represented lay-of-the-land designer Tom Doak's initial foray into desert golf, a
task he undertook with a team of inexperienced Indian laborers on a rolling, unspoiled
piece of desert 90 miles east of Phoenix. Its 7,519 yards shortened somewhat by 3,200
feet of altitude, the course tumbles across the, dry wash-dotted landscape, offering
high playing interest despite having no water and less than 50 man-made bunkers. The par-37
front nine opens with the huge 661-yard 1st but shows its truest colors at holes like the
427-yard 2nd (played over a dry wash-divided fairway), the driveable 325-yard 6th and the
456-yard 7th, which crosses more rough native terrain. The inward half begins with the
split-fairway 472-yard 10th before peaking at the 480-yard par-4 13th (a tempting dogleg
right) and the 186-yard 14th, a fine Redan replica situated atop a high ridge. From there,
play descends at the 614-yard 15th (a near 90-degree dogleg right), then features a pair of
dry wash-affected holes at the 510-yard 16th and the 230-yard 17th, before closing with
the 458-yard 18th, whose sharply downhill tee shot leads the golfer back to the casino.
The club weathered some tough financial times during its first decade, and it lacks much
of the flash that defines so many of Phoenix and Scottsdale's highest-profile facilities.
But for many purists, that may be its biggest quality – and ample reason to make the long
drive out. Though much overlooked, this remains among the top golf courses in Arizona.

Cobre Valle Country Club - Miami   ♦½

Unknown   www.cobrevallecc.com
4877 West Cypress Way, Miami, AZ 85539   (928) 473-2542
          3,338 yds   Par 36   Rating: 34.9 / 116   (1927)

One of Arizona's longest surviving courses, the nine-hole Cobre Valle Country Club dates to 1927, when it began playing over sand greens on a rectangular site flanked along its western edge by the tracks of the Southern Pacific Railroad. Though inevitably altered somewhat over the years, this remains a good-size nine which, despite being sparsely hazarded, is affected by enough mature trees (which often pinch lines of play) to remain fairly challenging. Play opens with the 420-yard 1st (whose green complex is bordered on three sides – with some buffer – by an often-dry water hazard) and later includes full-size holes like the 588-yard 6th, the 246-yard 7th (a long enough par 3 that its alternate second-round tee, plays as a 318-yard par 4) and the 550-yard 9th. No match for Apache Stronghold (its only local competition) but mature, functional stuff.

Hayden Municipal Golf Course - Hayden   ♦

Unknown
125 Golf Course Rd, Hayden, AZ 85235   (520) 356-7801
          2,795 yds   Par 35   Rating: 33.1 / 108   (1960)

A simple nine-hole loop serving this tiny mining town whose landscape is still dominated by the facilities of the American Smelting & Refining Company, the Hayden Municipal Golf Course is a short, barely hazarded track which actually lies closer to the adjoining settlement of Winkleman than to its own lightly populated downtown. Built on flat ground, it is strictly a rudimentary track which, after the incongruously imposing 565-yard 1st and the 385-yard 2nd, offers nary a hole over 330 yards in length. Very basic.

Payson Golf Club - Payson   ♦½

Frank Hughes & Russell Zakariasen   www.paysongolfcourse.com
1504 West Country Club Dr, Payson, AZ 85541   (928) 474-2273
           5,894 yds   Par 71   Rating: 66.0 / 111   (1959)

An undersized public facility built in 1959, the Payson Golf Club sits 4,800 feet above sea level, making its "real" yardage closer to 5,200. Mostly basic in its design (less than 10 bunkers are present throughout), its nines sit on either side of South Vista Road, with the stronger outward half running out to the east and featuring a pair of full-size par 5s, the 537-yard out-of-bounds-lined 4th and the 519-yard 9th, where left-side trees and a crossing creek enliven play. The hillier and shorter back nine then strikes out to the west where it opens with a trio of short, doglegging par 4s dovetailed (too) tightly together before ultimately finishing with the club's longest entry, the 525-yard dogleg right 18th. Functional golf but a layout hugely overshadowed by its nearby private neighbors, Chaparral Pines and The Rim, taking this off the radar of the connected one-day visitor.

YAVAPAI COUNTY

Capital Canyon Club - Prescott

Tom Weiskopf   www.capitalcanyonclub.com
2060 Golf Club Lane, Prescott, AZ 86303   (928) 350-3150
           6,622 yds   Par 71   Rating: 71.5 / 135   (1997)

As a summer resort retreat for Phoenix and Tucson's finest during the pre-air conditioned days of the 1920s, this, the former Hassayampa Golf Club, initially played golf over a nine-hole, sand-green layout which dated to 1919. This course was abandoned during the mid-1960s (its clubhouse taking on a ghost town-like presence) but before eventually being replaced by a brand-new Tom Weiskopf layout in 1997. At only 6,622 yards (and that at over a mile above sea level), this might in a sense be thought of as a sort of "Weiskopf light" – for there are few suggestions of Major championship grandeur here. It is, however, a scenic, semi-wooded track built below Thumb Butte, which opens somewhat tamely over a 3,270-yard (occasionally quite narrow) front nine, then amps up the action on the homeward half. The marquee holes are routed around a small residential neighborhood at the property's eastern end and include the 618-yard pond-guarded 10th, the 168-yard 11th (which plays across another small water hazard), the 454-yard 12th (where several trees narrow the tight side of the driving zone) and the 375-yard 13th, one final water-bothered entry. Also worth a mention are the 170-yard 16th and 204-yard 17th (a pair of back-to-back rugged-terrain par 3s set 400 yards apart) as well as the 421-yard 18th, a dogleg right requiring a long tee ball across some rough country.

Club at Prescott Lakes - Prescott

Hale Irwin   www.theclubatprescottlakes.com
311 East Smoke Tree Lane, Prescott, AZ 86301   (928) 443-3500
           7,216 yds   Par 72   Rating: 73.4 / 140   (2000)

The least celebrated of Prescott's three private golf facilities, the Club at Prescott Lakes is an engaging layout built by three-time U.S. Open champion Hale Irwin which, despite being shortened noticeably by 5,300 feet of altitude, can still hold its own challenge-wise. The course is expansively routed through a wide range of mostly low-density housing and features appealing mountain vistas in nearly every direction. The slightly shorter front nine initially offers the 330-yard downhill 2nd (driveable, but with water lurking left) as well as the 554-yard 3rd, where a narrow arroyo flanks the left side before crossing in front of the green. This same arroyo later keys a downhill quartet which closes the outward half: the steeply descending 454-yard 6th (fronting the green), the demanding 240-yard 7th (whose putting surface angles above it), the 601-yard 8th (which is affected on all three shots) and the 414-yard 9th, where the hazard both crosses the fairway and flanks the green. Lacking the arroyo, the back nine relies on man-made water to spice things up, first at the 539-yard 11th (a sharp dogleg left to a pond-guarded green) and the 180-yard all-carry 12th. But more tactically interesting is the 402-yard downhill 14th (with its multiple tee shot options and lakeside green) and the 190-yard creekbed-flanked 16th before play closes with the 537-yard 18th, which is lined by a series of right-side ponds.

Seven Canyons - Sedona   ♦♦♦½

Tom Weiskopf   www.sevencanyons.com
625 Golf Club Way, Sedona, AZ 86336   (928) 203-2000
          6,746 yds   Par 70   Rating: 71.1 / 139   (2003)

Nicely secluded within Coconino National Forest, several miles north of Sedona (and more than 100 miles from Phoenix), Seven Canyons sits upon an incongruously small tract surrounded by some truly imposing mountain and canyon scenery. The golf course acreage is actually quite limited, requiring Tom Weiskopf to utilize a notably compact, non-returning routing, resulting in a layout which, particularly at 4,600 feet of altitude, is palpably short by modern standards. But "short" can be deceiving, for with six par 4s measuring under 400 yards and a par of 70, there is plenty of room left for some substantial challenges to arise. The semi-blind 389-yard 9th is often viewed as the club's centerpiece but at least as much excitement can be found at the 175-yard 4th (a drop shot to a green sitting some 80 feet below the tee), the 305-yard dogleg left 12th (Weiskopf's obligatory driveable two-shotter, played over a bunker-divided fairway) and the 490-yard par-4 13th, another dogleg left where a lone pine defines the preferred left-side route. The closing run is of a larger scale and is led by the 500-yard dogleg left 15th (where a creek angles before the green), the 246-yard 17th (whose putting surface is fronted by a similar hazard) and the uphill 452-yard 18th. Indeed, Seven Canyons' lone blemish might be the water hazards that mar the otherwise natural landscape at the 6th and 7th, a pair of shorter holes which loop around behind the clubhouse. But the relatively limited housing presence, the splendid setting and some genuine variety within Weiskopf's design are more than enough to compensate. **(GD:** #23 State**)**

Talking Rock Golf Club - Prescott   ♦♦♦

Jay Morrish   www.talkingrockranch.com
15075 N Talking Rock Ranch Rd, Prescott, AZ 86305   (928) 493-2600
          7,350 yds   Par 72   Rating: 74.1 / 138   (2002)

Anchoring a low-density real estate development in a flattish stretch of desert far north of downtown Prescott, the Talking Rock Golf Club is an understated Jay Morrish design offering relatively little in the way of bells and whistles but a reasonable amount of tactical playing interest. The front nine, though the longer half, is slightly the less interesting, offering as highlights the tightly bunkered 428-yard 2nd and a trio of later entries: the 461-yard 5th (played downhill to another sand-squeezed fairway), the 641-yard 6th (an endless dogleg left) and the diminutive 163-yard 7th. The inward half, on the other hand, is rather more engaging, opening with the 416-yard 10th (whose approach is defined by a small centerline bunker) and the 563-yard 11th, where a narrow dry wash must be carried (or not) on the second. The 454-yard 14th is another sandy test and sets up a closing run led by the 337-yard 15th (driveable between several large fairway bunkers) and the 434-yard 17th, where more sand guards the favored left side off the tee. The 542-yard 9th and 589-yard 18th, meanwhile, occupy opposite sides of the club's lone water hazard, making for solid (if formulaic) finishers. At least in part due to its somewhat remote location – and, perhaps, its lack of wildly photogenic hazarding and island greens – Talking Rock draws a tad less national attention than one might expect. But there is plenty of strong, engaging golf here.

Sedona Golf Resort - Sedona

Gary Panks   www.sedonagolfresort.com
35 Ridge Trail Dr, Sedona, AZ 86351   (928) 284-9355
              6,646 yds   Par 71   Rating: 70.6 / 128   (1988)

Serving an adjacent Hilton hotel, the Sedona Golf Resort sports a 1988 Gary Panks design which, owing to its spectacular views of the region's famous Red Rocks, ranks among the most scenic in the American West. Lined by rows of varying-density single-family homes, the layout itself is relatively short (particularly given its 4,000-foot altitude) and largely manageable for the average player, though a number of engaging holes manage to appear throughout. On the par-37 front nine, these include the downhill 183-yard 2nd and the out-of-bounds-flanked 448-yard 8th, as well as a trio of par 5s: the 506-yard 3rd (downhill and easily reachable) the 623-yard 5th (uphill and seldom reached) and the 522-yard 9th, whose tree-narrowed approach allows it to fall somewhere in between. Best known, easily, is the 210-yard 10th, really only a functionally bunkered par 3 but one made famous by its dazzling, much-photographed Red Rocks backdrop. Subsequent favorites coming home include the 380-yard 11th (played sharply downhill to an arroyo-fronted green), the 394-yard pond-guarded 13th, the 439-yard arroyo-crossed 15th and the 336-yard 18th, a tempting par 4 guarded left by both sand and water. A healthy chunk of this rating is about the scenery alone, but the golf isn't too bad either.

Antelope Hills Golf Course (North) - Prescott   ◆◆

Lawrence Hughes   www.cityofprescott.net
1 Perkins Dr, Prescott, AZ 86301   (928) 776-7888
            6,844 yds   Par 71   Rating: 72.1 / 128   (1956)

A 36-hole public facility located on the north side of Prescott, Antelope Hills is squeezed in between Route 89 and Ernest A. Love Airport, where it offers a pair of full-size courses built nearly four decades apart. The older North course (which directly abuts the airfield) is a Lawrence Hughes design dating to 1956 which, as one might expect from Hughes, is eminently solid but entirely unspectacular. Mature enough to be tree-lined, it offers a parkland feel, particularly within a back-and-forth section of the front nine that features the 518-yard tree-narrowed 2nd, the 461-yard par-4 3rd (a very tough dogleg right), the 160-yard pond-crossing 8th and the 459-yard 9th. The shorter inward half leads with the 405-yard 11th (which climbs steadily to a well-bunkered green) then circles around the end of the airfield's primary runway where it finds two varied par 3s, the demanding 228-yard 14th (whose green is squeezed between sand and several trees) and the 132-yard 16th, whose greens sits behind a huge circular bunker. The 418-yard 18th, a slightly downhill closer bothered by still more trees, finishes things on a suitably high note.

Antelope Hills Golf Course (South) - Prescott   ◆½

Gary Panks   www.cityofprescott.net
1 Perkins Dr, Prescott, AZ 86301   (928) 776-7888
            7,014 yds   Par 72   Rating: 71.3 / 124   (1992)

Antelope Hills' Gary Panks-designed South course was built in 1992 on a mostly open, housing-dotted tract across Perkins Drive, where its far boundary nearly reaches the Pioneer Parkway. It is also the odd layout to be 36 years newer, 170 yards longer and yet still rated easier than its older sibling. But this rating seems a fair one, for this is a lightly bunkered test offering only sporadic strategic interest, with its most memorable holes being a pair affected by man-made lakes, the 359-yard dogleg left 7th (which dares a long over-water drive) and the 209-yard all-carry 11th. The rest is less-inspiring, though longer par 4s like the 467-yard 6th, the 456-yard 9th and 469-yard 18th do provide some challenge based on size alone. Longer hitters may find the drive at the 526-yard 3rd a bit tricky (water right, out-of-bounds left) but the South is the visitor's second option here.

Coyote Trails Golf Course - Cottonwood   ♦♦½

Unknown   www.coyotetrailsgolfcourse.com
1480 W Anna's Ave, Cottonwood, AZ 86326   (928) 634-1093
               2,223 yds   Par 33   Rating: 31.1 / 108   (1996)

Situated in a valley between the Mingus Mountains and the Coconino National Forest, the Coyote Trails Golf Course is another facility which cheats to gain regulation course status, reaching its par of 33 only by classifying the 214-yard 6th and the 367-yard 8th as a par 4 and par 5 respectively. But beyond such gimmickry, there is more worthwhile golf present here than on most similar-size layouts, this because despite the club falling far below the state's 90-acre turf limit, it has left the native desert terrain intact nearly everywhere but on fairways, greens and a modest buffer of rough. Thus while there is nary a man-made bunker in site, and a couple of later housing-flanked holes feel a tad generic, this is enjoyable – and challenging – golf of this type.

Oakcreek Country Club - Sedona   ♦♦½

Robert Trent Jones & Robert Trent Jones II   www.oakcreekcountryclub.com
690 Bell Rock Rd, Sedona, AZ 86351   (928) 284-1820
               6,824 yds   Par 72   Rating: 71.7 / 131   (1967)

Somewhat overshadowed by its near neighbor, the much newer Sedona Golf Resort, the Oakcreek Country Club began with nine holes built by the Trent Joneses in 1967, with the father and son duo returning to add nine more a decade later. Offering scenic views of the area's famed Red Rocks, it is a short layout (at 4,300 feet) with several similarities between the nines, including the use of uphill opening par 5s (measuring 560 and 565 yards) and strong par-4 closers, the 445-yard dogleg right 9th and the 450-yard lake-flanked 18th. The nines run away from the clubhouse in opposite directions and if their design isn't among the Joneses' period elite, it does feature a number of tightly bunkered doglegs, which add life to holes like the 450-yard dogleg left 12th, the 490-yard 6th (a creek-fronted par 5) and the 524-yard dogleg right 12th. More consistently engaging, however, is a set of par 3s led by the pond-guarded 160-yard 4th, the especially scenic 185-yard 13th and the downhill (and heavily bunkered) 205-yard 16th. Reliable period stuff from Trent, but with only a few of the strategic touches often injected by Bobby.

Prescott Golf & Country Club - Dewey   ♦♦

Milton Coggins   www.prescottgolf.net
1030 Prescott CC Blvd, Dewey, AZ 86327   (928) 772-8984
        6,655 yds   Par 72   Rating: 70.9 / 127   (1972)

Another early entry to the area golfing scene, the Milton Coggins–designed Prescott Golf & Country Club represents a fairly typical real estate-oriented layout of its period, being functional, playable, housing-lined and with just enough water present to occasionally dress up the landscape. While tactical questions are thus at a premium, this is steady enough golf, led by a quartet of par 3s which includes the 189-yard 3rd (routed past a mostly decorative lake), the 212-yard 12th (played slightly uphill to a green angled behind front-left sand) and the 199-yard 15th, another upgrade test played to a light-bulb-shaped putting surface. Par 4s like the 420-yard 8th and the 439-yard downhill 11th are strong enough, though the best of the longer holes may well be the two closers, as the 484-yard par-5 9th is a sweeping dogleg left with a prominent left-side tree guarding the lay-up zone, while the 510-yard 18th is a slight dogleg right where a right-side tree affects the second and a front-left pond threatens the approach.

Quailwood Greens Golf Course - Dewey   ♦½

Unknown
12200 E State Rd 69, Dewey, AZ 86327   (928) 772-0130
        5,430 yds   Par 69   Rating: 65.1 / 110   (1990)

Lying just across Route 69 from the Prescott Golf & Country Club, the Quailwood Greens Golf Course is an undersized par-69 layout which is frequently as limited as its statistics might suggest, but which also manages to sneak the odd engaging hole into play. But such occasions are pretty limited on a 2,524-yard front nine which opens with a 458-yard par 5, then plays through a run of very short, mostly uneventful holes before reaching the quirky 358-yard 8th, a 90-degree, pond-guarded dogleg left whose second is very tightly squeezed between trees. The longer inward half follows a clockwise path around a residential neighborhood, where highlights include the incongruously difficult 468-yard par-4 14th (which gently ascends to a very shallow putting surface) and the 487-yard 15th, a dogleg right with a single tree guarding the corner. Bunkering is sporadic throughout, though oversize putting surfaces (of which several appear) mostly are not.

StoneRidge Golf Course - Prescott Valley

Randy Heckenkemper   www.stoneridgegolf.com
1601 Bluff Top Dr, Prescott Valley, AZ   86314   (928) 772-6500
            7,052 yds   Par 72   Rating: 72.3 / 142   (2002)

Located three and a half miles west of Prescott Golf & Country Club, within the Prescott Valley city limits, the StoneRidge Golf Course is a demanding new millennium layout by Randy Heckenkemper which, though not gigantically long, is capable of consistently challenging even the better player. This is mostly because of the course's terrain, as it is routed over rolling, often hilly ground which is mostly covered with desert scrub. Accuracy, then, is at a premium, as balls hit more than a few yards off the fairway will frequently vanish without a trace. The front nine (which borders housing in several spots) opens with longer entries like the 638-yard 2nd, the 247-yard 3rd and the 433-yard uphill 4th, but hits its peak at a trio of shorter, hillier par 4s which begin atop a ridge: the downhill 383-yard dogleg right 5th (which, at 5,000 feet, dares one to take the tiger's line towards the green), the similarly descending 385-yard 6th and the uphill 324-yard 7th, a tightly bunkered dogleg right that offers several tee shot options. The back includes a pair of slightly awkward par 4s at the 430-yard desert-crossed 10th and the 402-yard 14th, but it also offers another noteworthy trio: the 230-yard 12th (an all-carry monster played over a small ravine), the sharply downhill 194-yard 17th and the 630-yard 18th, which descends to the finish. Not quite classic, but tough, often memorable stuff.

Verde Santa Fe Golf Course - Cornville

Stanton McCaw   www.verdesantafe.com
645 S Verde Santa Fe Pkwy, Cornville, AZ   86325   (928) 634-5454
            6,287 yds   Par 71   Rating: 69.3 / 116   (1997)

Built within Coconino National Forest just outside of Cottonwood, the Verde Santa Fe Golf Course is rather a quirky facility, being a short, housing-lined test which makes some use of the native desert but lacks even a single man-made bunker. In spots the design is awkward, particularly at both the 338-yard 6th and the 366-yard 17th, which have arroyos crossing their fairways at troublesome distances for the average player. There are, however, some stronger entries as well, led by the 549-yard 9th, an uphill three-shotter which makes a late left turn to a green tucked across an arroyo. A collection of man-made ponds separates the 354-yard 10th and the 502-yard 18th, with the 465-yard pond-flanked 12th and the 414-yard 15th otherwise leading the homeward charge.

Canyon Mesa Country Club - Sedona   ♦½

Arthur Jack Snyder   www.canyonmesacountryclub.com
500 Jacks Canyon Rd, Sedona, AZ 86351   (928) 284-0036
                1,450 yds   Par 28   Rating: 30.0 / 80   (1984)

Located half a mile east of both Oakcreek Country Club and the Sedona Golf Resort,
Canyon Mesa is a good-size par-3 course (with a single two-shotter thrown in) built by
Arthur Jack Snyder in 1984. Its property is a crowded one, with numerous condominiums
occupying the eastern half (two holes are actually encircled by them), and an access road,
two ponds and a creek also marking the landscape. Tree-lined but lightly bunkered, this
is a notch above many of this type, including its only direct local competition, the basic
par-3 nine at the Poco Diablo Resort, which lies just over the Navajo County line.

Mesa View Golf Course - Bagdad   ♦

Unknown   www.bagdadaztown.com
4 Ash St, Bagdad, AZ 86321   (928) 633-2818
                1,650 yds   Par 30   Rating: 29.5 / 89   (1989)

The only golf course in one of two remaining company towns in the state of Arizona
(Freeport-McMoran owning most every structure in sight – including the local copper
mine), the Mesa View Golf Course is a par-30 executive nine wedged into a triangular
property near the town's center. With but a single bunker present, this is basic
recreational golf that is in no way suited to a player of skill – but it must surely make a
nice amenity in so largely isolated a working community.

INDEX

500 C at Adobe Dam	54	Desert Mountain (Outlaw)	21
500 C at Adobe Dam (Futures)	96	Desert Sands GC	99
Adobe Family G Center	96	Dobson Ranch GC	60
Aguila GC	54	Dove Valley Ranch GC	61
Aguila GC (Par 3)	96	Duke at Rancho El Dorado	118
Ahwatukee CC	54	GC at Eagle Mountain	40
Alta Mesa CC	12	Encanterra CC	112
Ancala CC	12	Encanto GC	61
Antelope Hills GC (North)	135	Encanto GC (Exec)	99
Antelope Hills GC (South)	135	The Estancia C	22
Anthem G&CC (Ironwood)	13	GC of Estrella	62
Anthem G&CC (Persimmon)	13	Falcon GC	62
Apache Creek GC	116	Falcon Dunes GC	52
Apache Stronghold GC	127	Fiesta Lakes GC	99
Apache Sun GC	116	FireRock CC	23
Apache Wells CC	55	Foothills GC	63
Arizona CC	14	Fountain of the Sun CC	100
Arizona Biltmore GC (Adobe)	36	Francisco Grande G Res	114
Arizona Biltmore GC (Links)	36	Gainey Ranch GC	40
Arizona City GC	117	Glen Lakes GC	63
Arizona G Res & Con Cen	37	Gold Canyon Res (Dinosaur Mt)	115
Arizona Grand Res	37	Gold Canyon Res (Sidewinder)	114
Arizona Traditions GC	56	Gold Canyon RV & Golf Res	124
Arrowhead CC	14	Grand Canyon Univ GC	64
ASU Karsten GC	56	Grayhawk GC (Talon)	64
Augusta Ranch GC	97	Grayhawk GC (Raptor)	65
Bear Creek G Complex	57	Great Eagle GC	65
Bear Creek G Complex (Cub)	97	Greenfield Lakes GC	100
Bellaire GC	97	Hayden Muni GC	128
Blackstone CC	15	Hillcrest GC	66
Boulders Res GC (North)	38	GC at Johnson Ranch	118
Boulders Res GC (South)	38	Kearny GC	119
Briarwood CC	15	Ken McDonald GC	66
Camelback GC (Ambiente)	39	Kierland GC	41
Camelback GC (Padre)	39	Kokopelli GC	67
Canyon Mesa CC	139	Las Colinas GC	67
Capital Canyon GC	132	Las Sendas GC	68
Cave Creek Muni GC	57	The Legacy G Res	41
GC at Chaparral Pines	126	Legend at Arrowhead	68
Club West GC	58	Legend Trail GC	69
Cobre Valley CC	128	Leisure World CC (Coyote Run)	23
Coldwater GC	58	Leisure World CC (Heron Lakes)	100
Continental GC	98	Lone Tree GC	69
Copper Canyon GC	59	Longbow GC	70
Coronado GC	98	Lookout Mountain GC	42
Corta Bella GC	16	Los Caballeros GC	42
Coyote Lakes GC	59	McCormick Ranch GC (Palm)	43
Coyote Trails GC	136	McCormick Ranch GC (Pine)	43
Dave White Muni GC	117	McDowell Mountain GC	70
CC at DC Ranch	16	Mesa CC	24
Desert Canyon GC	60	Mesa View GC	139
Desert Forest GC	17	Mirabel	24
Desert Highlands GC	18	Mission Royale GC	119
Desert Mirage GC	98	Moon Valley CC	25
Desert Mountain (Renegade)	19	Moon Valley CC (Moonwalk)	101
Desert Mountain (Cochise)	19	Mountain Brook GC	120
Desert Mountain (Geronimo)	20	Oakcreek CC	136
Desert Mountain (Apache)	20	Oasis GC	120
Desert Mountain (Chiracahua)	21	Ocatillo G Res	71

Orange Tree G & Con Res	44		Sun City (Willowbrook)	105
Painted Mountain G Res	71		Sun City (Willowcreek)	81
Palm Creek G & RV Res	124		Sun City CC	81
Palm Valley GC (Lakes)	101		Sun City Grand (Cimarron)	83
Palm Valley GC (Palms)	72		Sun City Grand (Desert Springs)	82
PalmBrook CC	72		Sun City Grand (Granite North)	82
Palo Verde GC	101		Sun City Grand (Granite South)	83
Papago GC	73		Sun City West (Deer Valley)	32
Paradise Peak West	102		Sun City West (Desert Trails)	106
Paradise Valley CC	25		Sun City West (Echo Mesa)	106
Paradise Valley Park GC	102		Sun City West (Grandview)	31
Payson GC	129		Sun City West (Pebblebrook)	30
PebbleCreek (Eagle's Nest)	73		Sun City West (Stardust)	105
PebbleCreek (Tuscanny Falls)	74		Sun City West (Trail Ridge)	31
Peoria Pines	102		Sun Lakes (Cottonwood)	84
The Phoenician	44		Sun Lakes (Oakwood)	84
Phoenix CC	26		Sun Lakes (Ironwood)	85
Pinnacle Peak CC	26		Sun Lakes (Palo Verde)	107
Poston Butte GC	121		Sun Lakes (Sun Lakes)	106
Prescott G&CC	137		Sun Village GC	107
C at Prescott Lakes	132		Sunbird GC	107
Pueblo El Mirage GC	74		Sundance GC	85
Quailwood Greens GC	137		Sunland Springs GC	108
Links at Queen Creek	121		Sunland Village GC	108
Queen Valley GC	122		Sunland Village East GC	108
Quintero G&CC	75		SunRidge Canyon GC	86
Rancho Manana GC	75		Superstition Mt (Lost Gold)	113
Raven GC	76		Superstition Mt (Prospector)	112
Red Mountain Ranch CC	27		Superstition Springs GC	86
The Rim GC	126		Talking Rock GC	133
Rio Verde CC (White Wing)	27		Talking Stick GC (O'oodham)	45
Rio Verde CC (Quail Run)	28		Talking Stick GC (Piipaash)	46
Roadhaven GC	124		Tatum Ranch GC	32
Robson Ranch GC	122		Terravita	33
Rolling Hills GC	103		Tierra Grande GC	123
Royal Palms GC	103		Toka Sticks GC	87
San Marcos GC	45		Tonto Verde (Ranch)	88
Scotsdalle National (Bad 9)	103		Tonto Verde (Peaks)	87
Scotsdalle National (Mineshaft)	28		TPC Scottsdale (Champions)	46
Scotsdalle National (Other)	29		TPC Scottsdale (Stadium)	47
Scottsdale Silverado GC	76		Tres Rios GC	88
Sedona Golf Res	134		Trilogy GC at Power Ranch	89
Seven Canyons	133		Trilogy GC at Vistancia	89
Seville G&CC	29		Troon CC	33
Shalimar CC	77		Troon North GC (Monument)	90
The Short Course	104		Troon North GC (Pinnacle)	90
Silverleaf	30		Union Hills CC	91
Southern Dunes GC	115		Verde River G & Social C	91
Southern Ridge GC	77		Verde Santa Fe GC	138
Springfield G Res	104		Verrado GC (Founders)	92
Starfire GC	78		Verrado GC (Victory)	92
Stonecreek GC	78		Viewpoint G Res	48
StoneRidge GC	138		Viewpoint G Res (Exec)	109
Sun City (Lakes East)	104		Villa De Paz GC	93
Sun City (Lakes West)	80		We-Ko-Pa GC (Cholla)	48
Sun City (North)	79		We-Ko-Pa GC (Saguaro)	49
Sun City (Quail Run)	105		Westbrook Village GC (Lakes)	93
Sun City (Riverview)	80		Westbrook Village GC (Vistas)	94
Sun City (South)	79		Western Skies GC	94

Made in the USA
San Bernardino, CA
29 April 2018